Genocide
in Rwanda

*Complicity
of the
Churches?*

Genocide in Rwanda

Complicity of the Churches?

EDITED BY

CAROL RITTNER   JOHN K. ROTH   WENDY WHITWORTH

aegis

in association with

PARAGON HOUSE
St. Paul, Minnesota

First Edition 2004

Published in the United States by
Paragon House
2285 University Avenue West
St. Paul, MN 55114

Produced by Aegis Trust
Laxton
Newark
Notts
United Kingdom
http://www.aegistrust.org

Aegis is a non-governmental organization whose purpose is to help
reduce the incidence of genocide by promoting cooperation and
scholarship between and among all those who have an interest in
preventing genocide, including governments, national and international organizations, and the media.

Library of Congress Cataloging-in-Publication Data
Genocide in Rwanda : complicity of the churches / edited by Carol
Rittner, John K. Roth, Wendy Whitworth.
    p. cm.
  Includes bibliographical references and index.
  ISBN 1-55778-837-5 (pbk. : alk. paper) 1. Genocide--Rwanda. 2.
Genocide--Religious aspects--Christianity. 3. Rwanda--History--Civil
War, 1994--Atrocities. 4. Rwanda--History--Civil War, 1994--Religious
aspects. 5.   Ethnic relations--Religious aspects--Christianity. 6.
Rwanda--Ethnic relations. I. Rittner, Carol, 1948- II. Roth, John K.
III. Whitworth, Wendy.

  DT450.435.G474 2004
  261.8'33151'0967571--dc22

                                    2004014772

Manufactured in the United States of America
10 9 8 7 6 5 4 3 2 1

For current information about all releases from Paragon House,
visit the web site at http://www.paragonhouse.com

To the memory
of
Father Vieko Curic, O.F.M.,
Mr. Gabriel Mvunganyi
and
Sister Félicitée Niyitegeka,
who laid down their lives for their friends,
and for all Christians in Rwanda, known and unknown,
who before, during, and after the 1994 genocide in Rwanda,
defended humanity,
stood firm against a tide of unprecedented atrocities,
and
who did not leave God without witnesses.

TABLE OF CONTENTS

PREFACE

Genocide never happens by chance. Nowhere was this more true than in Rwanda between April and July 1994 when thousands of hate-inspired Hutu extremists carried out a well-organized campaign of killing that left more than 800,000 of their fellow countrymen and women dead. Most of those killed, raped, and mutilated during those 100 days were members of the minority Tutsi ethnic group – the rest were moderate Hutus who advocated peaceful coexistence with their Tutsi neighbors. Unlike the genocide of the Jews during World War II and the Holocaust (1939-1945), neither institutions nor individuals can say, "What could we have done? We did not know what was happening in Rwanda in 1994." Those of us living in Europe, America, and elsewhere *knew* only too well what was happening between April and July 1994, in that God-forsaken little country in the center of Africa, thanks to the miracle of modern communications technology.

Every evening the sights and sounds of genocide in Rwanda, the most "Christian" country in Africa – "89.8 percent of the population claimed membership in a Christian Church"[1] – came cascading accross our television screens. For the most part, the international community did little more than wring its collective hands while hundreds of thousands of Rwandan Hutus hacked to death nearly a million Tutsis and moderate Hutus, urged on by the extremist Hutu-power government. While so much is horrific about what happened in Rwanda in 1994, nothing is more horrific than the fact that many of that genocide's large-scale massacres took place in churches – most of them Roman Catholic churches – all across that tiny "Christian" country. Thus, it is not surprising that many people have asked, and continue to ask, "Were the Christian churches complicit in the 1994 genocide?"

According to Timothy Longman, "The church was implicated in the genocide in numerous ways. People who sought sanctuary in church buildings instead were slaughtered there." Longman's research in Rwanda after the genocide supports the assertion made by African Rights, formerly a London-based human rights and advocacy organization, now an African-based one, which stated that "more people were killed in church buildings than anywhere else."[2] But, terrible as that was, does it mean that the Churches were complicit in the genocide? To quote Longman again, "Numerous Tutsi priests, pastors, brothers, and nuns were killed, often by their own parishioners, sometimes by their fellow clergy... In some parishes Hutu clergy attempted to protect those gathered within their church, but in many others, clergy assisted the killers."[3]

Genocide in Rwanda: Complicity of the Churches? grew out of an international seminar, *The Church and Genocide: Rwanda 1994*, held in London in March 2003. Organized by Dr. Carol Rittner, R.S.M., one of the editors of this volume, it brought together scholars and practitioners, clergy, nuns, and lay people, Rwandans, Europeans and Americans in an effort to try to grapple with the question of the Churches and genocide in Rwanda in 1994. It was not an easy topic to explore. Emotions ran high; sometimes discussion was difficult. Still, no one abandoned the seminar, and many who participated in it re-wrote and developed their original "trigger papers" into thoughtful essays, which is not to say that the question(s) about the Christian Churches, particularly the Roman Catholic Church, has/have been definitively answered. That will take more time, more research and much more analysis. *Genocide in Rwanda: Complicity of the Churches?* is intended to encourage more sustained, more careful, and more substantive research about various challenging questions: Were the Christian Churches complicit in the 1994 genocide in Rwanda? If so, how and why? If not, why is there such a strong perception that they were? What must be changed in terms of Church structures, authority, teaching, and formation of adherents to prevent genocide from happening again in the future, in Rwanda or elsewhere? If the Christian Churches were complicit in the 1994 genocide in Rwanda, can they ever recover from such ethical and moral failure?

The editors of *Genocide in Rwanda: Complicity of the Churches?* want to thank all those who participated in the March 2003 London seminar about the Churches and genocide. Likewise, we want to thank those who wanted to participate but were unable to do so, yet, nevertheless, contributed essays for this volume. In a special way, we would like to thank Professor Hubert G. Locke who so graciously assisted us in numerous ways. We extend our thanks as well to Drs. Stephen and James Smith, Co-directors of The Aegis Trust (UK), Dr. Michael MacDowell, President of College Misericordia in Dallas, PA (USA), and Dr. Vera King Farris (former) President of The Richard Stockton College of New Jersey (USA) for providing funds that helped to make the London seminar possible. The priests and brothers of the Society of St. John the Evangelist, St. Edward's House, London, provided an atmosphere conducive for reflection and discussion during the seminar and for that we are very grateful. Dr. James M. Smith and Glen Powell allowed us to use their excellent and moving photographs of various memorial sites in Rwanda, so we want to thank them for their generosity. Sisters Jean Benoit, S.S.M.N. and Nancy Charlesworth, S.S.M.N. helped by tracking down information for us. Sister Marie Julianne Farrington, S.S.M.N., one of the contributors to this volume, provided both encouragement and invaluable help to Carol Rittner as she compiled the Chronology, and Noreen Vasilakis, a graduate of the class of 2004, The Richard Stockton College of New Jersey, gave timely, accurate, and willing assistance in compiling the Chronology, Videography, Websites, and Bibliography. The editors are extremely grateful for their assistance. Glen Powell, our dauntless and expert designer, has once again been a pleasure to work with collaboratively. Finally, we thank Dr. Gordon Anderson and his staff at Paragon House Publishers for their advice, patience, professionalism, and confidence in this project. We trust *Genocide in Rwanda: Complicity of the Churches?* will be a valuable addition to Paragon House's growing list of excellent books in the area of Holocaust and Genocide Studies.

Notes

1. See further, Timothy Longman, "Christian Churches and Genocide in Rwanda," revision of a paper originally prepared for the Conference on Genocide, Religion, and Modernity, U.S. Holocaust Memorial Museum, Washington, DC, 11-13 May 1997. Last accessed July 2003: http://www.holocaustrevealed.org/_domai...ca/ Rwanda/Christian_Church_Genocide.htm
2. Ibid.
3. Ibid.

The continent of Africa with the country of Rwanda highlighted.

INTRODUCTION

Stephen D. Smith

Genocide is extreme. We expect the worst, and invariably we learn something about the darkness of human creativity and behavior. At the beginning of the twentieth century, the Armenian genocide introduced us to the possibility of removing whole communities and *murdering them en route*. Toward the middle of the twentieth century, the Holocaust introduced us to *industrialized killing*. It was clean, efficient murder, conducted at arm's length, implicating very few people directly. It was total in its aim. And Rwanda in 1994 introduced us to *genocide as a state-controlled popular movement*. It was genocide executed in every province, district, sector, cell, street, and home. This time, virtually everyone was implicated.

As a genocide by popular consent, the experience in Rwanda introduced a new and disturbing question about human behavior. *How do you* persuade neighbors to kill neighbors, friends to kill friends, even family to kill their own family? *How do you* convince teachers to kill their students, doctors to kill their patients, employers to kill their workers? *How do you* convince clergy to kill their parishioners?

The question can, of course, be put another way: Why were neighbors, friends, families, teachers, doctors, employers, and clergy convinced that they were doing the right thing when they killed or facilitated the murder of people so close to them? Did they change character, or was the possibility of being perpetrators always latent within them?

Genocide in Rwanda: Complicity of the Churches? brings together essays by scholars, clergy, and practitioners who try to grapple with demanding and uncomfortable questions about the role of the Christian Churches, particularly the Roman Catholic Church, during the 1994 genocide in Rwanda, and the acts of practicing Christian people who were involved in that genocide.

Prior to 1994 and superficially, Rwanda appeared to be a model of national piety, a profoundly Christian country, with high levels of church attendance among both Catholics and Protestants. Yet when the influence of genocidal ideology made itself felt, it overwhelmed the people of Rwanda, successfully splitting Roman Catholic parishes and Protestant congregations down the middle, undermining the fundamental moral imperative of Christian teaching: "Love your neighbor as yourself" (Luke 10:24).

What was the reaction of the Christian Churches, particularly the Roman Catholic Church, whose baptized adherents comprised more than sixty percent of the population of Rwanda, to the events that were happening between April and July 1994?

At an institutional level in Rwanda, the Church was mute, providing little or no leadership that countered the genocidal force unleashed on 6 April 1994 when President Juvénal Habyarimana's plane was shot out of the night sky. There was little or no dissuading influence channeled through the hierarchy that might have given impetus for Christian clergy and parishioners to resist the genocidal urge. Why was this so?

At a parish level, clergy were largely masters of their own destiny and in many cases made surprisingly poor and disturbing choices. We know that there were clergy and nuns who lost their lives trying to protect the lives of their parishioners – the London-based organization African Rights has documented such cases (see, for example, their 2002 publication, *Tribute to Courage*). Still, the connivance of too many clergy either in supporting the genocide indirectly or in actually ordering the murder of their own congregants raises questions about the sincerity of ordained Church leaders in their adherence to even the most basic principles of Christian living. To teach, "Thou *shall not* kill," then to act out, "Thou *shall* kill," is beyond hypocrisy. It is evil.

At an individual level, there was dysfunctionality among those who professed to be followers of Jesus Christ and the Christian message which allowed genocidal ideology to overpower any sense of individual or communal moral responsibility. Some people ran to the churches, expecting them to be sanctuaries of safety, as they had been in the past when violence erupted. Others ran to the same churches, knowing that their fellow parishioners were hiding there, and these dysfunctional followers of the Son of God assisted the extremist Hutu militia in murdering them in the sanctuaries and between the pews where they had once worshipped together.

The authors of the essays in *Genocide in Rwanda: Complicity of the Churches?* have engaged in a courageous and demanding task. They have begun to ask the kind of questions of Christianity and Christian believers which should never have been required, but cannot be ignored. These authors are acutely aware that this is not the first time Christianity has failed in a situation of genocide, but that it must be the last time it does so, for the sake of God's people. Many of these authors are aware that their questions shake the foundations of the Church as an institution, if not the efficacy of Christian teaching itself. And yet, they know they must struggle to find a way forward because there is no way back.

Reading the essays in this book leaves the reader acutely aware that this genocide could have been prevented, but it would have taken the population of Rwanda – the *most Christian country* in all of Africa – to individually and collectively refuse to follow the genocidal command to kill their neighbors. But that is not what happened.

Reading *Genocide in Rwanda: Complicity of the Churches?* will make you think about how things might have been different in Rwanda in 1994, but why they were not.

The above map of Rwanda highlights some of the sites of massacres that took place in churches and convents, including the monastery of Sovu, during the 1994 genocide. The location of the Marian Shrine of Kibeho also is shown.

CHRONOLOGY

Carol Rittner

No chronology can be complete. This one simply tries to provide readers with a broad context for the essays that follow. It draws attention to the Roman Catholic and other Christian Churches, their leaders, institutions, and organizations, and to some of their actions and statements before, during and after the 1994 genocide in Rwanda.

DATE	EVENT
1885	In negotiations between the European powers at the Conference of Berlin, Rwanda is given to the Germans as part of their empire.
1899	Rwanda is incorporated into German East Africa.
1900	The Society of the Missionaries of Our Lady of Africa (*Pères Blancs* – White Fathers) arrive in Rwanda and establish a mission.
1910	At a conference in Brussels, the frontiers of the Belgian Congo, British Uganda and German East Africa are fixed.
1911	German troops, assisted by Tutsi chiefs, crush a popular uprising in northern Rwanda, leaving widespread bitterness among the northern Hutus.
1913	Coffee is introduced into Rwanda as a cash crop.
1914-1918	World War I.
1923	Under the Treaty of Versailles, Rwanda is designated a protectorate of the League of Nations and is to be governed by Belgium, which carries out its mandate by indirectly ruling through Tutsi kings.
1931	The Belgians depose *Mwami* (King) Musinga and replace him with his son, Charles Rudahigwa Mutara.

1933-1934	The Belgian administration in Rwanda organizes an official census, classifying all Rwandans as either Hutu, Tutsi, or Twa. Identity cards, specifying ethnicity, are issued.
1939-1945	World War II.
October 17, 1943	After fourteen years of religious instruction, King Mutara III Rudahigwa is baptized as a Roman Catholic Christian, unleashing a veritable torrent of conversions among Rwandans.
1945	In San Francisco, California, the United Nations (UN) Charter is unanimously adopted and signed on June 26. Four months later, it enters into force.
October 27, 1946	King Mutara III Rudahigwa consecrates Rwanda to Jesus Christ the King.
December 9-10, 1948	The UN General Assembly adopts the Convention on the Prevention and Punishment of the Crime of Genocide on December 9th and the Universal Declaration of Human Rights the next day.
June 1 1952	In Kabgayi, Rwanda, Monsignor Aloys Bigirumwami is consecrated the first black Roman Catholic bishop in Belgian Africa.
March 1957	A group of nine Hutu intellectuals, supported by the Catholic Church in Rwanda, publish a tract known as the *Hutu Manifesto*. Parmehutu – the Party for the Emancipation of the Hutus – is formed.
1959	King Mutara III Rudahigwa mysteriously dies in Bujumbura, Burundi, while under the care of a Belgian physician. His brother, Kigeri Ndahindurwa, succeeds him. The Hutu "social revolution" begins with a peasant revolt, supported by the Belgians; 20,000 Tutsis are killed; there is a mass exodus of Tutsis, mainly into Uganda. Belgium places Rwanda under military rule.
1959-1962	An emancipated Hutu elite takes power after the Belgian trusteeship administration withdraws its support from the Tutsi minority.
1960	Rwanda's first municipal elections result in overwhelming victory for the Parmehutu party.
1961	The monarchy is formally abolished by referendum;

a republic is proclaimed. There is a new wave of violence against the Tutsis; thousands flee the country.

1962 Proclamation of the independence of Rwanda. Grégoire Kayibanda of the Parmehutu party is declared the first president. There are armed attacks by Tutsi exiles, followed by internal reprisals; 2,000 Tutsis are killed.

1963 More armed attacks by Tutsi exiles, who are now called *inyenzi* (cockroaches), which contributes to deepening ethnic tensions in Rwanda. More Tutsis are killed and more Tutsi refugees flee to Uganda, Tanzania, Burundi, and Zaire (later re-named the Democratic Republic of Congo [DRC]).

1964 British philosopher Bertrand Russell calls the killing of Tutsis in Rwanda the most horrible extermination of a people since the killing of the Jews during the Holocaust. By the mid-1960s, half the Tutsi population live outside the borders of Rwanda.

1972 Massacres of Hutus in Burundi.

1973 In Rwanda, Major-General Juvénal Habyarimana, a Hutu, takes power in a *coup d'état*. He declares the start of the Second Republic.

1975 Habyarimana establishes the National Revolutionary Movement for Development (*Mouvement Révolutionnaire National pour le Développement* – MRND), a new political party. He purges Tutsis from the universities, imposes a quota on Tutsi employment in public service jobs and in educational institutions, and refuses to address the question of the return of exiled Tutsis to Rwanda. Public "salvation committees" organize "Tutsi hunts."

1978 MRND is declared Rwanda's only political party. Habyarimana is reelected president. He also is reelected in 1983 and 1988, with more than 99 percent of the vote.

1979 In Kenya, Tutsi refugees start the Rwandan National Union (RANU).

November 28, 1981 The first reported apparition in Rwanda by Alphonsine

Mumureke of the Blessed Virgin Mary at the College of Kibeho, Diocese of Butare. The next day, she reportedly has another apparition.

1982

February & March Two other students from the College of Kibeho also reportedly have visions of the Blessed Virgin Mary.

May 31 The first important popular gathering of pilgrims takes place at the Marian shrine at Kibeho.

August 15 20,000 people are present at Kibeho to witness the Marian apparitions.

July 30, 1983 Monsignor Jean-Baptiste Gahamanyi, Bishop of Butare, issues a pastoral letter about the Marian apparitions at Kibeho.

July 30, 1986 The Bishop of Butare issues a second pastoral letter about the Marian apparitions at Kibeho.

1988 In Washington, DC, an international conference on Rwandan refugees is held; in Uganda, the Rwandan Patriotic Front (RPF) is started.

August 15 The Bishop of the Diocese of Butare approves public Marian devotion linked to the Marian apparitions of Kibeho.

1989 The bottom falls out of the coffee market, leaving Rwanda in a severe economic depression.

1990

September Pope John Paul II visits Rwanda.

October The Uganda-based RPF invades Rwanda, demanding political reforms and the right to re-settle thousands of mainly Tutsi refugees; civil war follows. Several RPF leaders are killed; Belgium and France send troops to protect their citizens. RPF insurgents are repulsed. Thousands of Tutsis and opponents of the Habyarimana regime are arrested in Rwanda on suspicion of complicity with the RPF.

1990/91 The Rwandan army begins training civilian militia known as the *interahamwe* (those who work together).

1991

August 15 The government of Rwanda issues an analysis of a census taken earlier in the year: 89.8 percent of the population claim membership in the Christian Church:

	62.6 percent claim to be Catholic, 18.8 percent Protestant, and 8.4 percent Seventh Day Adventist.
November	A Committee of Consultation organizes political demonstrations in Kigali against the government and the one-party system. Some 10,000 people participate.
November 21	The Catholic bishops of Rwanda issue a letter to priests and religious on the "Pastoral Role in Rebuilding Rwanda." A central theme of the letter is the need to overcome ethnic divisions.
December	The Rwandan Catholic Church takes a political stance, calling for serious talks with the RPF and the formation of an independent transitional government. In December, priests from the diocese of Kabgayi published a forty-page document, "Let Us Convert to Live Together in Peace." In this document, they attacked the passive attitude of the Church in the face of "mismanagement of public funds, corruption, social injustice, individual freedoms, the war, and aids."
December 1	Bishop Thaddée Nsengiyumva, Bishop of Kabgayi and President of the Rwandan Episcopal Conference, acknowledges the Church's complicity in perpetrating ethnic divisions in Rwanda when he declares in a public letter, "the church is sick."
1992	
January	The Committee of Contacts is formed. Its members are Catholic, Protestant and Seventh Day Adventist. Six Catholic bishops and eight heads of Protestant churches, or their representatives, are present.
March	Creation of the *Coalition pour la Défense de la République* (CDR), an extremist Hutu political party. *Interahamwe* massacre Tutsis and others in the Bugesera area.
May	An RPF offensive in the north displaces approximately 350,000 people, many of whom flee to surrounding countries. On May 16th, the Rwandan bishops meet in Rome with Pope John Paul II. They draw attention to "this senseless war [which] has inflamed ethnic hatred and regionalism."

June 27-July 6 Cardinal Jozek Tomko, Prefect of the Vatican Congregation of the Evangelization of Peoples, visits Rwanda. He insists that the Church in Rwanda must fulfill its commitment to justice and human rights.

August A peace conference formally opens in Arusha, Tanzania. Militias massacre large numbers of Tutsis in the Kibuye region of Rwanda.

November Dr. Léon Mugesera, a prominent Hutu activist, calls for Hutus to "send the Tutsis back to Ethiopia" via the rivers of Rwanda. Extremist Hutu *interahamwe* respond with an escalation in political violence. Despite government attempts to stop it, a demonstration in favor of the peace talks takes place.

November 28 The first stone is laid by Bishop Augustin Misago for the "Shrine of Our Lady of Sorrows," the name given to the Marian sanctuary at Kibeho.

December In Arusha, President Habyarimana refuses to sign a protocol on power-sharing and a transitional parliament. In Rwanda, massacres of Tutsis and Hutu opposition members occur in the Gisenyi area. In an effort to provide stability in a country suffering the effects of a barbaric civil war, and to support the UN's effort to provide international humanitarian aid to the starving people of Somalia, American troops storm Somali beaches on December 9th.

1993

February Fighting continues in the north; thousands of Hutus go into exile. The RPF carries out summary executions.

May Cardinal Roger Etchegaray, President of the Vatican's Pontifical Council for Justice and Peace, visits Rwanda as Pope John Paul II's special delegate. An open letter addressed to him denounces "the poisoning of the Roman Curia" and claims that the Tutsi-dominated clergy have been very active in the war.

June The Bishop of Byumba, Joseph Ruzindana, condemns, among other atrocities, rapes that have occurred in his diocese.

July *Radio Télévision Libre des Mille Collines* (RTLM), a Hutu extremist radio station, begins broadcasting in

Rwanda. A new government is formed; Agathe Uwilingiyimana, a moderate Hutu politician, becomes Prime Minister.

August The Habyarimana government and the RPF negotiate and sign a peace accord in Arusha. A transitional government, which would include the RPF, is part of the agreement, as is a UN peace-keeping force.

August 3 The Arusha Peace Accords, which put an end to hostilities and provide a power-sharing agreement between the MRND, the democratic opposition and the RPF, are signed in Tanzania.

October Eighteen elite American troops, sent to help stop the fighting between rival warlords in Somalia, are killed. America announces it will withdraw its forces and urges other western nations to do likewise.

October 5 The UN Security Council creates the UN Assistance Mission to Rwanda (UNAMIR).

November 20 The bishops of Rwanda issue a statement declaring that "one of the reasons for our national tragedy is the desire to confiscate everything for the benefit of a single region and ethnic group."

November – December UNAMIR troops arrive in Rwanda, under the command of Canadian Major General Roméo Dallaire. General Dallaire and diplomats in Kigali receive an anonymous letter from within the Rwandan army warning them of a plan to kill Tutsis in order to prevent the implementation of the Arusha Peace Accords.

December 28 Bishop Wenceslas Kalibushi and clergy of the diocese of Nyundo, in northwestern Rwanda, issue a press release in which they note the distribution of weapons in their parishes and ask the authorities "to explain clearly to the public the use [intended] for these weapons that have been handed out recently."

1994

January On January 1st, Christians from all religious confessions march in Kigali, from Holy Family parish to Amahora Stadium. They pray and appeal for peace. They proclaim 1994 a year of peace. The march is organized by the ecumenical Committee of Contacts. During the same month, President Habyarimana takes the oath of office according to the provisions of the Arusha Peace Accords, but the transitional government is repeatedly blocked by the president and his "Hutu Power" allies.

January 3 Belgian UNAMIR troops seize hidden stocks of arms, ammunition, and explosives. They later return these weapons to the Rwandan army, which was said to have been their owner.

January 11 Major General Roméo Dallaire sends a coded-cable to the United Nations in New York warning of the danger of severe impending ethnic conflict in Rwanda. The warning basically is ignored.

February Violence escalates in Kigali and in north-central Rwanda.

April 6 A plane carrying Rwandan President Habyarimana, Burundian President Cyprien Ntariyamira and other government officials returning from negotiations in Tanzania is shot out of the sky as it approaches Kigali airport. Within moments of the crash, widespread massacres of Tutsis, opposition leaders, and moderate Hutus begin. Churches – once havens of sanctuary during outbreaks of violence – become sites of mass murder.

April 7 Members of Habyarimana's Presidential Guard kill Prime Minister Agathe Uwilingiyimana and ten Belgian peacekeepers who were supposed to protect her.

April 8 Former Speaker of Parliament Theodore Sindikubwabo announces the formation of an interim government and declares himself interim President and Jean Kambanda, interim Prime Minister.

April 9 French and Belgian paratroopers are sent to Rwanda to assist with the evacuation of their expatriates.

April 10 Ambassador David Rawson closes the American embassy in Kigali; the Papal Nuncio, Archbishop Giuseppe Bertello, leaves Rwanda. In Rome, the

African Synod of Bishops opens with Mass at St. Peter's Basilica. In his homily, Pope John Paul II pleads for an end to the "fratricidal killings" in Rwanda.

April 11   Relief officials estimate that as many as 20,000 people have been killed in Kigali during five days of violence.

April 12   France closes its embassy in Kigali.

April 14   In the presence of Pope John Paul II and the bishops assembled for the African Synod, Cardinals Francis Arinze, Christian Wiyghan Tumi, and Paulos Tzadua, Presidents of the Synod, read an appeal for peace in Rwanda: "We make a heartfelt plea to all concerned in the conflict to lay down their arms and stop the atrocities and killings."

April 20   Belgium withdraws its troops from UNAMIR.

April 21   UN Security Council Resolution No. 912 reduces the UNAMIR peace-keeping force in Rwanda from 2,500 to approximately 250.

April 27   At his General Audience, Pope John Paul II speaks about events in Rwanda: "I invite all in positions of authority to work generously and effectively to end this genocide."

April 30   In New York, there are intense discussions about the crisis in Rwanda; the UN condemns the killings, but fails to describe what is happening there as genocide. Relief organizations estimate that as many as 150,000 people have been killed since the violence began on April 6.

May 3   Pope John Paul II issues a strong condemnation of the genocidal slaughter in Rwanda. The next day, UN Secretary-General Boutros-Ghali states that there is "a real genocide" in Rwanda.

May 15   Pope John Paul II, prior to the noontime Regina Caeli prayer, makes a public statement broadcast to pilgrims gathered in St. Peter's Square, "Again today, I feel it is my duty to recall the violence to which the peoples of Rwanda are subjected. This is an out-and-out genocide, for which unfortunately even Catholics are responsible." May 15th also is the last recorded apparition of the Blessed Virgin Mary at the hilltop shrine of Kibeho.

May 22 The RPF captures Kigali airport; it also extends its control in the northern and eastern regions of the country.

May 24 The Vatican's Permanent Observer in Geneva, Archbishop Paul F. Tabet, during the Special Session on Rwanda at the UN Human Rights Commission, makes a strong intervention decrying the human rights violations and atrocities in Rwanda.

May 25 The UN Human Rights Commission appoints René Dégni-Ségui as its Special Human Rights Envoy to Rwanda.

June RPF soldiers kill the Archbishop of Kigali, Vincent Nsengiyumva of Kigali, two bishops, Joseph Ruzindana of Byumba and Thaddée Nsengiyumva of Kabagayi, and ten priests. On June 9th, Pope John Paul II addresses a message to all the people of Rwanda deploring their murder.

June 19 After the Sunday Angelus, Pope John Paul II again appeals for peace in Rwanda and decries the extraordinary suffering of its peoples: "I ask everyone to listen to the voice of God and reason: stop the violence!"

June 24-29 Pope John Paul II sends Cardinal Roger Etchegaray as his envoy to Rwanda. He calls on Rwandans to disarm and to seek peace. The culmination of the visit is a Requiem Mass celebrated in the cathedral of Kabgayi where the three bishops killed by RPF soldiers are temporarily buried. Only sixteen of the faithful attend, since the area has recently been evacuated.

June 26 and 28 Cardinal Etchegaray delivers a message in Gisenyi (June 26) to the interim president of Rwanda, and at Byumba (June 28) to the president of the Rwandan Patriotic Front: "... this senseless war must be stopped... I implore all the political and military authorities to meet once again and declare a ceasefire and to maintain it at all costs... cease-fire means laying down your arms – machetes and spears."

June 28 In Geneva, René Dégni-Ségui issues his report; it

states that the massacres in Rwanda were part of a pre-planned and systematic campaign of genocide.

July 4 The RPF wins control of Kigali and the southern town of Butare. The RPF leadership announces it intends to establish a new government in Rwanda, based on the Arusha Accords.

July 5 A French-led operation known as *Opération Turquoise* establishes a "safe zone," in the prefectures of Gikongoro, Cyangugu, and Kibuye. As the RPF advances westward, the influx of displaced persons in the zone increases from an initial 500,000 to an estimated one million people within a few days.

July 13-14 Approximately one million Rwandan Hutus flee to Goma in eastern Zaire, creating a severe humanitarian crisis.

July 15 Members of the extremist Hutu militia as well as former Hutu government officials escape to the French "safe zone."

July 17 The RPF takes the last government stronghold in Gisenyi, and declares an end to the war.

July 19 The RPF installs a new government of national unity with a Hutu President (Pastor Bizimungu) and Tutsi Prime Minister (Faustin Twagiramungu). Compulsory identity cards are abolished. Major General Paul Kagame is appointed Defense Minister and Vice-President.

July 20 During his General Audience on July 20th, Pope John Paul II again appeals for peace: "I appeal to the local, political and civil authorities and to international organizations: do not abandon this fleeing throng! And... strive to help create conditions that will foster a harmonious spiritual, moral and civil rebirth."

July 24 After praying the Angelus, Pope John Paul II makes another pressing appeal for solidarity to be shown to the people of Rwanda: "Today there are epidemics in addition to genocide and desperate flight. Who can remain indifferent?"

July 27 British and Irish Church leaders endorse an urgent appeal from the All-Africa Conference of Churches for a day of prayer and healing (July 31st), for an immediate end to all the killings and to acts of genocide, for aid for the unprecedented numbers of refugees, and for bringing justice to the perpetrators of crimes against humanity.

August 2 From a refugee camp in Goma, more than two dozen Hutu priests sign a long letter to Pope John Paul II, defending the Church and their behavior during the genocide.

August 29 The new government of Rwanda agrees to allow trials for Rwandan war criminals before an international court, although later the Rwandan government changes its mind about this.

September 23 Bishop Thaddée Ntihinyurwa of the Diocese of Cyangugu issues a pastoral letter reflecting on the genocide in Rwanda. Among other things, he comments on the seeming zeal of the people "to receive the sacraments" which he says "is in contradiction with the wounds carried by the Rwandan people."

November The UN Security Council creates an ad hoc criminal tribunal for Rwanda. The tribunal is known as the International Criminal Tribunal for Rwanda (ICTR) and is empowered to try individuals for genocide, crimes against humanity and war crimes. The tribunal is seated in Arusha, Tanzania.

December 24 Hutu refugees in Zaire form a government-in-exile.

1995

April 22 In Rwanda, RPF soldiers massacre refugees at the Kibeho camp for internally displaced persons.

August The National Unity government breaks up; officials flee the country.

September 20 At a Mass in Nairobi, Pope John Paul II urges an end to the bloodshed in Rwanda and Burundi.

1996

March A group of Rwandese Catholics address a memorandum to Pope John Paul II detailing the extent of the violations committed by Catholic clergy during the genocide, the history of their involvement in ethnic politics, and their virulent anti-Tutsi rhetoric.

May 14 Pope John Paul II publicly declares that "The

Church... cannot be held responsible for the guilt of its members who agitate against the evangelical law. They must be called to account as a consequence of their own actions. All members of the Church who have broken the law must have the courage to take the consequences of their own actions."

December By the end of December, the number of genocide suspects in Rwandan jails is approximately 100,000.

1997

January Beginning in January and continuing onwards, armed conflict escalates in the northwest: groups of former Rwandan soldiers and *interahamwe* militia launch frequent attacks and the RPA (Rwandese Patriotic Army) retaliates in counter-insurgency operations. Civilians are massacred on both sides.

January 10 Jean-Paul Akayesu, accused of ordering mass killings in his area and organizing troops, is the first case to come before the International Criminal Tribunal for Rwanda. The trial is held in Arusha, Tanzania.

February 4 Five human rights observers are killed in an ambush in Cyangugu, Rwanda. All human rights observers in Cyangugu, Kibuye, and Gisenyi are withdrawn by the UN to Kigali.

April The UN Security Council expresses concern about reports of massacres of Rwandan refugees in Zaire by AFDL (Alliance of Democratic Forces for the Liberation of Congo-Zaire), headed by Laurent-Désiré Kabila.

April 15 The Evangelical Lutheran Church in America announces that it will seek through appropriate action to respond to the "recurrent tragedies of the 20th century resulting from ethnic strife."

May 8 UN Secretary-General Kofi Annan accuses the AFDL of "killing by starvation" the Rwandan Hutu refugees who have been surrounded south of Kisangani, Zaire.

July In an interview with the *Washington Post*, Rwandan Vice-President and Minister of Defense Paul Kagame acknowledges the active participation of RPA troops in the war in Zaire. During the same month, the UN publishes a report about the massacres of Rwandan Hutu refugees between September 1996 and May 1997. The report denounces "crimes against humanity" committed by AFDL troops and the RPF allies. In another development, the ICTR arrests a dozen senior officials responsible for the 1994 Rwandan genocide who are in exile in Kenya, including former Prime Minister Jean Kambanda and Hassan Ngeze, former editor of the hate-propaganda newspaper *Kangura*.

1998

March 25 US President Bill Clinton flies to Rwanda for a short visit. He apologizes for the failure of the international community to stop the genocide. He does not, however, take personal moral responsibility for wrongdoing.

April 29 Thirty-five Catholic lecturers and students at the National University of Rwanda in Butare write an open letter to the Papal Nuncio in Kigali, Monsignor Janusz, admonishing the Catholic Church because of "wishing to evade its historic responsibility" when it comes to examining itself in regard to the 1994 genocide of the Tutsis.

May The Archbishop of Canterbury, George Carey, is accused of failing to hold a church inquiry into an Anglican bishop, Samuel Musabyimana, who has been arrested over his alleged role in the 1994 genocide.

May 13 Rakiya Omaar, Director of the London-based group, African Rights, publishes "An Open Letter to His Holiness, Pope John Paul II" admonishing him and the Vatican for exploiting "the concept of 'reconciliation' while being scornful of the need for justice."

July 17 A diplomatic conference in Rome adopts the Statute of the International Criminal Court (ICC), a permanent international forum to prosecute genocide, crimes against humanity, and serious war crimes. The Court will be headquartered in The Hague.

September 2 Jean-Paul Akayesu, a Hutu and former government official in Rwanda, is convicted in the first genocide case prosecuted before an international tribunal.

	The conviction is also historic because it establishes that rape, when committed with intent to destroy a group, in whole or in part, can amount to genocide.
December	The London-based group African Rights calls on the leaders of the Anglican, Free Methodist and Presbyterian Churches meeting in Harare to examine evidence that leaders of their Churches were implicated in the 1994 genocide in Rwanda.

1999

March	UN Secretary-General Kofi Annan announces an inquiry into the role of the UN during the 1994 genocide in Rwanda.
April 14	Bishop Augustin Misago of the Diocese of Gikongoro is arrested and charged with complicity in the genocide.
August	Bishop Augustin Misago's trial begins. Genocide survivors accuse him of working with the *interahamwe* Hutu militias during the 1994 genocide.
September	The first verdict by the ICTR is handed down: Jean Kambanda, prime minister of Rwanda during the 1994 genocide, is found guilty.

2000

June 15	Bishop Augustin Misago is acquitted of all charges of having organized and participated in Rwanda's 1994 genocide. Vatican spokesman Joaquin Navarro-Valls publishes an official statement expressing the Vatican's satisfaction after receiving news of the verdict of innocence.

2001

March	After several redrafts, the "*Gacaca* Law" is adopted and published. This law allows for an alternative system of participatory justice – a reworking of the traditional community conflict resolution system – in which "the whole of society would take part."
June	After a trial held in Belgium from April 17 to June 20, 2001, two nuns from the Benedictine Monastery of Sovu in Rwanda, Sister Gertrude (Consolata Mukangango) and Sister Kizito (Julienne Mukabutera) are convicted of genocide. They are given prison sentences of fifteen and thirteen years respectively. The Vatican issues a protest on their behalf.

October	Voting begins to elect members of traditional *Gacaca* courts.
2002	
April	Former Rwandan President Pasteur Bizimungu is arrested and charged with illegal political activity and threats to state security.
May 6	Flouting the advice of major allies and outraging human rights organizations, American President George W. Bush renounces any obligation to cooperate with the new ICC.
June	The International Court of Justice (ICJ) in The Hague begins to consider a suit filed by the Democratic Republic of Congo (DRC) against Rwanda and its rebel allies for genocide, armed aggression and human rights abuses.
July	Rwanda and the DRC sign a peace deal under which Rwanda will pull its troops out of the DRC and the DRC will help disarm Rwandan Hutu gunmen blamed for killing the Tutsi minority in the 1994 genocide. The Rome Statute to create a permanent International Criminal Court with jurisdiction over crimes against humanity and genocide comes into force.
2003	
May	Rwandans vote to support a draft constitution designed to prevent another genocide. The document bans the incitement of ethnic hatred.
August	Paul Kagame claims a landslide victory in the first presidential elections since the 1994 genocide.
October	First multi-party parliamentary elections; the Rwandan Patriotic Front (RPF) wins an absolute majority. European Union observers contend that the election is marred by irregularities and fraud.
December	The UN designates April 7, 2004 as the International Day of Reflection on the Genocide in Rwanda.
2004	
March	President Kagame rejects the conclusion of a French report alleging that he ordered the April 6, 1994 attack

on President Habyarimana's plane, thus sparking the genocide in Rwanda.

April 7 The 10th anniversary of the 1994 genocide is commemorated in Rwanda and around the world.

SOURCES USED TO COMPILE THE CHRONOLOGY

BBC News. "Timeline: Rwanda. A Chronology of Key Events." http://news.bbc.co.uk/go/pr/fr//2/hi/africa/country_profiles/1070329.stm

Berry, John A. and Carol Pott Berry, eds. *Genocide in Rwanda: A Collective Memory.* Washington, DC: Howard University Press, 1999.

Dialogue. Special Issue: *Eglise Catholique Au Rwanda: 100 Ans.* Mars-Avril 2000. No. 215.

Keane, Fergal. *Season of Blood.* New York: Viking, 1995.

McCullum, Hugh. *The Angels Have Left Us: The Rwanda Tragedy and the Churches.* Geneva: WCC Publications, 1995.

Melvern, Linda R. *A People Betrayed: The Role of the West in Rwanda's Genocide.* London and New York: ZED Books, 2000.

Ngomanzungu, Joseph. *Efforts De Médiation Oecuménique Des Eglises Dans La Crise Rwandaise: Le Comité de Contacts (1991-1994).* Kigali. Février 2003.

---- *L'Eglise Et La Crise Rwandaise De 1990-1994: Essai De Chronologie.* Kigali: Pallotti Presse, Novembre 2000.

Rittner, Carol, John K. Roth and James M. Smith, eds. *Will Genocide Ever End?* St. Paul, MN: Aegis in association with Paragon House, 2002.

Salzman, Todd. "Catholics & Colonialism: The Church's Failure in Rwanda." *Commonweal.* 23 May 1997: 17-19.

Sellström, Tel, et al. *The International Response to Conflict and Genocide: Lessons From the Rwanda Experience. Historical Perspective: Some Explanatory Factors.* Uppsala, Sweden: The Nordic Africa Institute, March 1996.

Sibomana, André. *Hope for Rwanda: Conversations with Laure Guilbert and Hervé Deguine.* London and Sterling, VA: Pluto Press, 1999.

THE
CHURCH
AND
POWER

"...I wish to recall now in particular the people and the Church of Rwanda, who these days are being tried by an upsetting tragedy linked in particular to the dramatic assassination of the Presidents of Rwanda and Burundi. With you Bishops here present, I am sharing this suffering caused by this new catastrophic wave of violence and death which, investing this well loved country, is making blood flow even from Priests, Religious Sisters and Catechists, innocent victims of an absurd hate.

With you, reunited in this African Synod, and in communion of spirit with the Bishops of Rwanda who could not be with us today, I feel the need to launch an appeal to stop that homicide of violence. Together with you, I raise my voice to tell all of you: stop these acts of violence! Stop these tragedies! Stop these fratricidal massacres!"

Pope John Paul II, Rome, 10 April 1994

PART I

THE CHURCH AND POWER

Raising Voices

John K. Roth

When the word *power* comes to mind, what kinds of power are likely to be mentioned first? Probably words such as *political* or *economic* or *military* come to mind immediately. Concepts such as *religious power* or *the power of Churches* are likely to be far down the list, if they come to mind at all. Those possibilities, however, do not eliminate the fact that there are significant relationships between Churches – or "the Church," as we sometimes say – and every form of power that the world contains. Indeed, as the Rwandan genocide shows, those relationships can be matters of life and death.

Preceding the words on this page, there is a statement from Pope John Paul II, that he made on 10 April 1994 as the killing escalated in Rwanda. The Pope indicated that he was raising his voice against those "fratricidal massacres," which, a few days later, he openly – and earlier than most – called genocidal. Every form of power includes, even depends upon, raising voices. Leaders have to raise their voices to state their principles, express their visions, and rally their supporters. Governments have to raise their voices to define policies, defend interests, and justify decisions. Supporters of leaders and governments have to raise their voices to back visions and policies; otherwise the power of principles and interests declines and even disappears.

Genocide depends on raising voices. It cannot exist unless divisions between people are constructed by speech, fears are expressed in ideology and propaganda, and killing is unleashed by voices that proclaim it to be necessary. Genocide also depends on "unraising" voices; it counts on the silencing of dissent and on the acquiescence of bystanders. Every voice unraised against genocide gives aid and comfort to those who call for and support that crime of crimes. Genocide can be prevented before it happens, and it can be stopped after it is under way. Neither prevention nor successful intervention, however, can happen without power. Rwanda's genocidal tragedy resulted from the fact that raising voices against it came too late and too little.

Here an objection may be raised: Raising voices may not count for much, because actions speak louder than words, and attention should be directed much more on what people do than on what they say. That point has validity, but it underestimates the relationship between raising voices and taking action. Genocide does not appear out of the blue. Intentions, plans, and many people are necessary to make it happen. Absent raising voices, the coordination of thought and action required by genocide will not and cannot be in place. The same can be said of resistance to genocide.

This book asks about the complicity of the Churches in the Rwandan genocide. Its first part particularizes that inquiry by considering relationships between Churches and power. Pope John Paul II's statement on 10 April 1994 indicates that a key aspect of religious power is its capacity and responsibility to raise voices against killing. As the chapters in Part I show, an important way to assess the performance of Churches during the Rwandan genocide must focus on the degree to which the Churches accepted or abandoned that responsibility. But the matter neither begins nor ends there, and that is why it is important to note not only the statement from John Paul II that precedes these introductory words but also this book's chronology.

Drawing attention to statements made and actions taken by Churches and their leaders before, during, and after the 1994 genocide in Rwanda, the chronology helps to underscore that religious power mixes and mingles with power that is political, economic, and even military. Religion can support, impede, or stand by as those powers do their work. The authors who contribute to this section on "The Church and Power" show that the complexities of those relationships must be clarified and focused if we are to answer well the many questions surrounding the Churches' responsibility regarding the Rwandan genocide. In their analyses, each and all, it will not be hard to see that much depended – and still does – on raising voices.

1

RELIGION AND THE RWANDAN GENOCIDE

SOME PRELIMINARY CONSIDERATIONS

Hubert G. Locke

Encounters between religion and the political sphere (or between Church and State as it is customary to depict such interactions in Western societies) have never lacked either intensity or complexity. The encounters, as we are witnessing in the present era, can involve severe clashes between what are essentially two competing arenas of ideology and authority. It is not surprising, therefore, to find that the outcomes of such encounters are not always predictable.

In the civil rights struggle in the United States, the Solidarity movement in Poland, and the collapse of the Communist regime in East Germany, religion is generally considered to have had a largely positive influence in the political sphere and on changes in state policy. In the latter two cases, religion had a decisive impact on the structures of the state itself. On the other hand, the account of religion's role in the rise of German National Socialism and the ability of the Nazi regime to maintain power for more than a decade is far less laudable.

Essentially, it is because of religion's normative role in society and the claims that are made for those values and principles which derive from religious teachings and traditions that religious institutions and their leaders find themselves under a special scrutiny whenever a society undergoes a major political crisis or upheaval. It was the obvious and immense contradiction between Christian principles and a state policy that resulted in the massacre of millions of European Jews that, in turn, stimulated interest in the role of the German Church during the Nazi era. Long before questions began to be asked about German universities, the German military, its courts, banks and other institutions, scholars, journalists and countless individual citizens were raising questions about the German Church and its response to the rise of the German Third Reich. A half-century later, a similar focus and similar questions – occasioned tragically by a similar catastrophe – are raised about the role of religion in the Rwandan genocide.

Questions regarding religion, of whatever sort, are inevitably questions about institutions – churches, mosques, synagogues, temples – and the people who participate in them. When seeking to establish what religious institutions do or fail to do, it is necessary to examine how the bodies of believers who make up the membership of the institutions behave. It is an unfortunate practice of many journalists and some scholars to assume and depict the behavior of clergy as a decisive reflection of what the religion's stance or posture is regarding political issues or situations. A fair appraisal of the role of religion in any societal crisis would take into account the response not only of clergy but also lay persons whose actions – positive or negative – if they are motivated by religious teaching or sentiment, are also expressions of the religion and its precepts.

Examining the actions and attitudes of the laity is but one of the more recent developments in the study of the German Churches during the Nazi period – a study that has proceeded apace for more than forty years. A great deal has been learned that should be useful to the more recent inquiries regarding the role of the Churches during the genocide in Rwanda. Principal among the lessons learned are the importance of asking the right questions – first about what actually occurred, then about what might have occurred, and finally about what can or should be expected of Churches in the aftermath of genocidal catastrophes.

A

The basic facts of what took place in Rwanda between April and June 1994 – that some 800,000 Rwandans, predominantly Tutsis, were massacred in a frenzy of bloodletting – is beyond dispute. These facts appear in a number of accounts of varying utility that are available to English-speaking readers. Factual details are a necessary beginning, but not the end-point for resolving the question of what occurred.

If, for example, we ask what it is that the Churches did in Rwanda during the course of the genocidal tragedy, we open up an enormous arena of dispute and confusion. In part, the confusion and the diverse responses reflect a lack of clarity regarding the question being asked. Were the Churches silent when they should have spoken? Did they back the wrong political regime? Did they help mastermind the genocide? Did clergy and laypersons – in their religious roles or capacities – actually participate in the slaughter?

It does not suffice to respond "all of the above" since there are clearly varying degrees of moral culpability in these four stances. The first suggests institutional timidity or indifference, the second possibly an inept political calculation or political naiveté, while the third and fourth responses imply a far more active, deliberate and sinister involvement. And if there are documented instances of clergy or other religious persons acting as actual participants in the slaughter (as there are – several members of religious orders and clergy have been indicted and convicted for their involvement), it leaves undetermined the precise nature of that participation, as well as whether the participation was an exceptional situation or part of a more pervasive pattern of religious complicity. Quite apart, therefore, from a concern for getting the facts straight is also the necessity of making explicit whatever the moral norm is by which the action or non-action of the Church is being measured.

These are the very problems that have presented themselves over the course of forty years of inquiry regarding the responses of the German Churches to the rise of the Nazi state. The broad outlines of what occurred in the first few years of the Church's encounter with the Nazi regime are well known – early opposition by many German Catholic prelates and clergy that was cut short by the signing of a concordat between the Vatican and the Nazi state; widespread initial support for the regime among Protestant leaders and laity followed by growing disillusion and dissent that led to a breach in the Protestant fold between Nazi supporters and those who took issue with that support. What is less clear, or less easily resolved, are answers to the same questions that are asked of the Churches in Rwanda – were the German Churches silent when they should have spoken? Was their dissent, where it did occur, directed against the political regime or only against their religious opponents? Was the Church in any way complicit in the genocide of the Jews and Gypsies? Were clergy or laity actually involved in the slaughter?

In part, these questions are factual but they are also questions of intent and, to some extent, of motive. The record of the Churches in Germany is largely the record of the main Protestant body – the Evangelical Church of Germany – and the Roman Catholic Church, together with that of several smaller bodies (primarily the German Methodist Church and the Jehovah's Witnesses). Seeking to determine whether the Churches in Rwanda helped mastermind the massacre that occurred requires examining the record of the Roman Catholic and at least a half-dozen Protestant denominations. It involves sifting through the testimonies of a large number of individuals who had various degrees of awareness of what was occurring in government circles, or being circulated by the media, or who were eyewitnesses to specific events. As one of the most insightful of the observers regarding the Rwandan genocide states: "… even with the wealth of information now available there is still too much that remains obscure. This is particularly true of the role of the Church in Rwanda, 1993-1994."[1]

B

If one then turns to the question or issue of what might have occurred in Rwanda, similar parallels and some significant differences with the saga of the Churches in Germany emerge. It is widely acknowledged that if the Churches were and are to play any meaningful role in genocide prevention, it must occur early in the sociopolitical process. This is the clear lesson in the case of Germany; it is an equally compelling conclusion regarding Rwanda. In Germany, the time for the Churches to act was in the years 1933-1938 – immediately after the Nazi seizure of power – when the first state-initiated policies of discrimination against Jews were being enacted, and before the government had managed to consolidate its reign of terror over German citizenry.

The potential significance of a strong stance by religious institutions at an early stage in the development of an unwelcome policy by a state is demonstrated most clearly in the German situation. In October 1939, a month after Germany's invasion of Poland and the beginning of the Second World War, Adolf Hitler signed a decree that authorized putting to death countless thousands of Germans who were mentally ill or physically handicapped and who were housed in state institutions.[2] Like many of the Third Reich's most notorious policies, this euthanasia decree was expected to be implemented surreptitiously with the least possible amount of public knowledge.

Word of the policy became known publicly and the outraged response of the Churches was widespread. In the Protestant camp, Bishop Theophilus Wurm twice sent blistering letters to the Minister of the Interior condemning the euthanasia edict. The director of the principal Protestant institution for handicapped persons at Bethel (actually, a cluster of institutions comprising an entire community) held the federal Minister of Health at bay for a year, utilizing various devices to avoid or postpone the policy's implementation. In the end, only a handful of persons at Bethel fell victim to the euthanasia decree.[3] (Ironically, the director of the institutions of Bethel had been elected in 1934 as bishop of the Evangelical Church, a post in which he proved unable to withstand the pressures of the Nazi government.) In the German Catholic fold, Archbishops Bertram and Faulhaber were especially outspoken. This combined reaction of the Churches sufficed to bring about the official discontinuance of the edict (there is some dispute as to whether the policy continued clandestinely in some regions but the government formally announced its termination).[4]

Unlike the German situation in which the majority of the populace belonged to one of the two principal Christian Churches, the Rwandan people were divided along both religious and socioethnic lines. The genocide in the German Third Reich was principally the slaughter of Jews – a tiny, non-Christian minority in Germany in a society that was overwhelmingly Christian (Jews were one-tenth of one percent of the German populace) – and the subsequent massacre of huge numbers of Jews in Nazi-occupied Europe, but again in countries that were predominantly Christian.

In Rwanda, the entire populace was chiefly Christian. The genocide did not occur along religious fault-lines. Instead, Christians who were Hutus murdered Christians who were Tutsis – in many cases members of the same denomination. Socioethnic divisions in Rwanda trumped Christian commitments and denominational affiliations. If one asks, therefore, what might the Churches have done in Rwanda to stem the slaughter, the question requires a recognition that Christianity, at best, appears to have been a thin veneer of religiosity over basic and deep-seated cultural, economic, and political realities. In this respect, the situation regarding religion in Rwanda may be much more akin to that of religion in Northern Ireland than in Serbia or Bosnia where religious affiliation also defines ethnicity and nationality, or Germany where religion in the Nazi era was an institutional feature of the state. If there is a lesson to be derived from the Rwandan experience, it is that religion, in the final analysis, may not be a sufficiently strong inducement to engage in ethically responsible behavior – strong enough at least to outweigh the influence of social class or ethnic and cultural tradition.

C

As to the question of what can or should be expected of Churches in the aftermath of genocidal occurrences, there has been a pattern of response that is similar in the cases of both Germany and Rwanda. In Germany, the Evangelical Church issued a series of confessions – the first was offered immediately after the war's end and, with each successive pronouncement, the Church became more direct in acknowledging its failure to speak out on the plight and ultimately the fate of the Jews. The Roman Catholic Church was slower in responding; its acknowledgements have come principally in statements issued by the pontiff, John Paul II.

Rwanda, in the case of at least one denomination, has followed the same course. On the same day that a Seventh Day Adventist minister and his son, a physician, were convicted as participants in the genocide by the International Criminal Tribunal for Rwanda at Arusha, the General Conference of the Seventh Day Adventist Church acknowledged "with sadness that some of our church members turned against their fellow members and their neighbors. We are saddened that the accused did not act in harmony with the principles of their church. We offer an apology."[5]

The Seventh Day Adventist Church provides a pertinent example of the problems and dilemmas faced by the Churches in Rwanda both during and after the genocide in that nation, as well as the questions that remain unresolved from the slaughter. The Adventist Church has received special scrutiny because of the conviction of one of its pastors; the conviction highlights the problem of trying to achieve closure in the aftermath of such an occurrence.

The approximately 350,000 members of the Adventist Church in Rwanda make it the second largest Christian Church in the country. Some 10,000 members and over 200 workers of the Church are said to have perished during the slaughter. Testimony given at the trial in Arusha indicates that 6,000-7,000 members perished in a notably brutal, single incident at the Adventist Church and hospital in Mugonero on 16 April 1994. The president of the West Rwandan Seventh Day Adventist Association is the pastor indicted and convicted for having conveyed perpetrators of the genocide to the church and hospital at Mugonero and then abandoned the churchgoers and their neighbors who were inside to "machete-wielding attackers."[6]

The pastor, the Reverend Elizaphan Ntakirutimana, is alleged to be "the first clergyman convicted of genocide in an international court of justice."[7] He has been sentenced to ten years in prison for aiding and abetting in the genocide. (His son, the medical doctor, received a twenty-five-year sentence for committing genocide and "crimes against humanity.") Both the prosecutor and witnesses at the trial, however, suggest that the pastor's guilt essentially stems from his failure to warn the people hiding in the church of their impending fate. He and his son, according to the prosecutor, owed those taking refuge in the church and hospital, "a duty of care." Their failure to do so constituted "extreme indifference" and "reckless disregard" for the lives of those sheltered in the two Mugonero institutions.[8] We have here, then, a standard of conduct sanctionable not only by law but under the most basic rules of religious leadership – the responsibility of a pastor for the nurture and protection of those who are in his charge.

This situation, however, puts the charge of genocide and participation in genocide in a new light. Here we do not have direct involvement in the murders or, as far as any testimony submitted in the trial shows, an indication of any participation in planning for the slaughter that occurred. In religious terms, the crime of Pastor Ntakirutimana was the sin of omission. In previous incidents of conflict between Hutus and Tutsis, the churches had served as effective refuge sites. Rwandans were accustomed to fleeing to churches and finding protection from invaders. In 1994, the places of refuge became scenes of slaughter and the fact that a religious leader did not, apparently, use his influence to forestall such made his lack of action reprehensible.

D

It is clear, then, that both in law and by the standards of religious teaching and practice, societies look to religious institutions and their leaders to display behavior that may not be expected or required of other leaders in the society. This, however, poses problems and questions that religion, in general, and the Christian Churches, in particular, have yet to resolve.

It may, for example, seem self-evident that religion in all of its variant forms should consider genocide a crime; if so, most major religious traditions have not seen fit to declare as much. Religion continues to operate, in this sphere, on moral assumptions developed and articulated three millennia ago. All major religions have proscriptions against murder or the act of taking an individual life, but genocide, especially in the century just past, presents the modern world with a new form of mass murder, instigated and implemented under official government auspices, that requires a new set of sanctions. Genocide received such in international law in the International Treaty on Genocide in 1950; it warrants the moral opprobrium that would come from specific proclamations by religious bodies to the effect that genocide is a monstrous violation of the most basic of religious principles and values.

Quite beyond this, other questions beg attention. Concepts of forgiveness and reconciliation are at the core of Christian teaching. Rooted as they are in the Christian Scriptures and reinforced by both liturgy and sacrament in some Christian traditions, forgiveness is seen as an essential step in healing breaches in trust and confidence that arise out of tragic circumstances, and in establishing the basis for new relationships. Reconciliation also is viewed as a means of overcoming past errors – either of omission or commission. As an act of reuniting or bringing back into harmony that which has been ruptured, reconciliation is considered essential if communities are to move forward in the aftermath of severe periods of crisis and upheaval.

In the aftermath of genocidal experiences, these concerns often become a principal preoccupation of the Churches. Too often, however, the Church finds itself caught up in the language and processes of forgiveness and reconciliation without having taken the harder, first steps of remorse and penance. Victims have a right to seek and expect authentic indications of sorrow – expressed in concrete, meaningful acts of contrition – before they are asked to consider forgiveness and reconciliation.

It may be, in one respect, that the Church and much of modern society along with it have become morally mesmerized by the examples of truth and reconciliation commissions that have operated with such power and influence in South Africa and in several Latin American nations. One cannot help but acknowledge and applaud these displays of individual and societal forgiveness; they should not be allowed, however, to displace or overwhelm the consideration of those situations in which some other kind of process to restore harmony and social balance is needed.

Victims of genocide will ask, for example, whether the concerns for forgiveness and reconciliation override or should be permitted to override the concern for justice – a concern that the Church also insists is an essential part of its mission and message. Justice may well precede – it may, in fact, preclude – forgiveness and reconciliation, at least until the perpetrators of genocide have been punished for their deeds.

Victims of genocide will also ask whether the Church can dispense forgiveness to those who commit genocide. This is one of the most difficult but necessary issues with which the Church must wrestle. Dispensing forgiveness is a power, according to the Christian Scriptures, that Jesus gave to his apostles. In one of the major Christian traditions, that power is bestowed on priests of the Church; in other Christian bodies, forgiveness is a pronouncement that automatically follows confession, in general recognition that those who acknowledge their sins are forgiven of them.

All of this, however, overlooks the situation of the person who has been aggrieved – the victim – in the process. Victims rightly ask if anyone has the right – not to mention the power (!) – to forgive the acts of perpetrators of genocide except those against whom those acts were directed.

These questions were first raised in considering the response of the Churches to the virtual destruction of the European Jewish community some sixty years ago. That they remain unanswered today is an indication of how far religion and, in the case of the Christian community, the Churches and their religious leadership have to go to address one of the modern world's most persistent problems.

Notes

1. Linda Melvern, "The Responsibility to Protect," a paper delivered at a Special Seminar on the Church and Genocide in Rwanda, 21-24 March 2003, St. Edward's House, Westminster, London.
2. Ernst Helmreich, *The German Churches Under Hitler* (Detroit: Wayne State University Press, 1979), 312. (The decree extended "authority to specified doctors that those incurably sick can be granted a 'mercy death'" and its implementation was placed in the hands of the Reich Public Health Officer in the Ministry of the Interior).
3. Ibid., 313-314.
4. Ibid., 313. (Hitler suspended the euthanasia program on 24 August 1941.)
5. Alita Byrd, "Searching for Truth in Reports of the Sabbath Massacre," *Spectrum* 31, No. 2, (Spring 2003), 41.
6. Ibid., 40, 26.
7. Ibid., 26.
8. Ibid., 36.

2
GENOCIDE IN RWANDA 1994 – AN ANGLICAN PERSPECTIVE

*Roger W. Bowen**

The genocide in Rwanda poses searching questions for all the Churches. In the 1991 census ninety percent of Rwandans called themselves Christians – how could this catastrophe have happened in such a predominantly Christianised country after years of evangelisation by both Catholic and Protestant missions? As the second largest Church in Rwanda, the Anglican Church, known as the *Eglise Episcopale au Rwanda,* has played a significant role in the nation's development. The Anglican Church has been involved with education, medical work, agricultural development, and training in industrial skills, as well as the work of evangelisation and planting new congregations. For many in the Anglican Communion, Rwanda was synonymous with a great movement of the Holy Spirit in the 1930s and 1940s which became known as the East African Revival. It swept through the whole of East Africa, but many would trace its source to events in both Uganda and Rwanda in the 1930s which brought new life to Protestant Churches throughout the region. How is it, people ask, that Churches marked by such a profound revival seem to have been drawn into this appalling slaughter, and by and large have been unable to deal with the ethnic and power issues within the Christian community itself, let alone in the wider society?

Nearly ten years after the genocide, some Anglican leaders remain in exile, at least one was arrested but died before being brought to trial, and a deep heart-searching continues. In this chapter I seek to explore the historical roots of the Anglican Church in Rwanda and offer some reflection on the situation within the Anglican Church in Rwanda which may have played a part in the catastrophic events of 1994.

*This essay originally appeared in *Anvil*, Volume 13, number 1, 1996, but it has been re-written and substantially developed for this book.

ROGER W. BOWEN

The background to the Anglican Church in Rwanda

To understand the Anglican Church in Rwanda, it is important to understand the context and background from which the British missionaries came who founded the Anglican Church there. Anglican missionary work in Rwanda began in the 1920s and the missionaries came out of a particular context in the Church of England at the time. They were heirs of theological controversy at home, which focused around the authority of Scripture and attitudes to Biblical criticism. It was the background to the splits between the Cambridge Inter-Collegiate Christian Union (CICCU) and the Student Christian Movement (SCM) in 1910, the separation of the Bible Churchman's Missionary Society (BCMS) from the Church Missionary Society (CMS) in 1922, and the establishing of the special relationship between the Rwanda Mission and its parent society, the CMS, in 1926. The more conservative attitude to Scripture, and the associated controversy, led to an emphasis on evangelism rather than any engagement with the public life of the nation or critique of the sociopolitical context. Indeed, the missionaries were dependent on the goodwill of the colonial administration and sought to be apolitical. This, in fact, was impossible, as a telling extract from Dr. Joe Church's diaries reveals. In 1959, as Hutu massacres of Tutsis took place, the missionaries sought to be outside of politics and Dr. Church writes, "[W]e protested in two memoranda our non-participation in politics as a Mission but our stations became places of refuge for those who were being hunted and killed. One of these was the Queen Mother who came as a patient to Gahini Hospital and became a refugee, and we did not allow her or any others to be molested. This drew the fire on us and seemed unavoidable."[1] In caring for the fleeing Tutsis, they were inevitably seen as political.

Besides being heirs of theological controversy, many of the Anglican missionaries were also influenced by the pietist tradition, the Keswick holiness teaching and the search for the "higher life." This hunger for a deeper experience of the transforming power of God in one's life was a deep undercurrent leading to the outbreak of revival. This is not the place to outline the history of the East African Revival (EAR), which has been done much more competently in other places. But it is interesting that one of the marks of that revival was that it did address very deeply the ethnic issue. First of all it addressed the issue of black and white, as "ground was level at the foot of the Cross." A new fellowship of forgiven sinners – African and European – was formed, who knew that they had been made brothers and sisters in Christ through being cleansed in His precious blood. Equally, the

38

emphasis on repentance and the Cross of Christ led to a new sense of identity "in Christ" where there is neither Jew nor Greek (Galatians 3.28), Hutu nor Tutsi. At its best, the revival movement spoke very directly to the ethnic issue. The movement was also characterized by fellowship meetings, which were marked by mutual confession of sin, Bible study, prayer and testimony, and mutual encouragement. Studies of the rise of African Independent Churches have described them as movements in search of "a place to feel at home." In the revival many African Christians did find such a place and a genuinely African expression of spirituality. This movement profoundly marked the Anglican Church in Rwanda at its foundation.

It is also clear that the founding British missionaries inherited the false anthropology which was later used to lay the foundations for ethnic conflict in the future. This false anthropology saw the Tutsis in Rwanda as migrants from Ethiopia. So, in Dr. Church's diaries he contrasts the Bahutu with the "tall dignified Batutsi, often called the giants of Africa, an ancient cattle people who were supposed to have migrated over the centuries through Africa from Ethiopia with their flocks."[2] In the official account of the beginnings of the Rwanda Mission, a similar assumption is made when the author writes, "Several centuries ago a tall, slender, haughty, aristocratic people known as the Tutsi began the second conquest of Rwanda. Reputed to have come from Ethiopia or the Nile Valley, the Tutsi were the outer fringe of a great southbound pastoral migration."[3] This false anthropology was to climax in the genocide in Rwanda with the appalling exhortation to "send the Tutsi back to Ethiopia by the Nyabarongo River!"

In what follows I want to reflect on some of the possible inadequacies in the theology which undergirded the Church in Rwanda, and some of the issues which are raised. These issues are very stark in the context of Rwanda, but are also deeply relevant to our own situations and a challenge to the integrity of our Christian witness.

1. Church and State

"A Church too closely identified with a regime shares its fate." The Roman Catholic Archbishop of Rwanda had sat on the Central Committee of the ruling party of President Habyarimana's government. Some members of the Anglican hierarchy were public supporters of the former President and courted his favor and patronage. There appears to have been little ability to maintain a critical distance vis-à-vis the government authorities. The Church hierarchies remained "too closely linked with the ruling regime to be a credible voice of protest. Their many declarations during the genocide were insignificant and inadequate. Church reaction was too late and too little."[4] From a Protestant perspective, one is bound to ask whether the theological foundations bequeathed to the newly independent African Church by the missionaries were adequate to deal with Church-State issues. I have already mentioned the pietist tradition of the missionaries and this was reinforced within the Anglican Church by Dr. Joe Church's frequent use of the Scofield Bible with its pre-millennialist interpretations. Dr. Church in his diaries makes reference to preparing the Bible readings for the Kabale Convention in 1935 "based as always on the Scofield Bible chain references."[5] Scofield's pre-millennialist perspective meant that, in his own words to a prophetic conference in Philadelphia in 1918, there was "no hope for humanity except in the personal return of the Lord of glory."[6] This theological combination can lead to one of two reactions: either the withdrawal from the public life of the nation into a spiritual ghetto, or a naïve and uncritical support of whoever is in power, with Biblical justification being frequently drawn from Romans chapter 13. Both these reactions are discernible within the life of the Anglican Church in Rwanda.

2. Injustice and impunity

In Rwanda the lesson had not been learned that an unresolved injustice in one generation would return to haunt the next. The Tutsi exiles from the early 1960s had never been allowed back to Rwanda and had remained in exile for thirty years as stateless people. The Church in Rwanda failed to plead their cause, perhaps because, in the Anglican Church at least, the leadership was exclusively Hutu. It raises the issue as to whether the Church should speak up for any group treated unjustly, or only when the Church's interests are threatened? In our own context, if a Muslim minority is being discriminated against and treated unjustly, do we protest on their behalf, or remain silent because we see Muslims as in competition with us for the religious allegiance of our people? Gross abuses of human rights were taking place within Rwanda long before the crisis of April 1994, yet the Churches by and large did not speak up. There has been a failure to see that abuse of human beings, created in the image of God, is a very serious issue that the Church cannot ignore if it is to be true to its Lord.

The history of Rwanda and Burundi is scarred by outbreaks of appalling ethnic conflict of an horrific nature. In all cases there has never been a bringing to justice of the major perpetrators. A climate of impunity has been created which gives the impression that people can get away with such behavior without fear of being brought to trial. There is little doubt that the assassination of President Ndadaye of Burundi in October 1993, and the fact that no one had been brought to justice for that event, gave the green light to the Rwandan government that they too could get away with their genocidal plans without fear of arrest and trial. Prior to the genocide in Rwanda, there had been outbreaks of ethnic violence and considerable abuse of human rights, yet the Churches failed to call for the perpetrators to be brought to justice, and for justice to be seen to be done. The climate of impunity created a climate of confidence for those bent on maintaining their power and influence at all costs.

3. Ethnicity and identity

In many parts of the world today, in situations of economic/social/ political stress, we see people falling back on their ethnic identity with often violent results. In Rwanda in a situation of insecurity and threat caused by the Rwandan Patriotic Front (RPF) invasion in 1990, by the imposition of Structural Adjustment Programs leading to high urban unemployment, by the imposition of multi-party politics, and by economic decline, people fell back on their ethnic identity, and were encouraged to do so by unscrupulous politicians. Sadly, within the Church itself the mutual fears between Hutus and Tutsis were not faced up to and dealt with. Within the Anglican Church it was hard for Tutsis to advance in leadership while the hierarchy remained solidly Hutu. The issue, which in the past in times of revival had been addressed so powerfully, was allowed to remain unresolved. The challenge to find a deeper, more fundamental identity "in Christ" where there is no Jew nor Greek, Hutu nor Tutsi, seems to have been forgotten by many. There were glorious exceptions to this where Christians who were also Hutu helped and protected their Tutsi neighbors from the *interahamwe* militias. By and large, however, the Church had allowed these ethnic tensions to continue unresolved, often below the surface, until conditions occurred where the issue exploded beyond their control in horrific violence. What happened in Rwanda is a salutary reminder that the fear and pain preventing the Church from addressing a painful tension within itself needs to be overcome if one is to avoid the far more horrific consequences of not facing it. I believe there may be lessons here for us around ethnic issues within our own Church, but also regarding such issues as sexuality.

4. What sort of evangelization?

Bishop Nsengiyumva (Roman Catholic) of Rwanda said, "The Christian message is not being heard. After a century of evangelization we have to begin again because the best catechists, those who filled our churches on Sundays, were the first to go out with machetes in their hands."[7] It is a heart cry which is relevant to all the Churches in Rwanda and perhaps elsewhere. I am reminded of a comment made to me by a French priest in Burundi, "We have sacramentalised the Barundi, we have not evangelized them." The catastrophe of Rwanda raises the issue of how deeply the Gospel has penetrated both individuals and the culture, and what sort of evangelism is needed in order to address the issues that really trouble Africans. From the Protestant side, the revivalism-style of evangelism can be very authoritarian, giving the impression that the evangelist knows what people need, and all they need to do is sit back and listen to him. In contrast, there is a need to listen to people's questions and concerns – a need for a humble, listening evangelism, which, like Jesus, asks of inquirers, "What are you looking for?" (John 1.38) Such an approach might help towards the Gospel being allowed to address the deepest anxieties and fears of people and then penetrate more deeply into the culture.

5. What sort of spirituality?

The pietist, pre-millennialist background of missionary founders of many of the Protestant Churches in Rwanda and the experience of revival have already been mentioned. These played their part in the spirituality which developed within the Rwandan Churches. A number of features of this spirituality give cause for concern and challenge the Church in our own context.

i) Converts not disciples

The revival background of the Church in Rwanda has been strong on the evangelistic task but often weak on the Christian training and discipleship. There would be many calls in preaching to "repent and believe the Gospel," but little teaching on how to live out Christian discipleship in the secular world and how to be "salt and light" in society. The Church needed David Bosch's reminder that "People are not called to repentance and conversion solely with the purpose of securing a seat on the train to heaven: the purpose of conversion is to become followers of Christ, to be enlisted in His service."[8] The Church in Rwanda had been growing in numbers, as it is widely in sub-Saharan Africa. However, it is a sharp reminder that mere growth in numbers, without a quality of costly discipleship, is empty and powerless to confront the pressures of evil.

ii) Inadequate view of sin

Perhaps because of the individualistic background of the missionary founders, or because of the surprisingly individualistic nature of Rwandan culture in contrast to other African cultures, the Church has operated with a very privatized and inadequate view of sin. The challenge to repentance has usually focused on a fairly limited range of private morality – lying, stealing, adultery, and drunkenness. However, there is little awareness of the solidarities of sin in which we are embedded as members of society. In his sympathetic critique of the East African revival, Max Warren comments that "sin tends to be simplified to the sin of the individual... the corporate nature of man is lost to view and the full magnitude of evil most seriously underestimated."[9]

In the same article, Warren reminds us of the "collective unconscious down into which stretch the roots of every individual life"[10] and this is horrifically revealed when the ethnic solidarities are manipulated in an act of genocide. Ironically, the revival doctrine of sin underestimates the power and depth of evil, and by focusing on personal/private morality is quite inadequate to tackle the hideous strength of structural evil and corporate sin manifested in an act of genocide.

iii) Use of Scripture

The experience of revival in the Rwandan Church sometimes led to the Church tacitly affirming the canon of the whole of Scripture, but in reality operating with a "canon within the canon." This is always a danger for any Church or individual to focus on favorite books or passages in the Bible rather than allowing, in Pauline terms, the "whole counsel of God" to inform our spirituality. Within the Rwandan Church, there has been a lack of teaching on the whole counsel of God, and exposing God's people to the whole revelation of His Word from Genesis to Revelation. In some cases, all Scripture is interpreted to give the same message, often interpreted through the lens of the revival experience, rather than letting the diversity within the Bible be heard. Inadequate exposure to the whole counsel of God has meant that Church leaders were often left without the theological tools to engage with the complexities of relating to newly independent African states, to issues of economics, development, justice, human rights, and ethnicity.

iv) Substitution of testimonies for Biblical exposition/teaching

In his study of revival movements in South Africa, Dr. Sundkler noted the danger of such an emphasis being put on sharing personal testimonies that Biblical instruction was neglected. Within the revival in East Africa the fellowship meetings put great emphasis on the sharing of testimonies and this was an enormous encouragement to one another. However, it did lead to a lack of Biblical input and instruction, with the danger that personal experience becomes more important than the Word of God. We need reminding that the Word of God may be challenging us to face up to and move into areas of human life we have not yet experienced, and our personal experience continually needs to be challenged in this way. Equally, we need reminding that the Truth as it is in Jesus is always greater than our personal experience of that Truth. The danger of an overemphasis on personal testimony is that it leads participants to feel that their grasp of truth is exhaustive and they are blind to other implications of the Truth. Max Warren's comment on meeting William Nagenda, one of the Ugandan leaders of revival, is worth noting here. "He is able with single-minded devotion to pursue what he sees to be true. But he is unaware that Truth is more than he can see."[11] The truth of Christ is indeed more than any one of us can see and it will be only with "all the saints" that we can come to know "how wide and long and high and deep is the love of Christ" (Ephesians 3:18).

6. What sort of obedience?

In Rwanda people killed because they were told to do so by the government, local burgomasters and the radio. Obedience to authority is inculcated within African culture and we need to ask whether the Churches have adopted the same approach. Within the Catholic tradition, there has been an unquestioning submission to Papal authority. Within the Protestant tradition in Rwanda, you are wise to obey your Bishop because your livelihood depends on his goodwill. More importantly, the whole teaching method in Rwanda, both in churches and the state education system, does not encourage reflection and questioning. It is often an exercise in rote learning, which can then be repeated back to the examiners on examination day. I remember an American colleague of mine in Burundi who was expelled from the country during a time of Church-State conflict. During his interrogation, one of the main accusations against him focused on his theological teaching method which provoked reflection and questioning, rather than giving the students the answers. The authorities saw this as highly subversive and duly expelled him from the country. In Rwanda, the Churches' authoritarian teaching style that encouraged little reflection avoided the crucial issues troubling the society, inculcated uncritical obedience to government authorities, and failed to teach Christians that situations can be so dire that "we must obey God rather than man" (Acts 5:29).

7. What sort of leadership?

Another of the tragic ironies of Rwanda was that as the nation was being pushed politically towards more democratic structures, the structures of the

Church and the style of leadership offered remained authoritarian. Prior to the genocide, some of the Anglican leadership had brought public shame and disgrace on the Church, to the despair of the laity, through an open and public conflict between two Bishops that nearly led to schism within the Church. Questions are raised about the accountability of Church leaders to the whole people of God, and what mechanisms there can be for the people of God as a whole to challenge and, if necessary, change their leaders. There are also questions about the lifestyle of Bishops and Church leaders and whether they lead to an alienation from the mass of people who, in a country like Rwanda, are very poor, peasant farmers. This has been acknowledged openly by the Roman Catholic Church in Rwanda, but in some cases applies within other Christian communities as well. "Having access to foreign currency for projects, many Church leaders developed lifestyles that alienated them from the struggles of common people and made them appear part of the exploitative upper class."[12] One might ask whether a Church leader visiting his diocese in Rwanda in a chauffeur-driven Mercedes really gives the right message about servant leadership modeled on the servanthood of Christ?

8. Role of media

The catastrophe in Rwanda has raised very sharply the issue of the enormous power and influence of media and disinformation, particularly in a context where the vast majority of the listeners are illiterate and have no other means of verifying the truth or falsity of what they are hearing. Both sides in the Rwandan conflict had their radio station. The RPF "Radio Muhabura" was very successful in communicating to the Western media a righteous image of a well-disciplined army with a just cause, doing battle with a corrupt and abusive government, bent on genocide as a means to maintain its power. The Rwandan government used the infamous *Radio Télévision Libre des Mille Collines* to pump out vicious and racist incitement to "kill more Tutsis, the graves aren't full enough." The unscrupulous manipulation of a largely illiterate peasant population was horrifyingly effective. Part of the policy was to demonize the enemy. The government propaganda referred to the RPF invaders as *inyenzi*, cockroaches, and you crush cockroaches! Once the enemy is demonized and seen as sub-human, you can do terrible things to them, which people could never bring themselves to do if they saw them as human beings like themselves, (cf. the Nazis' attitude to the Jews). In the Rwandan context, the Churches did not seem to have access to the media to counteract the lies and disinformation of the government-controlled media. It is an irony that in Africa generally, the Churches pioneered the written word in encouraging literacy and Bible translation, but have lagged behind on the use of modern electronic media. In the Rwandan context, "Pastoral letters alone were no match for professional radio propaganda."[13] Maybe this raises issues for us in the debate about religious broadcasting and the access to the media allowed to the Churches.

9. Land and population

Rwanda was the most densely populated country in Africa. There was a dramatic increase in population from 2.8 million in 1962 to an estimated 7.5 million in 1990, with a density of 285 inhabitants per square kilometer. Scarcity of land is a major issue in the conflict and often, perhaps at subconscious levels, the violence and mass murder of whole populations has been motivated by a desire for living space. Certainly in a society where the vast majority of the population lives off the produce of their plot of land, the issue of land is quite critical.

10. International dimensions

Within the global village in which we live, no nation can avoid being influenced by events and policies that are decided outside its borders. Many of these events are beyond the power of national Churches to influence. However, Churches such as the Roman Catholic and Anglican, which have international networks, do have both the opportunity and responsibility to make their voice heard. It is sad that through the Anglican Communion, and its observer at the UN, some of the issues affecting Rwanda were not brought to the attention of the world Anglican Communion and the international community before the crisis of April 1994. Like all African cities, Kigali was teeming with thousands of young jobless people living off informal economic activities, occasional labor, petty thieving, and prostitution. This hopeless situation of African urban youth has been made worse by Structural Adjustment Programs imposed by the World Bank/International Monetary Fund. This pool of jobless, urban youth with no hope for a better future was easy prey for political agitators and unscrupulous political extremists who recruited them for the *interahamwe* militias.

The involvement of foreign nations in the Rwandan conflict is also clear. The Ugandan government infringed the OAU (Organization of African Unity) charter by allowing part of its army to leave and attack a neighboring country. The French government actively supported the

Habyarimana regime and supplied them with weapons and military advisers. The UN decision to withdraw yet more of its pitifully small force in Kigali at the beginning of the massacres gave a clear message to the militias that no one was going to stop them killing. The situation has also raised again the questions about the international arms trade. Who has armed Rwanda, one of the poorest nations in the world, and provided them with weapons of destruction rather than the economic aid they need to build a stable and just society? As a world Communion, I wonder if the Anglican Church could have done more to bring the developing situation in Rwanda to world attention? As the representative at that time of the main Anglican mission society relating to the Anglican Church in Rwanda, I bear some responsibility for a failure in partnership, which leads to my last point.

11. A flawed partnership

As Anglican Churches in Africa and other parts of the world have become independent, a partnership relationship has been established with the founding Churches and their mission agencies. Partnership in mission is the dominant theme in Anglican relationships. But one may ask in the context of Rwanda, as perhaps elsewhere in Africa, whether the mission agencies at least have so leaned over backwards to avoid the charge of colonialism that they have failed to challenge their partner Churches? Within both Rwanda and the Rwandan Church, we were aware of many of these issues and yet, as their partners, we largely failed to challenge them as equal partners and to "speak the truth in love" (Ephesians 4:15). In Ezekiel 33 the prophet is challenged to be a watchman for the House of Israel to warn the people of God of impending danger. Both the national Church in Rwanda and its partners overseas have largely failed in this role of watchman. Sometimes it is easier for outsiders to perceive better what is happening than the nationals themselves, who are too close and too involved. This gives a special challenge to partners such as ourselves as we relate to Churches overseas. It also means that we in the Church in the UK need to be open to the challenge and prophetic insight of our partners from overseas. We need reminding that we are members one of another in the Body of Christ, and therefore have a responsibility to mutually challenge and encourage one another. We desperately need each other within the international community of the Church, because it is only "with all the saints" (Ephesians 3:18) that we can grow into Christian maturity and, hopefully, avoid some of the distortions in Church life that may have played their part in the Rwandan tragedy.

Notes

1. J. E. Church, *Quest for the Highest* (Carlisle, UK: Paternoster, 1981), 252.

2. Ibid., 33-34.

3. Patricia St. John, *Breath of Life*, (London: The Norfolk Press, 1971), 199.

4. Father Wolfgang Schonecke, "What does the Rwanda tragedy say to AMECEA Churches?", AMECEA Documentation Service 17/1994 No. 424, P. O. Box 21400, Nairobi, Kenya.

5. Church, 116.

6. Quoted in D. Carson (ed.), *Biblical Interpretation and the Church* (Carlisle, UK: Paternoster, 1984), 200.

7. Quoted by Richard Dowden, Africa Editor of *The Independent, Vocation for Justice*, Vol. 8, No. 2 (Summer 1994).

8. David Bosch, "Mission – An Attempt at a Definition," paper delivered to the Dutch Reformed Church in Southern Africa, printed in *Church Scene*, 25 April 1986.

9. Max Warren, *Revival – An Enquiry* (London: SCM Press, 1954), 77.

10. Ibid., 79.

11. Quoted by Kevin Ward in "Obedient Rebels – the relationship between the early 'Balokole' and the Church of Uganda: the Mukono crisis of 1941," *Journal of Religion in Africa* XIX, 3 (1989): 222.

12. Schonecke, 4.

13. Schonecke, 5.

3

THE CHURCH AND THE GENOCIDE IN RWANDA

Octave Ugirashebuja

> "...there will be more rejoicing in heaven over one sinner
> who repents than over ninety-nine righteous persons
> who do not need to repent."
> *(Luke 15:7)*

Introduction

From the beginning of its mission in Rwanda, the Catholic Church was deeply involved in all the events of that country's history. Unquestionably, the Church contributed to the religious, cultural and economic development of Rwanda, and that is to its credit, but one must recognize as well that the 1994 genocide of the Tutsis was also, in many ways, the Church's failure, and perhaps its sin. Until the Catholic Church in Rwanda, and beyond, can courageously accept this fact and humbly mourn with all Rwandan people, it will remain in a difficult position in regard to its mission today, and in the future.

The facts

"A Hutu Church in a Tutsi State"

"A Hutu Church in a Tutsi State" is how Ian Linden characterized the Catholic Church of Rwanda from 1900 to 1920.[1] Indeed, Catholic missionaries – like the German and Belgian colonizers of the twentieth century – considered Rwanda a country of two completely different human groups – which they later called "ethnic groups" and "races" – the Hutus, who made up the peasant masses, and the Tutsis, who were considered to be aristocrats. The Catholic missionaries and colonizers never took into account the specific unity of the Hutu and the Tutsi peoples, their common pride which made them Rwandan, nor the fact that ninety percent of the Tutsis belonged to the masses of poor peasants. As historian Jean-Paul Gouteux comments: "The 'racialization' or 'ethnicisation' of these communities is a modern, Western phenomenon. It results directly from the concept of the missionaries and colonizers, even if it was also adopted by the natives, both Hutu and Tutsi."[2]

From the beginning, the White Fathers (*Pères Blancs*) felt compelled to choose the ethnic group with whom they would collaborate. Cardinal Lavigerie, the founder of the White Fathers, the name by which the Society of the Missionaries of Our Lady of Africa is known, had given his priests clear instructions: "To have the sympathy of the chiefs, in order to convert them first." The White Fathers would have been willing to follow their founder's directive, but the first missionaries were discouraged after disastrous contacts with the court of Yuhi VI Musinga, the King who never converted to Christianity. We know that Father Alphonse Brard, Superior of the first mission station in Save, admired the Tutsis for their "intelligence, liveliness, and curiosity, and also for their discreet, appropriate manner" and that he despised the Hutus. But, as Ian Linden has written, "after a few months of frequent and frustrating relations with the Tutsi, their illusions disappeared. Father Brard started to hate the Tutsi and their *garagu*."[3] This was also the case for many missionaries who turned readily to the Hutus.

In 1910, the 4,500 Christians in Rwanda were largely Hutus and the seminarians preparing for the Catholic priesthood also were Hutus. This was the beginning of a relationship of "conflict and contradiction" between the Catholic missionary Church and the Tutsis. From the beginning, the missionaries would have liked "a Hutu Church in a Hutu State," but this was not immediately possible. It was necessary to wait until the advent of the first two Hutu-dominated Republics, in 1960 and 1973 respectively. These were the regimes which – under the Church's almost indifferent eye – prepared and carried out the genocide of the Tutsis.

For the German colonizers who sought collaborators during the years of their administration (from approximately 1899 to 1916), there was no doubt that it was necessary to work with the Tutsi royal court as well as the Tutsi people. The missionaries, however, remained convinced that their true partners were the Hutus. Thus, there were two points of view which should have been complementary, because each group of Rwandans certainly had its particular qualities. One commentator, the Canon de Lacger, for example, describes the importance of the Hutus in the country's development: "It is the farmer who seizes the land, transforms it, imposes a seal of humanity on it, creates the historical landscape. In Rwanda, this conqueror, this transformer was the bantu peasant, the muhutu. He was the one who cut back the forest, traced the first network of lasting pathways, scattered the countryside with green enclosures and homes... "[4] Rather than appreciating the merits of the two groups, the missionaries and the colonizers placed the Hutus and Tutsis in opposition to each other.

Admiration later turned to hatred, as was evident from the beginning of Catholic missionary-Tutsi relations. The same phenomenon was to be repeated at the end of the 1950s, at the time of the Hutu social revolution, but in a radical and definitive way, and this, after thirty years of collaboration and "mutual admiration." The hatred developed even to the point of accepting the extermination of the Tutsis. Monsignor Léon Classe was concerned about the anti-Tutsi animosity at the heart of the clergy and did everything in his power when he was Bishop of Rwanda to contain it, helped by the first resident German governor, Richard Kandt.[5] From the 1920s, the virulence of the hatred was momentarily stopped by a series of practical and pragmatic considerations.[6]

The doubtful years: exorbitant privileges granted to the Tutsis

Once the crisis of the First World War was over, a series of changes took place. The Germans were replaced as colonizers by the Belgians, and King Musinga, a man of weak character, obstinately opposed to the Christianization and modernization of Rwanda, lost much of his authority over his subjects. (He was deposed in 1931, with the Church's blessing, by the Belgian colonial powers and was sent into exile.) Mutara III Rudahigwa, the young prince chosen to succeed him, was open to Western ideas and was taught the principles of Christianity. Good relations were established between Rwanda's rulers and its colonizers. The King was baptized in 1943, with Governor General P. Riyckmans as his godfather.[7] The King's baptism unleashed a veritable torrent of conversions among the Tutsis, as well as among all Rwandans. Indeed, the conversion movement began from the time of Musinga's deposition and the coronation of a Christian prince.

The astonishing torrent of conversions marked a watershed in the religious, intellectual and political development of Rwandans, especially among the Tutsi elite. Thirty years later, this elite would be entirely rejected by the missionaries and colonizers, but one cannot deny the positive effects of this period, even if fate cast dark clouds on the horizon.

This was also a turning point for the Belgian colonial administration, particularly with the Mortehan Reform of 1926-1931.[8] The colonizers made a definite decision to recruit their collaborators from among the Tutsis of important families, since they were more educated, and thought to be more competent and reliable. Whereas in the traditional system, there had been many Hutu leaders, the Belgians unified all the administration to the profit of the Tutsis. The Hutus were dismissed from all public offices and, as Ian Linden writes, "what was formerly a fluid ethnic border, which the Hutus who wanted to could easily cross, became under Belgian administration an insurmountable barrier between castes which delimited access to public office."[9]

This arrangement very seriously decreased the number of Hutu leaders within a few years. "It was easier to direct a well-ordered, pyramidal feudal system from the top... [T]he Belgians wanted to rationalize the system in an attempt to sustain and consolidate the traditional framework of the leading batutsi class," as the Governor said, for the usual "hamitic" reasons: "their [the Tutsis'] great qualities, their undeniable intellectual superiority and their aptitude for leadership."[10]

The Belgian administration and the Apostolic Vicar, Monsignor Léon Classe, agreed it was absolutely necessary to take charge of young Tutsis. "If we want to consider the practical point of view," wrote the prelate, "and seek the true interests of the country, we have in Tutsi young people an incomparable element for progress, which all those who know Rwanda cannot underestimate... these young people are a force for good and the economic future of the country." He continued, "[W]e believe from our experience that the mututsi element is the better one for us; it is the more active, the more convinced, the more capable of playing a fermenting role among the masses."[11]

In addition, these young Tutsis felt an urgent need to be open to new things – to Christianity and to modernity. This convergence of will (between the Catholic Church, the colonial administration, and the new Tutsi generation) led to a staggering increase in the advantages reserved for Tutsis. The administrators believed that the existing social stratification had to be provisionally maintained, imposed on all and made more rigid. Mr. Servranckx stated that "a muhutu does not want to be ordered by a muhutu," and if Monsignor Classe could not conceive of a Rwanda administered by the Hutus, it was because nobody else envisaged it.[12] Thus, the Belgians not only recognized the traditional socio-political stratification in Rwanda, but they gave it a new definition[13] and new rigidity. Thus, from 1925 to 1955, excessive privileges were given to the Tutsi elite. They were considered the only group capable of offering substantial help in the work of Christianization and colonization.

This high esteem was not without its shadow side, but the administration obligingly overlooked the faults and abuses of the elite. A priest by the name of Father Pagès advised, "If a few abuses should slip in... injustices committed with regard to individuals... once aware of these abuses, the administration can only remedy them progressively, without overthrowing the current regime. With the leaders it has, on whose intelligence and docility it can count, the government will surely lead the country in the path of moral and material progress, the aim of all colonization."[14] Even if the missionaries were opposed to this development, they were asked not to draw attention to the leaders' faults or confront them in public. Thus, by order of the colonizers, a Tutsi Church did in fact exist in a Tutsi State.

Ian Linden points out in passing that some people found these instructions very disagreeable. "Several missionaries admitted that the Hutu were incapable of governing, that they were undisciplined and coarse. The Hutu Church flatly denied this, but faced with the Tutsi nobility and the triumphant Church, it was a negligible quantity."[15] This Hutu Church would bide its time.

As a result of this differentiation, a rift was gradually created – eventually, it became an unsurpassable abyss – between the two ethnic groups, especially between intellectuals. Monsignor André Perraudin, Bishop of Kabgayi, who devoted almost his entire life as a priest to the Church in Rwanda (1955-1994), apparently commented at the end of his life that all Rwanda's misfortunes resulted from developments during this period. The privileges reserved for the Tutsis during this period had made them more arrogant and self-important and favored their domination over the Hutus.

The volte-face towards genocide

Things changed around 1955. There was a definitive rupture with the Tutsis and an exclusive turn towards the Hutus. Once again, admiration turned to hatred, and this time without reversing itself. First, young colonial agents and young missionaries, mainly Flemish, arrived in Rwanda. They could not tolerate the overwhelming presence and influence of the Tutsis on Church and State in Rwanda, while the majority Hutu were almost totally absent. They compared the situation to the Walloon-Flemish injustice seen in Belgium, and they promised to change it without delay.[16] Second, there also was a new dynamic and attitude within the Roman Catholic Church, one which had become very sensitive to questions of social justice and the defense of the poor and weak in society. Third, the King and important dignitaries of the country's Higher Council[17] demanded immediate independence, which both the colonial administration and the Catholic Church opposed. The leadership of the Church became convinced that the Tutsi elite supported

Communism and freemasonry. And, finally, Hutu intellectuals clearly showed in their "Manifesto of the Bahutu" (March 1957) that they wanted their "share of the cake." Moreover, these intellectuals scarcely challenged the Belgian administration of Rwanda. They were submissive to the colonial authorities and did not claim independence.

In reality, the demonstrations of sympathy towards the Tutsis in the previous period were not sincere and thus could not last. Monsignor Classe regarded the Tutsis as useful "from the practical point of view," while the colonizers thought that the privileges of the Tutsis should be "provisionally maintained." The consequences of these attitudes were inevitable: the Tutsis were rejected by both the colonizers and the missionaries as soon as they no longer were needed, and the Tutsis also were rejected by the Hutus. As a result, the Tutsis were placed in opposition to everyone and eventually condemned.[18]

From 1959 onwards, events moved faster: the mysterious death of King Mutara III and the imposition of a new monarch, Kigeli V Ndahindurwa, without the agreement of the colonial authority. Acts of violence broke out between the new monarch and Hutu leaders. The Church defended the poor, that is, the Hutus. Belgium sent Colonel Guy Logiest[19] and a pitiless hunt began for Tutsis over all the country.[20] The Church considered this operation justified. Assassinations, plundering, and a thousand other acts of exclusion or persecution against Tutsis were regularly recorded until 1990. People became accustomed to them, and the Church's condemnation of human and civil rights abuses was only half-hearted.

With the "disappearance" of the Tutsis – many left and went into exile and others were killed, while the great majority remained within Rwanda, confined in a political and social non-existence – the Church achieved the realization of its dream: a Hutu Church in a Hutu state. The First Republic – that of the single "Parmehutu" party which was hysterically anti-Tutsi – was marked by an undeniable domination of Church over State. Monsignor André Perraudin became the intellectual guide of President Grégoire Kayibanda, who had been a seminarian and his secretary. In this exaltation of the Hutus, the young Flemish White Fathers found fertile ground for their apostolic mission. A deep hatred of the Tutsi regime (which no longer existed), and of all Tutsis was understood to be in complete accord with "sincere love" of the Church. These were not seen to be incompatible sentiments. On the contrary, they combined to inspire an apostolic and political line imbued with social Catholicism, and the majority of priests and religious Hutus were carried along in this river of mixed waters.

During the Second Republic (1973-1994), President Juvénal Habyarimana, freed himself from overt Church domination while allowing to continue in a subtle way the policy of marginalizing the Tutsis, which then culminated not only in their total societal exclusion but in their extermination during the 1994 genocide. Suffice it to say that the Church was perfectly at ease within this system and defended it without scruple. Church leaders were not concerned that the Tutsis were denied fundamental human rights, such as the right to education and employment, or that they were dispersed into refugee camps in neighboring countries and massacred at every moment of politico-economic unease. The Catholic bishops even went so far as to deny that there was discrimination against the Tutsis. In 1990, the Bishops of Rwanda wrote that "One sometimes hears people complaining that for reasons of ethnic origin, they have been refused employment or a place at school, they have been deprived of an advantage, or that justice was not impartial towards them. You are aware that the policy of ethnic balance in workplaces and schools is intended to correct this inequality, which could favor some to the detriment of others. The leaders are doing all they can to help the inhabitants of Rwanda to get along well... "[21]

The genocide

The attack in 1990 on the Hutu-dominated regime by the Rwandan Patriotic Front (RPF), made up mainly of young Tutsi refugees, was the occasion of a pact of self-defense between the Habyarimana regime and the Catholic Church.[22] Tutsis outside Rwanda, the RPF, and those within, were declared "the enemy to be fought without pity." Thus was the extermination of the Tutsis prepared.

The shooting down of the President's plane on 6 April 1994 gave the signal for the most rapid genocide in history. The Catholic Church witnessed the massacre in a kind of total paralysis. Only a few Hutu priests opposed this diabolic outburst (see further, *Tribute to Courage*[23]). After the genocide, there was the same embarrassed silence, and – worse still – churchmen tried to minimize, evade or trivialize the horror of the extermination.[24] It was only in 2000, with Pope John Paul II's initiative for repentance and forgiveness within the framework of the Jubilee year that the Church of Rwanda resolved to make certain statements and promote certain acts of dissociation from the perpetrators. But no bishop, priest, monk, nun, or ordinary Christian was condemned by the Church for his or her participation – close or remote – in the genocide. In fact, the Church did not recognize by name a single culprit within its institution of the genocide. Doing so was considered to be the exclusive affair of state justice.

The explanation
The "racialization" of Rwandan society

From the moment of their arrival in Rwanda at the beginning of the twentieth century, the Catholic missionaries supported the theory of "races" and "ethnic groups" which, according to racial theory, were considered incompatible because one race or ethnic group was inferior and the other superior. What is troubling in the Church of Rwanda is an attitude that resulted from this "racial theory," and that is a refusal to offer salvation to all Rwandans, whether Hutu or Tutsi. As Eric Gillet writes, "Whether it was a question of promoting the Tutsis – first – then the Hutus – the mental universe was the same: to create social classes in ethnic groups, to base the future of a country on racial cleavage, to exacerbate what divides, to refuse to focus on what unites, to inculcate a sense of fear... "[25]

What differentiated Hutus and Tutsis was not race or ethnicity but their traditional economic specializations – the Tutsis were cattle breeders, the Hutu farmers, and the Twa hunters. Moreover, far from bringing them into conflict, these economic functions made the groups complementary. Their social functions were also fluid; they were never closed compartments. With the development of a more Westernized Rwandan society, these specializations were gradually destined to disappear. The Hutu was no longer necessarily a farmer; he might also be a shopkeeper, a teacher, priest, etc., just as the Tutsi no longer only earned his living from his cows, but from all the new occupational possibilities. Interethnic marriages became more common and more numerous, although under the Hutu-dominated republics, racist laws unconditionally prohibited such marriages. Today, however, even after the terrible rupture of the genocide, numerous interethnic marriages are happening again, which only shows that such racist laws are actually against nature. Anyone entering Rwanda at the beginning of the last century would have been struck by the population's unity, as they had the same language, culture, religion, and habitat. As the Canon de Lacger put it, "The natives of this country really feel that they form a single people, the Banyarwanda... a patriotism which is affirmed in their loyalty to the reigning dynasty."[26]

One may question, therefore, why there was a determination on the part of the missionaries and the colonizers to separate and divide the Rwandan people. Was it to facilitate their work? Was it to further the "principle" of divide and rule? There were, of course, conflicts in Rwandan society, as there are everywhere – between governors and governed, rich and poor – and there also were prejudices. The colonists and missionaries certainly noted these "seeds of separation," which they catalogued with zeal, for reasons which are sometimes clear and sometimes obscure.

The role of the Church of Jesus Christ, however, is to reconcile all God's children. (As St. Paul writes in Galatians 3:28, "There is neither Jew nor Greek, slave nor free, male nor female, for you are all one in Christ Jesus.") Yet, the decisions made – first to ignore the Tutsis and turn towards the Hutus, then to overvalue the Tutsis at the expense of the Hutus, and finally to totally exclude the Tutsis from Rwandan society – were deliberate. By about 1955, the desire not to reconcile Hutus and Tutsis was even being theologically justified: "The Church's mission is not to please everyone but to preach the truth and justice."[27] Although this brief historical review does not excuse the leadership of the Church, it does help one to understand the immense difficulty for Church leaders to resolutely condemn the genocide of the Tutsis in 1994.

Clearly, I do not think either the colonizers or the missionaries acted with the intention of preparing genocide. They were guided by the immediate need to more easily and effectively carry out their tasks of administration and evangelization. The reproach which should be leveled against them – a serious one – is that of exploiting existing antagonisms between two groups of Rwandans and having done practically nothing to fight the virulence of those claims when they became bloody and murderous. "How difficult it is to break with the men and women with whom a tight network of friendships has been woven, when one still cannot believe that they killed a million people, destroyed the social structure of the country, dishonored a people, and pushed cynicism beyond the conceivable... "[28]

Social justice = racial justice

The social doctrine of the Roman Catholic Church speaks of the "preferential option for the poor." For the missionaries, there was only one class of poor in Rwanda, the Hutus. They chose to ignore the fact that ninety percent of Tutsis never belonged to the category of princes and chiefs. They were peasants just like their Hutu neighbors. In his "Letter for Lent, 1959," considered by some as the signal for the Hutu uprising, Monsignor André Perraudin wrote, "In our land of Rwanda, differences and social inequalities are largely linked to differences of race."[29] He thought that the social inequalities matched the races in Rwanda exactly, but this was a false generalization.

A. Mugesera shows very clearly that what predominated at this point in Rwandan history was not economic considerations, but politico-racist ideology. The Tutsi minority did not monopolize the country's wealth; they shared everyone's poverty.[30] The Tutsis were to be pursued and killed not because they were rich, but because they were Tutsis. Whilst vigorously taking the side of the poor against the rich, the missionaries felt very much in accord with this Christian idea. They could not see that they were preaching a preferential option for one race against another. And when the Tutsi genocide occurred, they had difficulty seeing anything wrong in it.[31] They were proud to see "social justice" finally reign in the form of "racial justice."

A long and insidious poisoning

To understand why the Church of Rwanda – no longer under the missionaries' influence – continues to behave on the Hutu-Tutsi question as in 1950-59, one must mention the long-inculcated indoctrination of Hutu extremists, which the missionaries supported and passed on to the native Church. This consisted in seeing the Tutsis as the source of all Hutu misfortunes. The Tutsi was the mortal enemy, the terrifying and foul animal, the snake. This mentality of the persecuted and constantly threatened, which haunts the Hutus, especially its intellectuals, is of course also that of indigenous Hutu clergy.[32] Indeed, during the period of "exorbitant privileges granted to the Tutsi," Hutu intellectuals (including priests) had to endure enormous frustrations. Admittedly, they should have understood that it was primarily the act of the colonizers and the missionaries, but the Tutsis certainly misused the power which was granted to them. That created inferiority complexes, insecurity, and threat. This may explain – but does not excuse – the obliging behavior of the missionaries and certain Hutu ecclesiastics with respect to the genocide and *genocidaires*, to whom the genocide appeared as a necessary evil.

The future?
A Rwandan Church in a Rwandan State

The wounds of the genocide will take time to heal – for the survivors, *genocidaires* and those suspected of complicity with the *genocidaires*. We Rwandans must have a great deal of patience with one another. Directly after the genocide (1995-1998), the Catholic Church resolutely denied the genocide; many ecclesiastics, both inside and outside Rwanda, considered it a simple mishap, a spontaneous reaction to the death of President Habyarimana. The Church then demanded an immediate dialogue between the new regime and the *genocidaires*, and advanced the thesis of the double genocide.[33] In addition, certain elements of the media openly accused the Church of participating in the genocide. There was also talk of the Church's persecution by the new regime.

Little by little, however, positions softened. The Church made declarations and moves towards understanding what really happened, and expressing compassion for the victims, thanks to Pope John Paul II's appeal in 2000 to make the Jubilee a time of repentance, reconciliation and seeking forgiveness.[34] There was also the example given by the French Catholic bishops asking the Jewish people for forgiveness in regard to the Holocaust (*L'Eglise de France demande pardon – The Church of France asks for Forgiveness*, Drancy 1995) as well as the actions of the German bishops on the 50th anniversary of the Second World War. The two Churches asked forgiveness for their weak and cowardly attitude at the time of the extermination of the Jews. The Rwandan Bishops Conference, 20-27 October 2000, invited bishops from countries that have also experienced division and are working towards reconciliation to come to Kigali to exchange their difficulties and hopes in an atmosphere of truth and prayer. South Africa, Germany, Northern Ireland and Burundi responded to the invitation.[35]

Since then, there has been participation – although still timid and tentative – in Rwanda's initiatives, for example, the "National Commission of Unity and Reconciliation," the "*Gacaca* courts," etc. The Church has created the "Special Diocesan Synod," devoted to approaching the reality of the genocide and the terrible faithlessness which Christians experienced, with a view to opening paths of reconciliation. One has to acknowledge, however, that there is still a long way to go.

Three topics merit reflection for the future: First, a more resolute recognition that a terrible genocide was committed in Rwanda in 1994, a country which is ninety percent Christian and sixty-five percent Catholic. From this fact follows the question, "Are we Christianized or simply baptized?" In Rwanda everything today is said and done against the background of memory of the genocide. Anyone who claims not to know about it, or tries to forget it, can undertake nothing of value. Pasteur Gatwa reports that the participants of the Protestant Council of Churches Conference declared that "the genocide constituted a failure not only of the Church of Rwanda, but also of the universal Church." "The Churches," they said, "must recognize their share of responsibility for the genocide, repent and humbly beg forgiveness of the nation and God."[36]

In 1999, I wrote in Rwanda's only Catholic weekly: "Our ambition is that the Church of Rwanda, with the confidence and grace which the Holy Spirit confers, will be the first to initiate real gestures of reconciliation between Rwandans: to recognize the truth of what happened, to bear the sin of the whole people and not only accept, but desire the demands of justice."[37]

The Church must help all Rwandans to grieve, to hide nothing of the horrors committed, but to accept that they happened so that this can never happen again. In this task of reconstructing the social fabric, the Church must support all efforts of justice. "One cannot speak of reconciliation without judgement of the guilty"[38] Only the recognition of the 1994 genocide will allow us to denounce and punish all the ensuing mistakes, including the RPF's acts of revenge.

Second, the need to avoid the rigid confines of the categories of Hutu and Tutsi. The Church must refuse to adopt language which continues to consider and judge everything in suspicious, aggressive terms, such as the language of provocation, demand, and ethnic injustice. An immense effort has begun in Rwanda to achieve unity and reconciliation in all fields. Church leadership must not ignore, and surely they must not disparage this effort. Rather, they must find a way to complement and contribute to it in a positive manner. Further, expatriate missionaries and their Hutu refugee friends must not continue to encourage their Rwandan Hutu friends to claim their rights in the name of their ethnic group. We know from past experience that this is the most direct path to another genocide. In Rwanda, we can no longer afford to play with this kind of fire. We must find better, more acceptable, more tolerant, respectful, and humane ways to relate to one another, if Rwanda is to have a future in the community of nations in Africa, and in the world.

Third, the Church must become a credible, critical authority for society as a whole. To achieve this goal, the Church has the light and principles of the Gospel of Jesus Christ to preach and live by, honestly, *opportune et importune*. The Church must make more of an effort to place itself above any and all opportunist ideologies, such as racism and ethnicism. In addition, the Church and its members must regularly and rigorously analyze and critique the political, economic and security development of Rwanda, in order to prevent any moves towards armed conflict of one group by another. In doing so, the Church must make sure its message is clear, fair, humane, and correct, above any sectarian or racial influence. The entire Church – by which I mean, bishops, clergy, religious, and laity, including intellectuals from among all these groups – must be exemplary in this effort. In view of the immense damage caused by so many years of siding with one ethnic group against another, and of collaborating with past political regimes which have been complicit in abusing or denying the human rights of the Hutu, Tutsi, and Twa peoples, the Church of Rwanda must be unfailingly vigilant that it becomes the humane champion of the human rights of *all* people. It must "shake off" old habits and emerge from its lethargy.

The excessively clerical, even episcopal-focused ecclesiology in which the hierarchy – popes, cardinals, archbishops, and bishops – alone was the repository of truth,[39] must give way to an open ecclesiology, one which is "attentive," as T. Gatwa would say,[40] open to all the members of the Roman Catholic Christian community. This will require a fundamental reform of what up to now has been a hierarchical, one-way, top-down model of communication – that is, archbishops and bishops to the rest of the Church – if Church leadership genuinely wants to encourage all capable members of the Christian-Catholic community to participate in a critical and effective manner, both in terms of conceiving and implementing Church initiatives. It is a challenge worth undertaking for the sake of the Church in Rwanda, and beyond.

Translated by Wendy Whitworth

Notes

1. Ian Linden, *Christianisme et Pouvoirs au Rwanda (1900-1990)* (Karthala, 1999), 101-129. In the preface, the author says that his book describes "*the antecedents of the genocide of 1994,*" 5. My emphasis.

2. J.-P. Gouteux, *Un Génocide Secret d'Etat: La France et le Rwanda 1990-1997* (Paris: Editions Sociales, 1998).

3. Linden, 63. The word "*garagu*" means "servant" or "customer."

4. L. de Lacger, *Rwanda* (Kabgayi, 1939), 32.

5. He wrote to his colleagues, "We must absolutely work to destroy government opinion that we are the men of the Hutu." Quoted by Bernard Lugan in *Histoire du Rwanda. De la préhistoire à nos jours* (Paris: Bartillat, 1997), 308-9. In reality, many missionaries refused to support a policy which aimed to serve the interests of the court, which in their view was powerless. Some also considered that the Christian religion was for the poor.

6. It was easier for them to govern with the Tutsis who already had a traditional command structure.

7. Significantly, Ian Linden used a photograph of this baptism on his book cover.

8. In 1926, Mortehan, the resident governor, undertook a territorial reorganisation and dismissed a significant number of Hutu leaders, in order to put in place young Tutsi leaders trained in the official schools, see Bernard Lugan, *Afrique: De la colonisation philanthropique à la récolonisation humanitaire* (Paris: Bartillat, 1995), 305.

9. Linden, 246.

10. Report on the Belgian administration of Ruanda-Urundi, 1938, 38. Classe's Letter to Mortehan, 21 September 1927, cited by Linden, *Christianisme et Pouvoirs au Rwanda*, 217.

11. Cited by B. Muzungu in *Des prêtres rwandais s'interrogent* (Bujumbura, 1995), 142-143.

12. Linden, 218-19.

13. "Between the two wars, the principal characteristic of education was to be at the service of the Tutsi and to respond uniquely to the short-term needs of the Belgian administration. In this system the Church was the servant of the State," Linden, *Christianisme et Pouvoirs au Rwanda*, 260.

14. Letter of Pagès to Philippart, 6 November 1933, cited by Linden, *Christianisme et Pouvoirs au Rwanda*, 251.

15. Linden, 223.

16. "It is not a question," they said, "of recommending simple alterations or a partial reform which would not go to the root of the evil. The Church must aim at a true social transformation." See also J.-P. Chrétien, *L'Afrique des Grands Lacs. Deux Mille Ans d'Histoire* (Paris: Flammarion, 2000), 264.

17. Adminstrative body which helped the *Mwami* (King) to govern and was principally made up of Tutsis.

18. The Tutsi elite, feeling that they were losing everything, rebelled against the colonizers, the missionaries and the Hutu elite. They made some mistakes, and consequently became the enemy to be destroyed.

19. Logiest was a Belgian army officer, sent from the Congo to Rwanda in 1959 to bring order to the country. In practical terms, he had all administrative and military power at his disposal, see Chrétien, *L'Afrique des Grands Lacs*, 266.

20. Logiest wrote that he had come "to give a people back its dignity," but that "it was perhaps just as much out of a desire to reduce the pride and expose the duplicity of a fundamentally oppressive and unjust aristocracy" in *Mission au Rwanda* (Brussels, 1988), 135.

21. Catholic bishops, *Message aux Chrétiens*, February 1990, 5.

22. See the "Letter of the Expatriates," written and signed by 115 missionaries in 1991, affirming that they had opted for the Hutu ethnic group against the Tutsi enemy.

23. African Rights, a human rights organization, has just published a list of nineteen people who without question devoted themselves to the defence of the Tutsi pursued by the murderers. Among them were seven Rwandan priests and a missionary. This is the document entitled *Hommage au Courage* (Kigali: African Rights, 2003).

24. See *Osservatore Romano*, 19 May 1994, especially the article "Rwandan Genocide: last act" (*Génocide rwandais: dernier acte*) which claims that there were two genocides. The Catholic agencies Fides, Misna and Nigritia determinedly offer the strongest denial of the genocide of the Tutsi.

25. E. Gillet, "Le génocide devant la justice", *Temps Modernes. Les Politiques de la Haine*, No 583, July-August 1995, 234.

26. Louis de Lacger, *Rwanda. Première Partie: Le Rwanda Ancien* (Grands-Lacs Namur, 1939), 36.

27. P. Adriaenssens, cited by Linden, *Christianisme et Pouvoirs au Rwanda*, 341.

28. Gillet, 235.

29. A. Perraudin in *Lettres Pastorales et Autres Documents des Evêques Catholiques du Rwanda* (1956-1962), 31-32.

30. A. Mugesera, "Prépondérance de l'idéologie sur l'économie dans la crise identitaire au Rwanda (1957-1962)" in *Rwanda: Identité et Citoyenneté* (Butare: National University of Rwanda, 2003), 108.

31. Already in 1959, Father Alvoet wrote when witnessing the massacre of the Tutsis, "I have experienced the Hutu revolt in a very painful way because there were corpses. *But on the whole I was happy*. Something historical was occurring: the liberation of a people." Quoted in *L'Eglise Catholique à l'épreuve du Génocide*, (Canada: Les Editions Africana, 2000), 112. (My emphasis.)

32. Father Erny describes "a quasi-obsessional defense reaction and an obvious sense of inferiority."

33. See Footnote 24.

34. Pastoral Letter at the close of the Jubilee 2001; Letter introducing the *Gacaca* legal system (participatory and reconciliatory justice), 2003; Letter commemorating the 10th anniversary of the genocide, 2004; Conference organised by the Bishops of Rwanda entitled, "The Church and Rwandan society confront the genocide and the massacres, 10 years on," 29-31 March 2004.

35. See the Proceedings: *Colloque international d'échange d'expériences en vue du Processus de Paix et de Réconciliation au Rwanda* (Kigali, 2000).

36. T. Gatwa, *L'Eglise: victime ou coupable; Les églises et l'idéologie ethnique au Rwanda 1900-1994* (Yaoundé: Clé, 2001), 285.

37. O.Ugirashebuja, "Mon ambition pour l'Eglise de Rwanda," *Kinyamateka*, N° 1520, 9.

38. M.A., "Les divisions de l'Eglise du Rwanda", *Temps Modernes. Les Politiques de la Haine*, N° 583 (1955), 101.

39. This is why very often criticism leveled at the Church of Rwanda is aimed mainly at the behavior of the hierarchy: dependence on the political powers, embarrassed silence or vague comment on the genocide.

40. Gatwa, 184.

4

THE CHURCH AND POWER

RESPONSES TO GENOCIDE AND MASSIVE HUMAN RIGHTS ABUSES IN COMPARATIVE PERSPECTIVE

Jerry Fowler

> "He stood up to read and was handed a scroll of the prophet Isaiah. He unrolled the scroll and found the passage where it was written: 'The Spirit of the Lord is upon me, because he has anointed me to bring glad tidings to the poor. He has sent me to proclaim liberty to captives and recovery of sight to the blind, to let the oppressed go free, and to proclaim a year acceptable to the Lord.'"
>
> *(Luke 4:8-9)*

On Sunday, 23 March 1980, the Archbishop of San Salvador, Oscar Romero, delivered what would be his last Sunday homily. In a land steadily descending into civil war, state-sponsored violence was increasing daily. Each morning saw a new crop of mutilated corpses littering the roadsides, left by death squads closely tied to the nation's military. In the first three months of 1980, the Church documented 900 civilians killed by government forces.

Archbishop Romero incited the anger of those wielding power by denouncing the murders and broadcasting the names of the assassinated and disappeared. In his March 23 homily, he once again directly addressed those ruling the tiny Central American nation: "In the name of God, in the name of this suffering people whose cries rise to heaven more loudly each day, I implore you, I beg you, I order you in the name of God: stop the repression."

The next evening, as he celebrated a memorial mass for a friend's mother, Archbishop Romero himself was assassinated, felled by a sniper's bullet.[1]

'The Spirit of God has led me to this'

It may seem anomalous to begin an essay on the Church and the Rwandan genocide with a recollection of Archbishop Romero's murder, occurring as it did on a different continent in a different decade under different circumstances. But the thread that connects them is the basic issue of the relationship between the Church and its leaders, on the one hand, and the temporal power on the other, in cases where that power is being violently abused. Examining this thread is important for several reasons. First, by acknowledging that there are other cases where the Church and its leaders have not responded adequately, it helps avoid the alibi that the case of Rwanda is a product solely of conditions in Rwanda. On the other hand, by considering cases in which the Church and its leaders have chosen to speak with a prophetic voice in response to massive human rights violations, it gives rise to hope that the failures in Rwanda are not predetermined.

The Catholic Church has a significant presence in numerous countries where there have been massive and systematic human rights abuses. In many of those countries, the Church is objectively identified with the targets of the abuses, as in Sudan, or is itself the target of persecution, as in the Eastern bloc before 1989 and in China today. The willingness and ability of the Church and its leaders to oppose human rights violations in those circumstances is not surprising, and probably does not help illuminate the conduct of the Rwandan Church. But there is another category of cases, those in which the Church and its leadership have a choice to make in reacting to human rights abuses – that is, they must choose whether to identify with the victims and speak out against or otherwise oppose the persecution. Stated another way, the Church has a choice in defining its relationship to political power and violence.

Archbishop Romero faced such a choice. When he was appointed archbishop, he was perceived as a conservative, friendly to the wealthy elite that ruled the country. In a stint as editor of the archdiocesan newspaper in the early 1970s, he redirected its focus from broad issues of social justice to more traditional concerns of personal conduct, such as alcohol abuse and pornography. As a bishop, he avoided publicly confronting the government or landowners over human rights abuses.

Only after becoming archbishop did he choose to speak out publicly and persistently in a prophetic voice, using the pulpit to advocate liberty for the captives, freedom for the oppressed. He was transformed by the violence and by his own awareness of the country's vast inequities into a passionate and articulate witness for the suffering of the people. He told a *New York Times* reporter that he "evolved rather than changed... The circumstances of the country led me to overcome my timidity and come closer to the people... The spirit of God has led me to this."[2]

Archbishop Romero was not the only Church leader in El Salvador who chose the path of confronting power, nor the only one who sacrificed his life for doing so. His close friend, the Jesuit priest Rutilio Grande, was murdered three years before him; three American nuns and an American lay worker – Dorothy Kazel, Maura Clarke, Ita Ford and Jean Donovan – were raped and murdered nine months after him. Indeed, between the killing of Father Grande and the four Americans, sixteen Church leaders were slain. And before the violence ended, many others died, including six Jesuit priests who were murdered in 1989 along with their housekeeper and her daughter on the campus of the University of Central America.

Though one might say that "the Church" in El Salvador chose to speak with a prophetic voice and suffered for doing so, it was also true that there were important members of the Church hierarchy who aligned themselves with the forces responsible for most of the violence. One member of the bishop's conference was in fact chaplain of the armed forces. Another outspokenly conservative bishop, Pedro Arnoldo Aparicio, who denounced unnamed priests and nuns as Communists, was caustically praised by a former military dictator as one "who wags his tail when you give him something."[3]

The Red Cardinal

On 11 September 1973, the armed forces of Chile, under the command of General Augusto Pinochet, overthrew President Salvador Allende, ending over a century of almost uninterrupted constitutional government. Allende, a Marxist who had been elected in 1970, died during the coup, an apparent suicide. Pinochet's takeover of power ushered in an era of violent human rights abuses in which several thousand Chileans were murdered or simply disappeared, while many others were imprisoned, tortured or exiled.

Raul Cardinal Silva, the Chilean primate, adopted a somewhat ambiguous stance toward the new regime. In his first public statement, issued two days after Pinochet seized power, Cardinal Silva expressed regret over the blood that had been shed, without appearing to assign blame or criticize the military's actions. On the other hand, he specifically called for respect "first of all, for the one who until Tuesday, September 11 was the President of the Republic." The following week, he sponsored a national mass of reconciliation. He seemed to adopt toward the military regime, that already was undertaking systematic murder of real or suspected political opponents, the same attitude that he had adopted in the preceding fifteen years toward democratically elected governments: an attitude of neutrality.[4]

A statement issued by the bishops the following April retained an air of ambiguity. The statement reiterated the theme of reconciliation, which is problematic in an environment in which one party is overwhelmingly responsible for sustained and substantial violence, and approved the regime's ostensible commitment to Christian values. It underscored the importance of "the full observance of human rights" as well as the need for democratic approval of any new constitution after open debate, implying that the regime was falling short of these standards. The military's campaign of murder, torture and disappearances seemed to be subsumed in criticism of "the climate of insecurity and fear" and references to "arbitrary or excessively long detention" and "interrogations that use physical and moral pressures."

If Cardinal Silva's public language did not match Archbishop Romero's passionate denunciations of the killers in El Salvador, he nevertheless began to take concrete steps to give succor to the regime's victims and ultimately to create space for dissent. He took the lead in establishing with other Churches the Committee of Cooperation for Peace in Chile (COPACHI), a focal point for supporting targets of human rights abuses. COPACHI organized the relatively few lawyers willing to represent victims of persecution, handling over 7,000 cases in two years. Government pressure resulted in COPACHI's being disbanded in 1975. But Cardinal Silva acted to continue its work in 1976 by creating under his direct sponsorship the Vicariate of Solidarity, which became an important voice of resistance against the Pinochet regime's violations of human rights. He subsequently told a journalist that from then on he broke off relations with the regime, which began calling him the "red Cardinal."[5]

"Wouldn't Christ want the armed forces one day to reach out beyond their job?"

The record of Church leaders in Argentina during that country's "dirty war" stands in stark contrast to the experiences in El Salvador and Chile. There, the Church hierarchy largely sided with the military government that perpetrated massive and systematic human rights abuses against huge sectors of the population perceived as "subversives." Indeed, the night before seizing power in March 1976, coup leaders met with the bishop's conference and received advice on the forthcoming dispensation. One of the members of the conference, Archbishop Adolfo Tortolo, was (and continued to be after the coup) chief vicar of the military and a childhood friend of top generals.

Another military vicar, Monsignor Victorio Bonamin, had publicly encouraged the military to seize power: "The army is purifying the dirtiness in our country. Wouldn't Christ want the armed forces one day to reach out beyond their job?" Monsignor Bonamin also reportedly chastised from the pulpit Bishop Enrique Angelelli, one of the few bishops who spoke out against the impending coup, musing on "the justifiable death of the anti-Christ even dressed as a bishop." Five months after the coup, Bishop Angelelli was murdered in a car "accident" subsequently determined to have been staged by military intelligence.[6]

As many as 30,000 Argentines were murdered or disappeared from 1976 to 1983. One target of this violence was the "Church of the People" – those elements of the Church, such as Bishop Angelelli and a number of other priests and catechists, who spoke out against the military regime. The response of the Church's hierarchy was muted and passive. In essence, the divisions in Argentine society were reflected and reproduced within the Church, with the same unfortunate results. In September 2000, the Argentine bishops apologized for the Church's conduct during the dirty war.[7]

"A small flare of hope"

The struggle and division evident in the cases above find an echo in Rwanda's neighbor to the west, now called the Democratic Republic of Congo. The Church there has more than 30 million members, accounting for some sixty percent of the population. For most of the time since the country obtained independence, the Church has been divided against itself, largely along ethnic lines. During the kleptocratic Mobutu regime, the government successfully pursued a 'divide and rule' strategy that largely prevented the Church from being a focal point for opposition to Mobutu's despotic rule. Dissident Archbishop Christian Munzihirwa complained that most of his episcopal colleagues were practically part of Mobutu's entourage.[8] The stress and challenge for the Church's leaders have only intensified with the catastrophic wars that resulted in Mobutu's overthrow in 1996 and then the fragmentation of the country since 1998.

Archbishop Munzihirwa, though, in many ways was a Congolese Romero. He had a long history of defying Mobutu's government, extending back to the early 1970s. On one occasion in the mid-1990s, he commanded rampaging troops, in words that eerily echo Romero's last homily, "Here before me I see these soldiers. I see the colonel. Stop troubling the people! I ask you, I order you: Stop it!"[9]

As Hutu refugees flooded his archdiocese in 1994, he insisted on extending his protection to them, recognizing that most were innocent, even as their number included *genocidaires*. It was this concern for the refugees that cost him his life. As Rwandan troops swept into eastern Congo in October 1996, intent on wiping out the *genocidaires* without regard for the civilians in whose midst they had established themselves, Archbishop Munzihirwa attempted to stand up to the Rwandans as he had stood up for so long against Mobutu. A final message to the outside world on 28 October expressed his "hope that God will not abandon us and that from some part of the world will rise for us a small flare of hope." The next day, he surrendered to a squad of Rwandan soldiers who executed him.

The small flare of hope that Archbishop Munzihirwa longed for has proved elusive for his people and the Congolese Church. Since the second phase of the war began in 1998, it is estimated that more than three million civilians have perished, either from direct violence or as a result of the collapse of social infrastructure.[10] And the Church leaders have faltered in fashioning a robust response. In an April 2001 article in the Jesuit publication *America*, Timothy Longman reports that Archbishop Faustin Ngaba of Goma was outspoken in denouncing anti-Tutsi violence in 1996, but has had relatively little to say about human rights abuses by the mostly Tutsi Rwandan soldiers and their rebel allies, the Congolese Rally for Democracy (RCD). His critics ascribe this to his Hema ethnicity and to the fact that many of the diocesan priests are Tutsis. Even from Archbishop Munzihirwa's region of Bukavu, there are allegations that the Church has not spoken out against abuses against Congolese Tutsis in the diocese.[11]

"I was certainly not an accomplice"

It is one thing for the Catholic Church to have at the core of its message, as it has had at least since Vatican II, an explicit commitment to defending human dignity against the abuses of power.[12] It is quite another effectively and consistently to fulfill that commitment, especially in light of a competing and longstanding institutional interest in stability and order. A preference for the latter compromises the former.

Also competing with the commitment to denounce abuses is the commitment to reconciliation, which flows from the basic principle of forgiveness and the overarching commandment to love one's enemy as oneself. But the aspiration of reconciliation is perverted if it becomes reconciling the captive to captivity, or the oppressed to oppression, or the slaughtered to slaughter. Yet that is often the case if reconciliation is promoted in lieu of changing the relationship that offends human dignity in the first place. That is why Cardinal Silva's mass of reconciliation, offered the week after Pinochet's coup and as the torture and murder of political opponents was in full swing, seems so amiss.

But perhaps the greatest challenge in meeting the commitment to defend human dignity, especially when it is most under assault, is that the leaders of the Church are, after all, human. As such, they must contend with the internal divisions and weaknesses that afflict all humans, even as they look to God for strength and inspiration.[13] The faith and courage of a Romero or a Munzihirwa are special gifts indeed. And Church leaders are themselves subject to the very forces that cause their societies to be in conflict in the first place. They may have a choice to confront the forces of power, but that choice is not made in a vacuum. Tugging at the longing for unity, as preached by the Church, are forces of division, the pressure to take sides against the threat of Communism, or an alien ethnic group, or whatever other category is used to define and exclude the other. There is also the reality, as Jesus recognized, that "no prophet is accepted in his own native place."[14] Church leaders, no less than the faithful, are at risk of being stuck in the same unending moment of conflict that produces massive human rights violations to begin with.

But in this regard the Church has the potential, often underused or, worse, not used at all, to help unstick its members, to focus them on the requirements of human dignity. Church leaders and the faithful are "citizens of two cities,"[15] that is, where they reside physically and where they reside spiritually. When conflict in the former leads to abuses of human dignity, their fellow citizens in the latter can come to their assistance.

This would suggest that there is a special obligation on the Church hierarchy outside a conflicted society to help the hierarchy inside respond effectively to affronts to human dignity. In particular, the Holy Father's representative has the potential to play a constructive role, both in his interaction with the government to which he is accredited and in his interaction with the local hierarchy. The record, unfortunately, is not entirely reassuring.

Former US Ambassador to El Salvador Robert White is a Catholic whose official duties included witnessing the disinterment of Sister Ita Ford and the other American churchwomen from the hastily dug grave in which their broken bodies had been dumped. He observed that the Vatican's first concern during the 1970s and 1980s, when dictatorships in heavily Catholic countries in Latin America were abusing human rights on a massive scale, was often order and stability, even as some local Church leaders like Archbishop Romero and Bishop Angelelli were paying a high price for speaking out against state-sponsored repression: "The papal nuncios usually had a very different viewpoint than the local bishops. The nuncios lived in a world where any kind of social conflict disturbed what they see as that tripartite order of the rich, the military, and the church working together."[16]

One of the most notorious examples of this was the papal nuncio in Argentina during the military dictatorship, Pio Laghi. Laghi's main public image at the time was established for the people of Argentina by press reports of his daily tennis match with one of the members of the ruling junta. He also spoke publicly in support of the junta. Three months after the military seized power, he effectively endorsed the dirty war on the ground that "Christian values are threatened by an ideology that the people reject. The church and the armed forces share responsibility. The former is an integral element in the process. It accompanies the latter, not only by its prayers but by its actions."[17]

U.S. government documents that came to light in 2002 make it clear that Laghi was aware of the scope of human rights abuses. When Patt Derian, the Assistant Secretary of State for Human Rights, met with him in 1977, he discouraged her from putting too much pressure on the junta leaders because, according to a memo written by an American after the meeting, "they knew they have committed evil in human rights and do not need to be told of their guilt by visitors." He was concerned it would be "rubbing salt into their wounds." He depicted himself as privately but strongly protesting human rights violations to the generals.[18]

In 1997, the Mothers of the Plaza de Mayo, an association of women whose children were "disappeared" by the military, petitioned the Italian government to prosecute Laghi for actively assisting the dictatorship in the dirty war. He stoutly denied the allegations, and charges never were brought.

Laghi's counterpart in Chile, Angelo Sodano, similarly cozied up to the military dictatorship there, establishing himself as a counterweight to Cardinal Silva and orchestrating the appointment of bishops friendly to the regime. Pinochet ultimately rewarded these efforts with the "Grand Cross of the Order of Merit." As a postscript, when Pinochet was arrested in London in 1998 and faced possible extradition to Spain, Sodano, by that time a Cardinal and Vatican Secretary of State, pushed for his release.[19]

A second, more ironic postscript occurred in January 2004, when Sodano officiated at the funeral mass for the first papal nuncio to be murdered in the line of duty. Archbishop Michael Courtney, the Pope's representative in Burundi, was shot to death in an ambush on 29 December 2003. Although it remains unclear whether he was specifically targeted by his killers, he was in harm's way as a direct result of his sustained efforts to end human rights abuses and bring about a lasting peace in Burundi.

Laghi and Sodano very much had choices in whether to confront abuses of power or to accommodate them. One can only wonder what effect the choice of confrontation might have had in galvanizing (or reinforcing) the local Church to do the same. One wonders, as well, what reflection there has been on their failure to do so. While the Argentine bishops have apologized for their actions during the dirty war, Laghi has been rather more ambiguous: "Perhaps I was not a hero, but I was certainly not an accomplice."[20]

"You are my witnesses"

Papal nuncios are not the only members of the international hierarchy who can play a potentially positive role. The late Father André Sibomana, a courageous defender of human rights, made an interesting observation about the visit to Rwanda in May 1993 of Cardinal Roger Etchegary, president of the Pontifical Council for Justice and Peace: "The fact is that when Cardinal Etchegary came to Rwanda, the massacres stopped wherever he went."[21] His presence made a difference.

This calls to mind God's admonition in Isaiah, which is also carved in the main hall of the United States Holocaust Memorial Museum: "You are my witnesses."[22] Professor Ervin Staub has observed that "[b]ystanders, people who witness but are not directly affected by the actions of perpetrators, help shape society by their reactions." By what they do, these witnesses "can define the meaning of events and move others toward empathy or indifference. They can promote values and norms of caring, or by their passivity or participation in the system they can affirm the perpetrators."[23] This is a powerful role that members of the international Church hierarchy can play – they can choose to be witnesses who affirm principles of human dignity when those principles are being violated. But the converse is equally true; their failure to do so affirms and encourages the perpetrators.

"The kind of love you don't often find"

As a general matter, the Church hierarchy in Rwanda was closely aligned with the government in the years before the genocide. Most infamously, Archbishop Vincent Nsengiyumva served at one point as a member of the central committee of President Habyarimana's ruling party. In addition to the leadership's close identification with the regime, Rwanda's ethnic divisions were reproduced inside the Church.[24] Far from being a force for social unity and respect for human dignity, the Rwandan Church in fact was at least as divided as the society itself.

After the genocide began, the Church hierarchy explicitly endorsed the interim government. As the killing continued, Rwanda's bishops ultimately issued "many declarations... [that] were insignificant and inadequate."[25] Some local clergy gave at least tacit support to the genocide[26] and some more actively assisted in the violence.[27] Others, including Archbishop Nsengiyumva himself, gave protection to many, while allowing death squads to cull and murder particular targets (including priests and nuns).[28]

By the same token, there were clergy who did all they could to try to save others, even to the point of sacrificing their own lives.[29] One such priest was Father Jean-Bosco Munyaneza, who tried in vain to save thousands who fled to his church in Kibungo. Foregoing several opportunities to save himself, Father Munyaneza ultimately perished with most of the refugees he was trying to protect. One of the few survivors recalled his sacrifice: "He chose to die for us when he had every opportunity to stay alive. He showed the kind of love you don't often find."[30]

"Let the oppressed go free"

As this brief essay suggests, one can marshal evidence from an array of cases in the recent past that some Church leaders have confronted abusers of power, while others have consorted with them, and some leaders have even done both. And even in the story of Rwanda, where there may be more of those who consorted, there are at least some who confronted. In any particular case, there can be a variety of historical, social and theological explanations for the actual choices made by the individuals involved.[31] But beyond that, this mixed record stands as an enduring challenge to national and international Church leaders, as well as to lay persons, to ask, "What does it mean, living in an 'age of genocide,' 'to proclaim liberty to captives and recovery of sight to the blind, to let the oppressed go free'?"

Notes

1. Raymond Bonner, *Weakness and Deceit: U.S. Policy and El Salvador* (New York: Times Books, 1984), 177-79; United Nations Commission on the Truth for El Salvador, *From Madness to Hope: The 12-Year War in El Salvador* (New York: United Nations Security Council, 1993), available at www.usip.org.

2. Bonner, 71.

3. Ibid., 72.

4. Paul E. Sigmund, *The Overthrow of Allende and the Politics of Chile, 1964-1976* (Pittsburgh: University of Pittsburgh Press, 1977), 251-53.

5. Pamela Constable and Arturo Valenzuela, *A Nation of Enemies: Chile Under Pinochet* (New York: W.W. Norton & Co., 1991), 119-20; Thomas Quigley, "The Chilean Coup, the Church and the Human Rights Movement," *America* (11 February 2002), available at www.findarticles.com/cf_0/m1321/4_186/82671261/print.jhtml.

6. Martin Edwin Andersen, *Dossier Secreto: Argentina's Desaparecidos and the Myth of the "Dirty War"* (Boulder: Westview Press, 1993), 188-91.

7. Carlos Ares, "La iglesia argentina pide perdón por sus 'pecados' durante la Junta Militar," *El Pais* (10 September 2000), available at home.t-online.de/home/effi.schweizer/arg-iglesia.htm.

8. John L. Allen, Jr., "Faith, Hope and Heroes," *National Catholic Reporter* (23 February 2001), available at www.natcath.org/BCR_Online/archives2/2001a/022301/022301a.htm.

9. Ibid.

10. International Rescue Committee, *Mortality in the Democratic Republic of Congo* (New York: International Rescue Committee, 2003), available at www.theirc.org.

11. Timothy P. Longman, "Congo: A Tale of Two Churches," *America* (April 2001).

12. Pope John XXIII, *Pacem in Terris* (11 April 1963) ("As a human person, [man] is entitled to the legal protection of his rights, and such protection must be effective, unbiased, and strictly just."); Pope Paul VI, *Populorum Progressio* (26 March 1967) ("Sharing the noblest aspirations of men and suffering when she sees these aspirations not satisfied, [the Church] wishes to help them attain their full realization.").

13. Pope Paul VI, *Gaudium et Spes* (7 December 1965) ("Pulled by manifold attractions [man] is constantly forced to choose among them and renounce some. Indeed, as a weak and sinful being, he often does what he would not, and fails to do what he would. Hence he suffers from internal divisions, and from these flow so many and such great discords in society.")

14. Luke 4:11.

15. Pope Paul VI (1965).

16. Margaret O'Brien Steinfels, "Death and Lies in El Salvador: The Ambassador's Tale," *Commonweal* (26 October 2001), available at www.findarticles.com/cf_0/m1252/18_128/80787129/print.jhtml.

17. John L. Allen, Jr., "These Paths Lead to Rome," *National Catholic Reporter* (2 June 2000), available at www.natcath.org/NCR_Online/archives2/2000b/060200/060200a.htm.

18. Arthur Jones, "Documents Reveal Nuncio's Cautious Human Rights Stance," *National Catholic Reporter* (30 August 2002), available at www.natcath.org/NCR_Online/archives2/2002c/083002/082002m.htm.

19. Allen (2000).

20. Ibid.

21. André Sibomana, *Hope for Rwanda: Conversations with Laure Guilbert and Hervé Deguine* (Sterling, VA: Pluto Press, 1999), 124.

22. Isaiah 43:10.

23. Ervin Staub, *The Roots of Evil: The Origins of Genocide and Other Group Violence* (Cambridge: Cambridge University Press, 1989), 86-87.

24. Timothy Longman, "Christian Churches and Genocide in Rwanda," in Omer Bartov and Phyllis Mack, eds., *In God's Name: Genocide and Religion in the Twentieth Century* (New York: Berghahn Books, 2001), 152.

25. Father Wolfgang Schonecke, "African Churches Draw Lessons from Rwanda War" (Rome: Jesuit Refugee Service, December 1994), 1.

26. Human Rights Watch, *Leave None to Tell the Story: Genocide in Rwanda* (New York: Human Rights Watch, 1999), 246.

27. Longman, "Christian Churches and Genocide in Rwanda," 156.

28. Ibid.; Human Rights Watch, 247. Nsengiyumva was in turn murdered along with twelve other clergy by Rwandan Patriotic Front soldiers on 3 June 1994. Gerard Prunier, *The Rwanda Crisis: History of a Genocide* (New York: Columbia University Press, rev. ed., 1997), 270-71.

29. African Rights, *Hommage au Courage* (London: African Rights, 2002), 178-237; Human Rights Watch, 247-48.

30. African Rights, 163.

31. E.g., Timothy P. Longman, "Empowering the Weak and Protecting the Powerful: The Contradictory Nature of Christian Churches in Rwanda, Burundi, and the Democratic Republic of Congo," *African Studies Review*, Vol. 41 (April 1998), 49-72.

"From the heart, I ask you to pray with fervor and deep conviction for Rwanda. The tragedy of those people seems relentless: acts of cruelty and revenge, murder, the shedding of innocent blood, horror and death everywhere. I invite all in positions of authority to work generously and effectively to end this genocide. It is time for brotherhood! It is time for reconciliation."

Pope John Paul II, Rome, 27 April 1994

THE
CHURCH
AND
PEOPLE

"Again today, I feel it is my duty to recall the violence to which the peoples of Rwanda are subjected. This is an out-and-out genocide for which unfortunately even Catholics are responsible. Day after day I am close to this people in agony and I would like to make a fresh appeal to the consciences of all those who plan and execute those massacres. They are bringing their country to the brink of the abyss. Everyone must answer for their crimes to history and, indeed, to God. Enough bloodshed! God expects a moral renewal from all Rwandans, with the help of friendly countries, and the courage of forgiveness and brotherhood."

Pope John Paul II, Rome, 15 May 1994

PART II
THE CHURCH AND PEOPLE

A Small Country No More

John K. Roth

This book has a map of Africa on page xiv. Rwanda occupies about 9,600 square miles of that vast continent, but it is a small country. Prior to 1994, most of the world's people had never heard of it. Many who knew of Rwanda's existence would not have been able to pinpoint its geographical location, let alone describe its history. Genocide, however, made Rwanda a small country no more. Its name is familiar because Hutus slaughtered hundreds of thousands of Tutsis in a matter of months in 1994 while most of the world stood by.

This book also contains a map of Rwanda on page four. As its caption explains, the map – in addition to delineating provinces and situating towns – highlights some of the sites of massacres that took place in churches and convents. In a country whose 1991 census found 89.9 percent of the population claiming membership in the Christian Church, including 62 percent identified as Roman Catholics, the sites of the mass killing that ensued three years later included churches and convents not because Christians targeted non-Christians but because Christians murdered one another.

Christians often speak of the Church as the people of God. Such thinking is problematic, even dangerous and lethal, if it leads Christians to deny that non-Christians are the people of God as well, a temptation to which Christians have often fallen. Understood better, the idea of the Church as the people of God has a very different meaning. It underscores that Christians are to be those who not only follow Jesus' commandment to "love one another" (John 15:12, 17) but also obey his admonition to "love the Lord your God with all your soul, and with all your mind... [and] your neighbor as yourself" (Matthew 22:37-38). During the Rwandan genocide, those commandments were massively violated by people who identified themselves as followers of Jesus and as members of Christian communities.

During the Rwandan genocide the identities of Churches and their people were turned upside down and inside out. Places of worship became sites where human life was desecrated. Sites that should have been characterized by words of healing, love, and peace became places where brutality and murder reigned instead. Christians who had once said, "The peace of Christ be with you," betrayed that hope by wielding death-dealing machetes. Christians who had once responded, "And with you also," saw their families slaughtered if they were not butchered first.

The reflections that follow in Part II, "The Church and People," sensitively combine anguish and analysis. How did it come to pass that so many Rwandan Christians chose, as Marie Césarie Mukarwego puts it, "to put the Gospel aside" and to become mass murderers? How did Christianity become embedded in Rwanda's ethnic rivalries and their lethal intensification? Are there senses in which some Christian teachings – even "love your neighbor as yourself" – left Christians defenseless and thus all the more vulnerable when the onslaught came? What teachings should a post-genocide Christianity emphasize or reject?

Philippe Gaillard rightly warns against turning the Rwandan genocide into a "case study." That approach runs the danger of reaching too easily for "lessons" to be learned from Rwanda and of jumping too quickly to conclusions about the Church and people. Before lessons are identified and conclusions drawn, the need is to encounter the catastrophic suffering and grief that Christians inflicted on one another during the Rwandan genocide and to ponder the conditions that made that devastation possible.

What happened in Rwanda in 1994 raises questions as important as they are large. None is more basic than the one that links the essays that follow in Part II: What parts did Christian identity play in its Rwandan self-destruction, and can there be a post-genocide resurrection and redemption of that identity that would show once again, and better than ever, that Rwanda is a small country no more.

5

THE FAILURE TO CONFRONT EVIL – A COLLECTIVE RESPONSIBILITY
A PERSONAL REFLECTION

*Charles Petrie**

> My God, my God, why hast thou forsaken me?
> (Matthew 27:46)

During and some months after the 1994 genocide in Rwanda, as I came upon church after church filled with the putrefying corpses of the worshipers who had sought and expected protection, a variant of the words introducing this contribution were ever present in my mind... "My Lord, my Lord why hast thou forsaken them?" In a number of cases the representatives of the Church themselves had led the killers to their prey, some even participating in the murders. A number of these individuals continue to celebrate the sacraments in parishes around the world, protected by the very institutions whose teaching should promote universal peace and forgiveness. Why is this so? And is the Church alone to bear the responsibility for not having lived up to its mission, then and after?

In mid-1994, the (at the time) unimaginable struck Rwanda. From early April to mid-July, a small group of people tried to retain political power by eliminating all who opposed them. What defined this crime as genocide was the fact that not only were individuals targeted based on their ethnicity, but also all those who had any physical resemblance were similarly eliminated. For 100 days, Hutu extremists successfully mobilised a population to systematically and ruthlessly slaughter members of a different ethnic group – Tutsis – for the "crime" of existing, and to kill moderate members of their own ethnic group because they disagreed with them.

---

*Charles Petrie offers these comments as a personal reflection. The paper, therefore, does not reflect the official views or positions of the United Nations or any of its agencies.

The genocide introduced an unprecedented level of nihilistic violence to the region. Once the genocide detonated, it produced a shock wave of terror, which, as it expanded over time and geographical space, triggered a number of secondary explosions. Events in Rwanda ultimately led to large-scale violence in what is now the Democratic Republic of the Congo (DRC), and some analysts argue that the impact of the genocide was felt all the way to Brazzaville (the capital of the Republic of Congo, also known as Congo/Brazzaville), a distance of almost two thousand kilometers. Some contend that it was in the Rwandan refugee camps near Brazzaville, made up of eighty percent Rwandan men and older boys between the ages of fifteen and thirty, that such militia groups as the Ninjas, Koikoi and Cobras[1] were able to find the necessary resources and expertise to wage the first 1997 civil war in Congo Brazzaville.

Many of the major humanitarian organizations in the international community had representatives present in Rwanda at the outset of the genocide. In fact, in the years leading up to the genocide some international donors viewed Rwanda as a development success story, at least as concerned the ease at mobilizing community involvement in the implementation of aid projects. As soon as the killings started, however, most fled, leaving behind a small group of United Nations (UN) peacekeepers, a few representatives of the humanitarian community (most notably among whom were the International Committee of the Red Cross (ICRC) and *Médecins Sans Frontières* (MSF)), and those in Roman Catholic Church structures. Against the backdrop of the international community's failure in Somalia and preoccupation with events in the Balkans in the early 1990s, the unseemly and frantic departure of almost all international personnel, coupled with the flagrant abandonment of communities to the murderous Hutu extremist militia at the gates of compounds from which international staff left, the situation in Rwanda between April and July 1994 represented the total opposite of what the UN and most international humanitarian organizations should stand for in times of conflict – the protection of innocent civilians.

Although the Roman Catholic Church wields the greatest influence, many religious denominations exist in the region. Likewise, although individual priests, nuns and related religious workers have been, and continue to be, exemplars of moral courage, many of their religious institutions have been unable to assert moral authority. Instead, much as the other international players, many of the Christian denominations, particularly the Roman Catholic Church, are perceived as inextricably embroiled in local realities and politics. The result is a perception that the

Catholic religious orders are blind to the evil around them. At times this perception even seems to be translated into fact by the actions and statements of individuals working for or representing those institutions.

In late 1994, for example, a senior Church official in Bukavu, a town in South Kivu (Rwanda), introduced me to the *Préfet* of Kibuye, Dr. Clement Kayishema, later condemned by the International Criminal Tribunal for Rwanda in Arusha for acts of genocide, but who at the time was the medical coordinator for the Order of Malta's[2] operations in one of the refugee camps near Bukavu. This Church official explained that it was only in this way that I would learn "the truth" about the 1994 genocide. For three hours I listened to the *Préfet* explain to me that the Tutsi bodies I had seen in his *Préfecture* during those horrific weeks were those of terrorists, however young they may have looked. I remember that some were nothing more than babies, others in fact babies on the backs of their mothers, but he explained that all were bent on eliminating the Hutu majority.

The *Préfet* told me that the genocide was an event triggered and basically managed by the Tutsis themselves in order to manipulate and gain the sympathy of the international community. Supposedly, it was widely known how well prepared the Tutsis had been. The *Préfet* maintained that it was common knowledge that every Tutsi family in Rwanda, prior to the 1994 war, had dug in the central room of their house a very deep pit within which were to be placed the bodies of their Hutu neighbors, once killed.

I felt physically sick at the time and fought hard to remain lucid. As the conversation continued, I became obsessed with the need to find a way to avoid shaking the *Préfet's* hand at the end of the meeting, a futile attempt at trying to retain some integrity. A concern obviously not shared by the accompanying religious leader who had arranged this meeting for me as a good opportunity to learn the truth about what really happened... Five years later, I would hear similar arguments made in the course of a discussion with the Roman Catholic Archbishop of Bukavu and his entourage.

How different from that afternoon in Kigali in May 1994 when a Missionary Sister of Charity, one of Mother Theresa's Sisters, asked me to pray that she and her children, 150 orphans, be shot rather than hacked to death. Though she was willing to die to protect her wards (it was, she said, part of her calling), she could not bear to watch and hear the cries and supplications of her children "macheted" to death. She had seen too many people die in that way. A few days later, I was to learn that her prayers had been answered and the request "honored" for many of the children.

That Missionary Sister of Charity is an example of extraordinary courage and integrity. When I met her, the *Interahamwe* militia (the Rwandan Hutu militia whose name means "those who work together"), for three days running, had come by and subjected her to sessions of humiliation and intimidation. They were convinced that she was hiding the ethnically mixed members of a moderate Hutu politician's family (a man they had murdered in April). That morning they had stood her up against a wall and acted out a mock execution. This had seriously shaken her. She "admitted" hiding the family to me. We spent two hours talking, trying to find a solution, a way to get the family out in order to save their lives and avoid bloody reprisals against the orphans. Roadblocks manned by extremists surrounded the orphanage. It was even reported that present at one of the barricades was a member of the UNDP (United Nations Development Program) national staff, previously entrusted with the care of the office after the departure of the internationals. We covered every option and finally had to admit that nothing could be done. Somewhat overwhelmed by the implications of the situation, I did not know what to say or to do, and on leaving expressed my sorrow and profound despair at not being able to help her and the children. She looked at me with clear eyes and asked that I pray for their painless death.

I can imagine that my interlocutors in Bukavu would have argued that the Sister should have revealed the hiding place of the family rather than risk the lives of her wards. But that calculation was never considered in our discussion. She believed that her responsibility was towards all in her keeping, and she placed her trust in divine support. She only asked to have the courage to confront the indescribable. Though I understand that she did survive, shattered and tormented, I am not sure how many of the children escaped death.

More than in almost any other context, the term 'evil' is the appropriate one to use. Possibly only the current conflict in Liberia and Sierra Leone can compare to the Great Lakes in the level of senseless nihilistic violence, though some would argue that however totally senseless and extremely violent these contexts are, devoid of a genocidal premise, the violence or evil is different in nature. General Roméo Dallaire, the Commander of UNAMIR (United Nations Assistance Mission to Rwanda) once reportedly said that now he was sure of the existence of God, because in Rwanda he had seen the work of the Devil.

I am convinced, given certain economic and social conditions of need and tension, that any people can be led into committing the crime of genocide. The history of the twentieth century has clearly demonstrated that the propensity to commit genocide is not defined by culture, and definitely not by race. In the course of that century, political groups in different corners of the world have been accused of – and some condemned for – committing genocide: the Ottomans of the Armenians, the Nazis of the Jews and other minorities, the Khmer Rouge of their Cambodian brothers and sisters, and the Hutu-extremist Habyarimana regime of the Tutsis.

My experiences in Rwanda, both during the genocide and more recently in the three years spent in the eastern parts of the DRC, have allowed me to observe some of the dynamics accompanying the execution of genocide and related nihilistic crimes. Possibly what affected me most while witnessing genocide is how ordinary the people committing it were. True, they may have been drugged and worked up, but not all the time. In many sites, the killings took days of hard "manual labor" to complete – after all, hacking a person to death with a machete is very physical – and yet everyone involved was so normal. In the Congo today, as in Rwanda in 1994, it is the ordinary person who has internalized the ideology of extermination. It is the everyday person who killed, and continues to kill, the very neighbor whom, according to religious teachings, he/she is to love.

In the fall of 1995, while undertaking a six-week assessment of conditions in all refugee camps located around Rwanda, I attempted to ask local religious leaders what message they were preaching and whether they received guidance from their superiors. None of those queried were preaching peace and reconciliation. One Baptist clergyman, in fact, argued that it was too early for such messages. Similar positions could be found among the aid community operating in the region. While those in Rwanda were arguing for the rapid repatriation of the refugee populations, those in the camps would not consent to such a return. Thus for more than two years, the international community maintained its support towards a refugee population that rapidly came under the control of the perpetrators of the genocide. The seemingly intractable nature of the "stand-off" further clouded the ability of many national and international actors to view the initial act of genocide for what it was, and thereby understand the longer-term consequences of not confronting it.

Such confusion over the way forward contrasted starkly with the position taken by Father Vieko Curic, a Croatian Franciscan priest, one of the notable examples of moral and physical courage who remained in Rwanda throughout the genocide and saved hundreds of lives. I frequently crossed paths with Father Curic during that period. During the genocide and a number of months later, he refused to provide the sacraments to his flock, finding it inappropriate to do so while they were in the throes of madness; and then after the genocide, only once they had undertaken such acts of collective penance and reconciliation as, for example, rebuilding the houses of their victims. Unknown assailants murdered Father Vieko Curic in early 1998.

The populations of the Great Lakes have not only been desensitized by the violence that prowls through the region, but they have also been dehumanized. The dehumanization process is not a spontaneous one; individuals and communities have to be prepared and conditioned to commit the crime of genocide. Genocidal leadership needs a base of social suffering and tension from which to work. It is only through a sense of personal injustice that individuals can be made to overcome their moral conscience or education and be taught to channel their grievances towards a particular group. The transformation of grievances into active hatred comes through the demonization of the targeted group... a process that takes time. The level of education of a people does not seem to inhibit this process: it only defines the level of sophistication required to mobilise it. The Nazis' manipulation of the German people attests to this fact. One essential factor in leading a people to commit such horrific crimes is the ability to corrupt moral values and beliefs. To make events of real cruelty seem fairly straightforward and natural.

In early 2000, I chaired a coordination meeting in south-eastern Congo. In the course of the meeting, an elderly Roman Catholic missionary of European origin explained that the Banyamulenge had forfeited their right to stay in the Congo. The assertion was based on the fact that "these people" were arrogant. Though they had lived in the Congo for generations, they had refused to intermarry. The missionary could not accept that they refused to mix, that they spoke their own language, and went to their own churches. The conclusion of this foreign spiritual advisor was that the Congolese of Tutsi extraction had no other option but to leave; they would not be allowed to stay. This was presented as a simple statement of fact.

In response to this presentation, an older man working for an Italian NGO (non-governmental organization) remarked that he had heard those very same arguments when he was a very young boy. He had heard such justifications as he fled what he believed to be his home, Poland. He had been forced to run away from a country whose population, or a significant part of it, would not accept that a Jewish boy could be Polish.

The tragedy of Rwanda and the Great Lakes is particular. My experiences in Afghanistan and the DRC have provided me with instructive comparisons to Rwanda. A most recent assignment in Afghanistan, almost eighteen months from early 2002 to mid-2003, brought closer the extent of human suffering the Afghan people have endured through twenty-five years of conflict as a result of international interests, local warlordism and fundamentalism. The suffering continues today as large numbers of Afghans continue to be abused, face real economic deprivation, and suffer extreme hardships. At the time I was there, levels of destitution were desperate. In order to survive, some families were devastated as they had no other option but to give their daughters away in marriage – some as young as seven years old – to ruthless Afghan militia commanders. Others had to painfully accept that their young sons become human mules for powerful drug lords. Despite the ongoing efforts of the international community to assist the Afghan people and attempts to develop legitimate state structures, lawlessness, human rights violations and violence remain rampant throughout many parts of Afghanistan.

While the large-scale human suffering and abuse in Afghanistan reminded me of that witnessed in other horrific situations, Afghan society seemed to have preserved a level of social cohesion. There seem to exist invisible moral or societal codes that helped prevent communities from entering a state of social madness and destruction. Thus, however extreme the situation in Afghanistan, it is different to the one that existed in Rwanda during the horrific 100 days of genocide in 1994, and to the situation which continues to prevail in eastern DRC today.

Attitudes I saw during my subsequent years in Burundi and the eastern portions of the DRC bore an ominous resemblance to the genocidal conditions of Rwanda. Both these areas were engulfed in extraordinary levels of violence, which displaced or consumed the voices of reason of local and traditional authority. Individuals and political extremists were – and continue to be – able to manipulate and escalate relatively harmless misunderstandings into deadly conflict based on a genocidal premise. They were able to brutally exacerbate and exploit traditional social and ethnic tensions and grievances in order to advance their individual economic and political agendas. The continued evolution of armed mercenary elements in the region, some of which participated in the 1994 genocide, has meant that individuals have the power to silence dissenting community leaders.

A particular facet of the current Congolese violence is the articulation of extremist ideologies in everyday social and political discourse. In 1994 the *interahamwe*, and the ex-FAR (*Forces Armées Rwandaises* – the Hutu-dominated army of Rwanda), the orchestrators of the Rwandan genocide, entered an environment already rife with ethnic tension in eastern Zaire, a direct outcome of a policy of political violence promoted in the early 1990s by then President Sese Seko Mobutu. Thus, local political leaders had partially prepared their constituencies to respond to violence against others. As a result, in the DRC politicians and extremist leaders of one group are able to promote the violent displacement, if not even the elimination, of the other, while other extremists argue that large-scale preemptive violence is the only way for the community to survive. In such an environment of hate, too few individuals are able to rise above the violence and appeal for restraint, and most who do are left unsupported.

There is no doubt that the Church should not bear the responsibility of providing support against the voices of hatred alone. The United Nations system and the broader aid community must also question the continued inability to support the courageous voices of reason. More importantly, the UN and many of the member states must acknowledge the full extent of their failure in this region. Acknowledgement of such guilt must go further than an apology. At the very least it should provoke internal reflection and investigation in order to identify the deficiencies that not only promoted inertia but also may have protected individuals accused of participating in the murder of colleagues.

As concerns the Roman Catholic Church, there is no escaping the fact that it failed in Rwanda. Unless the Church recognizes this fact and acts on it so as to avoid a similar situation in the future, it will continue to be unable to fulfill its responsibilities in the region. At a minimum, the Church needs to find the strength and courage to:

- Provide moral guidance to those under its direction and to those entrusted with the responsibilities of moral leadership. Senior officials of the Catholic Church cannot be allowed to continue to explain evil only in terms of ethnic confrontation, thereby insinuating, and even at times arguing explicitly, that there are "good" and "bad" victims. The Church must understand what is at stake in the region, in order to lead those entrusted to its care to freedom.

- Show love and compassion towards those within the Church who helped organize and participated in the killings, while at the same time insisting that justice be prosecuted, rather than letting impunity prevail. That the Catholic Church continues to protect some individuals from secular authority is troubling to believers and unbelievers alike. Such individuals should not be allowed to continue to celebrate the Mass or to administer the other sacraments of the Church. More importantly, they should be helped to confront the sins they have committed, be willing to accept the judgment of law courts, and to do penance – that is, if convicted, to serve their sentence and to make whatever restitution is required.

- Study and draw lessons from the involvement of some of the members of the Church in the Rwandan genocide. Will we have to wait numerous decades before hearing a future supreme Church leader – the Pope – admit responsibility for the failure of his institution to confront the forces of evil that led to the genocide and that continue to roam through the region?

Although special responsibility for failing those under their protection lies with institutions claiming to protect human life, respect for human dignity and the promotion of peace and justice, unless individuals are willing to fight the forces of darkness – of evil – with passion, conviction and courage, there is little hope that those forces will ever be dominated.

Notes

1. Militia groups at the origin of much of the fighting in and around Brazzaville.
2. The Sovereign Military Order of Malta, often referred to as the Order of Malta or Knights of Malta, was founded in Jerusalem in 1099 during the First Crusade. It is one of the oldest lay religious orders of the Catholic Church, an international hospitaller and relief organization. Its motto has been the same since its beginnings, *Tuitio Fidei et Obsequium Pauperum* – to defend the faith and to serve the poor.

6
RWANDA – 100 DAYS – 1994
ONE PERSPECTIVE

Marie Julianne Farrington

On 6 April 1994, the plane carrying Juvénal Habyarimana, President of Rwanda, and Cyprien Ntaryamira, President of Burundi, was shot down in Kigali, Rwanda, and both Presidents were killed. Thus were unleashed the forces that led to the genocide of Tutsis and the elimination of moderate Hutus, that were responsible for the massacre of approximately a million people, all within 100 days.

Even now, nearly ten years later, profound and difficult questions remain. These exist on many levels. It is still not known who shot down the President's plane; other factual matters are unclear. Yet there are still more difficult and painful questions such as: what accounts for the failure of the human community outside of Rwanda to respond to genocide? Relevant to this book's subject is the terrible question: how could such a thing have happened? How could a people predominantly Christian, (sixty-three percent Roman Catholic), have descended into genocide?

It is critical to continue to ask the question. Perhaps it will never be answered satisfactorily, but each attempt should lead us a little closer to understanding, and to changing what needs to be changed so that such a horror is less likely to happen again. The Gospel itself and the true nature of the Church demand that the memory of genocide be kept alive and that the question be endlessly and objectively pursued.

On 6 April 1994, my religious Congregation, the Sisters of St. Mary of Namur, was holding an international meeting of leaders at Vankleek Hill, Canada. I was present at the meeting as Superior General of the Congregation.

We have had Sisters in Rwanda since 1959 when a community of three, two Belgians and a Canadian, arrived in Mubuga, diocese of Nyundo, in north-west Rwanda. On this day in April 1994, we had six convents and forty-three Sisters and novices. Thirty-one were Rwandan, two were from

Zaire and ten were European or American. The numbers of Hutu and Tutsi Sisters were nearly equal.

Those Sisters at the Vankleek Hill meeting who knew Rwanda well, and the tensions that had been building there, immediately feared the consequences of the death of President Habyarimana. The same day, we heard of the attack on "Centre Christus," a Jesuit retreat facility near Kigali airport, where in a frequently repeated pattern, the Tutsis – priests and lay people – were separated from the Hutus and murdered.

From 4-16 April we had telephone contact with the Sisters at our convent in Kibuye, a provincial city in north-west Rwanda where the Sisters from four of our convents and several Sisters from other Congregations were regrouped. Thus we heard directly of the day and night hunt for Tutsis, the searching of the convent, the murder of many people in the area. We recognized the fear in the Sisters' voices and we were frantic in concern and a sense of helplessness. We were grateful to be in touch nearly daily with UNAMIR (United Nations Assistance Mission for Rwanda) in Kigali, and were told of the ongoing massacres there. In addition, there were bulletins coming from various religious sources and the testimony of some returning Canadian missionaries.

From Kibuye, we learned that one of the Sisters had been lost in the forest, hunted by the *interahamwe* (extremist Hutu militia). We had just about given up hope for her survival, when she was brought to the convent, having been hidden and protected for two weeks by Hutu neighbors.

From Belgium we heard that the government was announcing the return from Rwanda of Belgian expatriates, and that we could expect our Sisters who were stationed there. It was with immense relief and gratitude that the Sisters meeting the planes in Brussels found none of our Sisters on them. I believe that the decision of our European and American Sisters to remain in Rwanda was a significant contribution to the safety of our Rwandan Sisters.

On 16 April the phone lines to Kibuye were cut and we entered a period of greater darkness, in which we could no longer express tangibly the throbbing communion of the whole Congregation. At this time, the first Synod of African Bishops was convened in Rome. The Rwandan Bishops who had gathered in Kigali for their departure to Rome were unable to leave because of the violence.[1] On 11 April 1994, six days after the beginning of the genocide, they issued, through the Vatican, the promise of their support of the interim government.[2] In addition, they also denounced troublemakers and requested that the armed forces protect everyone, regardless of their ethnic identity. On 17 April, the Bishops called for an end to bloodshed, holding responsible both the government and the RPF (Rwandan Patriotic Front). On 25 April, they asked all Christians to refuse to kill.[3]

In April 1994, there were nine Bishops in Rwanda, seven of whom were Hutus. The Archbishop, Vincent Nsengiyumva, was extremely close to President Habyarimana, even having been a member of the central committee of MRND (*Mouvement Révolutionnaire National pour le Développement*) for many years, until he was asked by other members of the Church not to take so political a role. He regularly wore a portrait pin of the President on his vestments while celebrating Mass.[4]

Catholic missionaries, in numbers, had gone to Rwanda when the country became a protectorate of Belgium. In this way the Church was associated in the minds of many with the Belgian presence. It was the Belgian administration that instituted identity cards, designating people as Hutu, Tutsi or Twa. Some members of the Church had first favored and promoted the Tutsis, while later missionaries awakened the Hutus to sense an injustice in their situation.

So many burning questions arise for all of us in the Church: to what extent is it important and healthy for the hierarchy to be deeply involved with a government in power? The Archbishop and some of the hierarchy in Rwanda in 1994 had obviously lost their objectivity with regard to the government.

The Church must examine its preaching, pastoral functions, and formation to see how it had confronted conflict between Hutus and Tutsis before the genocide. Frequently, in various countries, we have seen that silence, or looking the other way, is an easy but ineffectual response to ethnic or social conflict. The Church is the traditional advocate of justice, but has not always modeled justice well. In Rwanda, did the institutional Church help Christians to understand and to recognize structural evil, as well as personal sin? Everywhere in the Church, this understanding seems slow to enter Catholic moral teaching and practice.

Beginning on 10 April, the Pope issued a series of anguished and passionate calls for the cessation of violence in Rwanda. In officially expressing his sympathy on the death of President Habyarimana, the Pope addressed himself to the Prime Minister, Mme. Agathe Uwilingiyimana, thereby acknowledging her as acting head of state.[5] On 27 April, the Pope was one of the first world leaders to characterize the events in Rwanda as "genocide,"[6] and he continued his strong appeals through May and June. On 15 May, the Pope spoke of this 'out-and-out genocide.'[7]

On 24 May, the Vatican Permanent Observer at the UN, Geneva, Archbishop Paul Tabet, addressed the Special Session on Rwanda at the UN Human Rights Commission, Geneva. He called for immediate action, saying, "the facts are obvious to all, and to the genocide of a people has been added the systematic extermination of members of the opposition, and of those who attempted to assist those who were being hunted down."[8]

Though the Pope and his representative reacted and spoke strongly and clearly, it is surprising to find so little reaction from the African Synod of Bishops. A general statement on 14 April expressed sadness and pleaded for a peaceful resolution of differences, and was signed for the Synod by the Presidents' Delegate.[9] It is also notable that while various persons or groups wrote or were quoted in *L'Osservatore Romano*, none used the term "genocide" except the Pope and Archbishop Tabet.

On 25 April Cardinal Roger Etchegaray, President of the Pontifical Council, "Cor Unum," called a meeting attended by about thirty representatives of Catholic relief organizations and UNHCR (United Nations High Commissioner for Refugees) and discussed ways to deliver humanitarian aid to the Rwandan and Burundian people. They also appealed for diplomatic mediation and concrete measures to ensure long-lasting development.[10]

While still in Canada, I applied for visas for Congo (then Zaire), for Burundi and for Rwanda. I hoped to find a way into Rwanda to be with our Sisters, and possibly to find a means for them to leave the country until peace could be restored.

Returning from Canada to Namur, Belgium (our Congregation's center), with another Sister, I stopped in New York City to meet with Archbishop Renato Martino, then the Vatican's Permanent Observer to the UN. When Archbishop Martino received us, we presented the list of our Sisters in Rwanda. With it we attached a petition asking the UN to do everything possible to implement the Arusha Accords, to guarantee human rights, etc. We called for an emergency session of the Security Council to strengthen the mandate of UNAMIR in order to enable it to stop the bloodshed. We asked the Security Council to encourage the Organization of African Unity to take action. Archbishop Martino listened to what we knew of the situation in Rwanda and promised to do what he could.

While we were in New York, we also contacted the American and Belgian missions to the UN, presenting the same papers that we had given to Archbishop Martino. We were given access only to minor American officials who gave us perfunctory responses. The Belgian representative seemed more concerned and attentive to our information.

Once back in Namur, I began contacting other religious congregations who had Sisters in Rwanda and discovered that the Superior General of the Assumption Sisters was planning to go to Rwanda. I contacted her and we flew together to Bujumbura, Burundi, on 16 May. There we quickly encountered a Canadian religious who had been based in Butare, south-central Rwanda. Since the beginning of the genocide, she had courageously ferried many people at risk across the border into Burundi. She offered to drive us to Butare and at the border left us in the car while she effectively negotiated with the border guards to permit our passage into Rwanda. This area at the border within Rwanda was then empty and desolate – the scene of some of the largest massacres, the rivers full of cadavers – our Sister driver told us.

Close to Butare we began to meet hostile roadblocks, but finally arrived at the Assumption Sisters' convent. This community, who had lost some of its members, was astonished, overcome and overjoyed to see their Superior from Paris. Sister then drove me to our closest convent, at Kiruhura, about twenty miles north of Butare.

We pulled up before a house locked and shuttered. When no one came, I left the car to walk around to the back of the house. One Sister was coming around the side and I glimpsed others running into the fields. The arrival of a vehicle in the weeks following 6 April had repeatedly signaled demands for money, threats, and attacks. When the Sisters realized that I and the driver were there, they gradually drifted back, amazed and very happy to see us. No one had dared to leave the property since 17 April. There were eight professed Sisters and eight novices, as well as four Sisters from another Congregation at Kiruhura. They were traumatized and drained by constant fear and the expectation of the worst. The mission complex was comprised of small and simple accommodations for the Sisters. There were no walls or protection and they had frequently been "visited" by gangs of militia, sometimes wearing banana leaves – intent on doing their "work." The Sisters had heard and witnessed the murder of many neighbors. Nevertheless, deeply united, the Sisters were trying their best to carry on the community schedule, particularly of prayer in common. They were hiding a woman who had been badly wounded by a machete, and two neighbor children whose parents had been killed.

Over several days, the Sisters had the occasion to tell me what they had been living, and I was able to talk with them, together and in private, and to tell them how deeply the whole Congregation was affected, and also to deliver the mail I had brought.

Kiruhura was in contact with the mission at Ruyenzi (twelve miles from Kiruhura) and with Kibuye, our two other communities. The Sisters had kept contact by wireless as part of the daily routine for many years. I wanted to reach both these convents.

As a result, I went to Butare with the Superior of Kiruhura, in an ancient jeep, to find out how we could achieve this. We went first to the Bishop's residence. Bishop Jean-Baptiste Gahamanyi was imprisoned in his own home. He knew that his sister had been killed close to the mission at Ruyenzi. His office, maintained by a dedicated Belgian laywoman, was a busy place. People came seeking direction and help of all kinds. Many of these persons had been witnesses to terrible massacres of even thousands of people. They spoke hesitantly of their experiences in hushed and incredulous tones.

It was here that I first began to understand the confusion in trying to determine who was responsible for the atrocities. A soldier seemed to be guarding the gate of the Bishop's residence, and yet gangs of militia or *Interahamwe* had already attacked. The Bishop was hiding a number of persons who were in danger.

We quickly realized that if I wanted to visit Ruyenzi or Kibuye, a written permission (travel pass), detailing who could be in the vehicle, had to be issued by the Prefect. We went to the Prefecture, which was surrounded by hundreds of people seeking protection. Later we learned that these people had either been driven back to their communes to be massacred or taken to one of several designated spots in Butare to be slaughtered.

We met with the Prefect, Sylvain Nsabimana, who had succeeded Jean-Baptiste Habyalimana. The latter had been replaced, had disappeared and was eventually executed because he had tried to assure the security of his Prefecture and had resisted the genocide. Prefect Nsabimana gave us the requested permission to go to Kibuye.

There remained the question of a vehicle. The mission at Kiruhura did not have one that was reliable. The Bishop's secretary, by means of strong persuasion, obtained the loan of a vehicle from the Seminary. When we went to pick it up, we found another strongly enclosed community attempting to protect a number of priests. Giving up the vehicle even for a short while was a real sacrifice. Before the end of July, fifteen priests of the diocese of Butare had been killed. The diocesan secretary insisted it was not safe for two Sisters to go alone cross-country. She managed somehow to obtain a military escort comprised of two soldiers and a military chaplain. Only later did I discover that these men had no will to intervene even if trouble arose at the checkpoints. We had decided to return to Kiruhura that evening, the eve of Pentecost, and to come back the next day to complete our business. However, the Suzuki would not start and there was no one to repair it. Many businesses had been pillaged and were closed.

Back at the Bishop's residence, the secretary obtained lodging for us at the African Catechetical Institute (ICA). We walked the several blocks through nearly deserted streets. All the vegetation had been cut down so that it could not provide shelter for anyone being hunted. At each corner checkpoint, we were halted by persons who demanded our destination and checked our passports.

When we reached the ICA, it was entirely in darkness. Sometime after we knocked, there was a very tentative response and inquiry of who we were. Inside, the building was in complete darkness except for some carefully placed candles. The setting was permeated by the smell of fear. A dozen or so persons, some of them injured and fleeing, were clustered in one room listening to a radio. My companion translated for me: one of the visionaries of Kibeho was announcing that President Habyarimana had been received into heaven. Exhausted, full of information and images that were profoundly disturbing, we went to our designated rooms, disgusted with this last detail, to pass a night of troubled sleep.

The next morning, Pentecost, we joined the Bishop for mass in his small chapel in the residence. Returning to Kiruhura, we found the Sisters deeply agitated and saddened. During the night, a gang had descended on the convent, seeming to know that there were persons hidden there. They searched every inch, and had taken away the injured woman and the children the Sisters were hiding. The children were killed, and the woman again cut with a machete and left to die in a latrine. Friends came to tell the Sisters that her cries could be heard for two days.

On 23 April, with one of our Hutu Sisters, I set out to drive from Kiruhura to Kibuye. At that time I intended to return to Kiruhura within a few days. Our escort preceded us. There were then no good roads to Kibuye and we crossed rough and dusty terrain, encountering forty-five roadblocks en route. At each one, a group of men – or sometimes young boys – stopped the jeep and looked at the travel pass, our identity cards and the vehicle ownership. There was obviously a set routine. Some had difficulty – holding documents upside down, unable to read. All were armed either with machetes, spears, or clubs of various kinds, some studded with glass or bits of metal. At every checkpoint one of the group was holding and listening to a radio, which seemed to be of good quality. Here and in other situations at Kibuye, we experienced what a powerful factor the radio was in inciting to continuing violence.

At each checkpoint the men were suspicious, unresponsive; some outright angry and hostile. We were taking sacks of food to Kibuye as well as our own bags. In several places all of this was thoroughly searched. Some men, especially as the day grew later, seemed to be under the effect of a kind of intoxication. With others, a sort of frenzy appeared in their eyes and in their manner. We saw first-hand that once one has killed, a sickness takes hold, which in certain persons is hard to dislodge. At the first very difficult barrier, I left the vehicle to appeal to the soldiers in the jeep ahead of us. They kept their eyes fixed forward, making no response to my requests.

Our route passed by the mission of Birambo, where the Sisters of the Assumption were stationed. I particularly wanted to stop as we had heard that there had been a massacre there. When we pulled up in the cluster of the devastated school and convent buildings, the place seemed deserted. We left the jeep and began investigating. A Belgian Sister came to meet us. On 21 April, three of their Sisters had been taken and killed; two priests, as well as many people of the parish, were also murdered. The remaining Sisters, three Rwandans and two Belgians had arranged the kitchen of the school. They stayed there day and night with a couple of laywomen, sleeping there on the floor. Though they had little food, they offered us something to eat. We gave them news of the outside world and were able to share with them what we had in the vehicle. They told us that some people occasionally dared to come out from the forest to bring them food.

Leaving these Sisters reluctantly, we continued on to Kibuye. In late afternoon we drove up the hill toward the convent and school. Some of the Sisters were in the road outside of the house to welcome us. They knew from the wireless that we were on the way.

What great joy and emotion! There were twenty-two Sisters of St. Mary at Kibuye, including the communities of Mubuga and Kibingo. Also with them were eight Sisters of other Congregations and fifteen secondary students from Mubuga, as well as one child. As it was a boarding school, there were a number of substantial buildings, a water supply and food that had been stocked for the coming trimester. The Sisters had moved to the students' dormitories and only emerged briefly from these buildings to go to the dining room.

On 13 April there had been explosions around the mission. On 15 April, the school secretary was led away and murdered. Some people came seeking refuge at the convent. The Prefect, Clement Kayishema, ordered that they must either go to the church or to the stadium, where he alleged that they would be protected. In previous ethnic conflicts this had proven true. The Sisters saw neighbors, friends, and family leave. All day long on 16 April, the Sisters heard arms fire and explosions coming from the stadium. On the night of the 17th, they heard continuous grenade and other explosions from the church. It was clear that mass murders had occurred.

In and around the beautiful stone church of Kibuye, more than 5,000 defenseless people were slaughtered and bulldozed into mass graves. (In 1996, I visited the UN forensic team, at the time excavating one small section of these graves. The director, later at Arusha, in 1997, told me that three-fourths of those exhumed were women and children, and over thirty percent were children under ten years of age.)

After the massacres in the church and stadium, the militia had come to the convent nearly daily, particularly at night, to harass the Sisters and students. They separated the ethnic groups and threatened the Tutsis with death, on one occasion even leading a group down to Lake Kivu, explaining that they would dispose of the bodies in the lake. The Sisters and students held firm in their unity. One of the Hutu Sisters became spokeswoman for the group, arguing, reasoning, and pleading with the militia and *interahamwe*.

When we arrived from Kiruhura, we found a courageous group of Sisters and students. The Tutsi Sisters were aware that they were the only members of their ethnic group left in the region. Of course, they were horrified, confused, and terrorized. I was able to hear their stories in groups and personally. We wept, reflected, and hoped together. The regular routine of common meals and extended common prayer together steadied and strengthened us. From children in schools in the US, Canada, and Belgium I had brought messages of support and sympathy. The Sisters read these, over and over, and found strength and consolation. Some board games we had with us, played in the dark at night, keeping quiet so as not to attract attention, occasioned some of the first laughter in weeks.

From the beginning, I was searching for the means for all the Sisters and the others at the mission to leave the country temporarily until peace would be re-established. So on the day after my arrival, I went with two other Sisters to the Prefecture. The Prefect was not present that day, but the sub-Prefect began a diatribe against the Sisters, inferring that particular ones were actively discriminating against Hutus. His behavior was unsettling and frightening.

On the next day, we met the Prefect, Clement Kayishema, in his office on the lake. He spoke of protecting the mission, and said that the Sisters and students should not attempt to evacuate by road. His advice was good as many fleeing Tutsis were killed at the checkpoints. He also counseled against boats on Lake Kivu, which he said would be intercepted. That night, a friend of the Sisters came secretly to the convent. He told them that he knew the name of the person who had been designated to kill the Tutsi Sisters and that that man would be returning to Kibuye the next day. He said that the only hope for the Sisters would be if their Superior General remained there.

The next morning, hoping to evaluate the reliability of Prefect Kayishema, I returned to the Prefecture with two other Sisters. Almost immediately, Kayishema began a frenzied justification of the "war." He said that most of the local civilian population was actually in league with the RPF to overthrow the government and that they had to be eliminated. He continued in the same tone for nearly two and a half hours. It was clear that I could not leave.

I wrote to the Sisters at Kiruhura, saying I was unable to return at that time, and said goodbye to the soldiers. The military chaplain drove the jeep belonging to the Butare diocese, in which we had come.

In the days and weeks following, we were constantly seeking possible ways for the Sisters to leave the country, but in every case we were always in doubt as to who could be trusted.

Various events punctuated this time. Once, with the permission of Kayishema, we went to visit our two abandoned missions at Kibingo and Mubuga. The first was completely destroyed. Mubuga had been substantially pillaged, but the structures of some buildings had remained standing. In the jeep on the mountain road to Mubuga, I experienced for the first time the totally unfamiliar odor, descending like a suffocating fog, of the cloyingly sweet-sour smell of mass human decay.

The church at Mubuga had been the scene of another terrible massacre and here the bodies had been left for many days before being thrown into mass graves. When we arrived, some efforts had been made to clean up the church, but holes in the roof, the grenade burns, the stain of blood on the walls, and the odor of death and decay were irradicable. Standing in the church, we felt the utter horror and absurdity of all that had happened.

There were very few people to be seen. Though the Sisters were well-known to the people of Mubuga, the few we glimpsed kept their distance. Who knows what they felt – hostility, shame, a mixture of many emotions.

Later in Kibuye, on several occasions we heard groups of soldiers running in step in the direction of the mission. The first time, we were sure they were coming to take the Tutsi Sisters. Then we heard them singing. They were returning from Bisesero where in the mountains many Tutsis had gathered and were resisting. Singing, the soldiers recounted how many they had killed that day.

As the days passed, it became clearer that it was not possible from the interior of the country to find a way for the Sisters to leave. There were no means of communication either within the country or to the world without. We found a brave driver and I asked Prefect Kayishema for a travel pass. I told him that I would be gone for one day to Goma, Congo, passing through Gisenyi in north-west Rwanda. With two companions, a Rwandese and a British Sister, I set out along the rough route to Gisenyi. There were the usual roadblocks. At one of these, the tire of the jeep was speared, but fortunately we had a replacement.

To reach Gisenyi/Goma, we passed close to Nyundo, the diocesan center. Thirty-one priests of the diocese were eventually killed during the genocide, nineteen of them between 7-9 April near or at Nyundo, where they were having a meeting on 6 April. It is ironic that on 28 December 1993, Bishop Wenceslaus Kalibushi of Nyundo and the clergy of his diocese had issued a press release in which they had noted the distribution of weapons in their parishes and asked the authorities to explain their use.[11] The answer came only in the events of July 1994.

Bishop Kalibushi had always refused to identify himself by his ethnic origin, though he was in fact a Hutu. In the early days of the genocide, he was led outside the city, forced into a mass grave and the militia prepared to shoot him. For some unknown reason, they relented at the last moment and after some weeks he escaped to Goma, Congo. We had the opportunity to talk with him there on two occasions. He was devastated by what was happening to his people and by the death of so many of his clergy.

One heroic example of a Hutu who resisted genocide was Sister Félicitée Niyitegeka, a member of the Auxiliaries of the Apostolate stationed in Gisenyi. She helped many to safety in Congo, for which her life was threatened. Her brother, an army colonel, asked her to stop her activities, but she said she could not. On 21 April, she was taken to a cemetery to be executed with forty-one others. Because of her brother, she was several times given the opportunity to escape. However, she refused to leave her companions and was killed with them. Félicitées has been named among the "heroes of the nation."[12]

As we passed through Gisenyi, we stopped at the convent connected with the cathedral. Three of the Sisters from there had been killed in May.

The doors were locked and the curtains drawn. We knocked and were admitted to find several Brothers and Sisters. The atmosphere was extremely tense.

After a short visit we left to continue to Goma. As we were leaving the house, one of the Sisters called me aside, and looking right and left, led me silently to a small shed. Inside was the fragile eighty-year-old mother of one of our Sisters. Her son had been killed in April, and these Sisters had since been hiding and caring for this woman. She was later brought out of Rwanda and reunited with her daughter.

We had to leave the driver and the vehicle at the border, and after some harassment by the customs officials, we crossed on foot into Congo. We walked into Goma and found the convent of the Bernardine Sisters. Their welcome was warm and gracious.

In Goma I was able on 9 June to telephone to the Generalate in Namur, Belgium. It was the first contact since 17 May. I gave what news I could, and asked that a Sister Councillor who was American (Belgians were also being threatened) come to Goma and then on to Kibuye, in order that I could come out to look for some help – though what help there could be was unclear.

Returning to Kibuye on 10 June, we found the Sisters even more tense and frightened. On the 9th, word had reached Kibuye that a soldier of the RPF had killed the Archbishop and three other Hutu Bishops, as well as at least ten priests at Kabgayi. Several persons had already been to the convent to warn the Sisters that reprisals against them could be expected.

Early in the genocide, toward the middle of April, three priests of Kibuye had been killed. In June a priest arrived in Kibuye from Nyange. Several times he celebrated masses and gave homilies for the Sisters. His behavior and his words were very ambiguous. Later in 1994, he was arrested and charged with alleged crimes committed in Nyange. He was taken to the prison in Kibuye, where in 1998 he was tried, convicted and eventually condemned to death. In October 2000, the Court of Appeals of Ruhengeri acquitted him of all charges and released him.

During these June days the fear and tension continued to grow. The Sisters had been restricted to the convent buildings since the early days of April. It began to seem that the situation would never end, or would only end tragically. Stories and rumors of the advance of the RPF, and the consequent frenzied statements and actions of the authorities then in place were very threatening.

Fear was certainly a huge, if imponderable, factor in the genocide. There can be little doubt that many who were not instigators of the drama were nevertheless drawn into it by fear, either for themselves or for their families. Without living in a similar situation, it is hard to imagine what a strong catalyst fear can be.

On 21 June, an indirect message arrived that a Sister was waiting for me in Goma. With the same two Sisters, I set off again for Gisenyi/Goma carrying a travel permit from Kayishema. In Goma, the Belgian Provincial Superior for Africa and the American Assistant were waiting. The Bernardine Sisters again welcomed us.

At the same time, French troops arrived in Goma and were preparing to mount their military operation – code name *Opération Turquoise* – with its mission "to protect people at risk, but not necessarily to disarm the RGF [Rwandan Government Forces]... to take down the barriers and disarm the self-defense forces and the *Interahamwe.*"[13] We were originally uncertain of the French because among the people we knew in Rwanda, there was the suspicion that the French intended to shore up the government in power. However, a Spanish Carmelite Father, acting as Consul for his country, urged us at least to talk with some French officers who had come to his residence. Our first conversations were brief and very tentative. The French were seeking information on the roads, on local conditions from Gisenyi to Kibuye.

The interim Rwandan Government, having fled from its temporary quarters in Kabgayi, was then established in Gisenyi, and we had an indication that we might receive safe passage out of the country for our Sisters from the interim President and ministers gathered there.

In what now seems a kind of blindness, we wanted to continue to negotiate with this totally discredited government so that the Sisters could leave "legally" and under the "protection" of the same people who, at the very least, countenanced the genocide. Part of this was due to the Rwandan Sisters' insistence that their departure should be only temporary and that they would return to Rwanda as soon as possible. A big factor was the difficulty of discerning truth, with no means of communication in an atmosphere permeated with fear.

On 23 June, with my Assistant and another Sister from Texas who had joined us, and with an interested American and an English journalist, we crossed the border and proceeded toward the hotel on the lake in Gisenyi, where the interim government was struggling to hold on. The atmosphere in the city was surreal. Groups of schoolchildren had been commandeered to stand on the sidewalks of the major thoroughfare, waving Rwandan and French flags to welcome the "saviors" they expected. We were taken for an advance group of the French and hailed. In fact, as far as I know, the French had not yet entered Gisenyi, at least not officially.

What a troubling contrast there was between the beauty of the hotel's setting on Lake Kivu and the hostility and extreme strain of the atmosphere. We expected to meet with some government ministers. However, we were left to wait some time on the terrace and then were taken to the office of Daniel Mbangura, whom we were told was Cabinet Chief. It was immediately evident that he was absolutely opposed to the Sisters' departure. Having made that clear, in a kind of fury he launched into a defense of all that the interim government had done, as justified by the "war," caused by the invasion and advance of the RPF. His discourse was nearly textually a repetition of what I had heard from Prefect Kayishema at the end of May.

We left his office feeling under threat and eager to get away as fast as possible. Our fear for the Sisters at Kibuye had grown even greater. While still at the hotel headquarters, the two Sisters received a travel permit to go to Kibuye and they left shortly after, with the intention of remaining there until some help arrived – or best, if the Sisters could leave the country.

Back in Goma, we again had conversations with the French officers and gradually accepted that their concern was real and that we could trust them. Eventually, we deeply appreciated these men. Finally, we explained what we had witnessed happening in Rwanda and the dangerous situation of our Sisters and others at Kibuye. On 24 June, French troops arrived by helicopter at Kibuye. With Prefect Kayishema they went to the convent. Of course, the Sisters were reticent in expressing their fears.

On 25 June, Cardinal Roger Etchegaray, on a mission for the Holy Father, came to Kibuye. A priest, who had preceded him to prepare his visit, had arranged for the Cardinal to stay at the convent. However, when he arrived, Prefect Kayishema took over all the arrangements and insisted that the Cardinal stay in a motel on the lake. That evening, there was a tightly controlled public meeting, and the Sisters had no opportunity to talk privately or freely with the Cardinal. He was travelling throughout the country in the short period of a few days, and in two locations – with the interim government and with the RPF leadership – he issued an appeal for peace, forgiveness, and reconciliation. Perhaps the Cardinal's activities and contacts were so restricted that he did not see the depth of the genocide and hence condemn the effort to exterminate the Tutsis. Or perhaps he feared that too direct a condemnation would cause further violence and suffering.[14]

In Goma, we tried to explain the constraints the Sisters were under in the presence of Kayishema. On 26 June, the French went again to Kibuye and took some reporters with them. This time several French soldiers were left at the mission. The next day, again trying for an "approved" departure from the country, the Assistant and two other Sisters went again to the Prefecture. Prefect Kayishema once again passionately defended his government's actions. Early on the morning of the 28th, six French helicopters landed on the grounds of the mission at Kibuye and evacuated the Sisters and students, in all forty-seven persons who were taking refuge there. Those being evacuated thought they were being taken to Bukavu, Congo. It seemed like a dream for all of us when we were able to meet them at Goma airport.

In the south, on 30 June, the advancing RPF soldiers reached Kiruhura, where the other group of our Sisters was located. Eventually, they took our Sisters to the mission at Save, to join other Sisters that they had assembled there. When the RPF had fully occupied the area and taken control of the country, they permitted the Sisters to return to their missions, circulate freely in the country, or move out of the country if they wished.

Over a period of time, all of our Sisters left Rwanda, dispersing for some months to our houses in Congo, Cameroon, Belgium or Canada. After a period of healing and recuperation, all have returned to Rwanda.

The first months and years were extremely trying. Much was in ruins. The memories of violence and death were vivid and always present. As did other persons, the Sisters sought the places where their families had been killed. Many recovered bodies and were able to clean, clothe, and rebury their dead with dignity. Places of interment were identified and blessed.

In September 1997, I testified against Clement Kayishema at the International Tribunal at Arusha, Tanzania. I witnessed to the fact that he had clearly exercised authority during the time I was at Kibuye. His defense had affirmed that he had not been able to control events. I was also able to tell of the conditions and situations I had witnessed in my time in Rwanda.

I have been back to Rwanda four times since 1994. In 2000 and in 2003, I led a retreat and workshop which dealt directly with questions of reconciliation in a general way, and also specifically among the Sisters. The Sisters wanted directly and openly to confront painful memories and past history. Their determination, in spite of the inherent difficulty, is to live and to work together in the charity of Christ. Their courage and grace in struggling for genuine unity is an inspiration. They are all fully engaged in ministries of education, health, or pastoral care. After a hiatus of five years, when we decided not to admit any candidates to the Congregation, we now have a number of young women in preparation for religious life.

Though many people were profoundly disillusioned with the Churches during the genocide, and gave up religious practice, in these recent years, there has been a gradual return to the ecclesial community. Now churches are often full and prayer groups flourish.

In the years 1995 and following, the Bishops who had been killed or disappeared in the genocide, and those who died of natural causes, were gradually replaced by the Vatican, thus almost completely reconfiguring the hierarchy. Through the years, many letters have been issued by the Conference of Bishops or by individual Bishops to their dioceses. For example: "We again seize this opportunity to condemn the genocidal acts and the massacres which were committed in Rwanda. We condemn criminal acts which aim to kill innocent people."[15]

On the occasion of the centenary celebration at Save on 8 February 2000, the Archbishop of Kigali, Bishop Thaddeus Ntihinyurwa, asked pardon in the Church's name for the evil caused through lack of courage by some members of the Church, and for crimes committed by some Christians.[16]

On 3 September 1997, Bishop Alexis Habiyambere addressed the Christians of Nyundo. He recognized that violence was continuing. The Bishop condemned all such activity and in the name of the Gospel he called on the people of his diocese to renounce every action and attitude that undermined peace. The Bishop exhorted his people to open their hearts to others as brothers and sisters. The role of parents in forming their children was emphasized. "When a Hutu finds himself in the privacy of his own home, what does he say of the Tutsi? When a Tutsi knows that no Hutu can hear him, how does he speak of him?"[17]

No doubt the gradual transformation of hearts and minds will have to take place in the formation of priests and religious, in the catechesis of children and youth, in schools, in the associations formed on the hills, and those of Hutu and Tutsi widows, as well as in the basic communities favored by many parishes.

Of course many terrible and trying questions remain. I simply mention some here as central to an ongoing analysis. Certain commentators, seeing the moral collapse of the government, of the academic world, of the army, etc., will claim that the Church was neither worse nor better than these other institutions. In all of these groups there were villains and heroes. And yet it would seem that because of the Gospel, the Church's teaching on justice and charity, the claim to grace through prayer and the sacraments, that the Church should hold itself to a higher standard and acknowledge its sinfulness in its participation in the genocide in Rwanda, while continuing always to point to the possibility of conversion and transformation.

A claim that an incomplete evangelization was a factor in the Church's failures needs to be examined. Was preparation for baptism too summarily practiced? In some countries, north and south, it is alleged that Christians adhere to a kind of superstitious dependence on sacraments, without regular clarifying and powerful preaching of the Gospel.

The whole issue of the practice of obedience to God, to elders, to authority needs to be examined. Only a long and enlightened initiation leads from a concept of blind obedience to free, faithful, critical obedience.

The Church in all its institutions and members must denounce extremism in every form. Christians can be helped to recognize this tendency in their own hearts, in others, and in groups and movements. Once extremism is manifested, immediate and radical action must be taken to discredit and uproot it.

The work of various sciences, as well as religion, is required to find the relation – in theory and in practice – of truth, remembering, forgiveness, and reconciliation. A true rebuilding of the nation will depend on this continuing work, and the faith communities have a large part to play.

In 1995, Archbishop Desmond Tutu of South Africa visited Rwanda. He addressed a rally at Kigali where the President and other political figures were present, and spoke some difficult truths: "I reminded the Tutsi that they had waited thirty years to get their own back for what they perceived as injustices done to them. I said that the extremists among the Hutu were also quite capable of waiting thirty years or more for one day when they could topple the new government, in which the Tutsi played a prominent role, and in their turn unleash the devastation of revenge and resentment... I told them that the cycle of reprisal and counter-reprisal... had to be broken and that the only way to do this was to go beyond retributive justice to restorative justice, to move on to forgiveness, because without it there was no future."[18] Archbishop Tutu recounts that President Kagame and others present received his sermon with considerable magnanimity.

In South Africa, in Guatemala, and in various other countries, types of "truth and reconciliation commissions" have done thorough, difficult and efficacious work in the restoration of true national unity. The time for this may not yet be right for Rwanda. However, Rwandans who belong to the Church, and those of us who care deeply about Rwanda and its people, journeying together in the search for truth and in the repeated decision for charity, will help to prepare the future of peace and prosperity for which all long.

Notes

1. The Apostolic Nuncio, Archbishop Giuseppe Bertello, had denounced human rights abuses, disappearances, and assassinations between 1990-1994. He was targeted in the first days of the genocide and barely escaped with his life.

2. Agence France-Presse, "Les Evêques du Rwanda promettent leur soutien au nouveau gouvernement," BQA, No. 14190, 12/04/94, 29, as quoted in Alison Des Forges, *Leave None to Tell the Story* (New York City: Human Rights Watch, 1999), 245.

3. Missionnaires d'Afrique, Guy Theunis and Jef Vleugels, fax no. 10, 25 April 1994, and no. 15 and annex, 26 May 1994, as quoted in Des Forges, 246.

4. Des Forges, 43-44.

5. *L'Osservatore Romano*, 13 April 1994, Weekly Edition in English, pp. 1, 8, 12.

6. Ibid. 4 May 1994, p. 23.

7. Ibid. 18 May 1994, p. 1; 15 June 1994, p. 1.

8. Ibid. 18 May 1994, p. 1.

9. Ibid. 27 April 1994, p. 13.

10. Ibid. 10 May 1994, p. 4.

11. "Kalibushi, Monsignor Wenceslaus and priests of Kibuye and Gisenyi," Communiqué de Presse, 28 December 1993 (ADL), quoted in Des Forges, 146.

12. Des Forges, 248.

13. Roméo Dallaire, *Shake Hands with the Devil* (Canada: Random House, 2003), 450.

14. *L'Osservatore Romano*, 20 July 1994, p. 2.

15. Message de la Conférence des Evêques Catholiques du Rwanda, in Charles Ntampaka, "Controverses sur la Responsabilité de l'Eglise Catholique au Rwanda," *Dialogue*, no. 215, (Bruxelles: Mars-Avril 2000), n. 24, pp.48-49.

16. Ibid., p.50.

17. "Pastoral Letter of Bishop Alexis Habiyambere to the Faithful of the Diocese of Nyundo," *Dialogue*, no. 200, (Bruxelles: Sept.-Oct., 1997), pp. 60-64.

18. Desmond Mpilo Tutu, *No Future Without Forgiveness* (New York: Doubleday, 1999), 259-260.

7

MEMORY NEVER FORGETS MIRACLES

Philippe Gaillard*

"Die Sprache spricht als das Geläute der Stille."
"Language speaks like the peal of bells of silence."
Martin Heidegger, *Unterwegs zur Sprache*

In 1994, before, during and after the genocide in Rwanda, during which around one million people – mostly civilians – were killed, I gave hundreds of interviews, reports and conferences to all kinds of audiences – newspapers, television, radio stations and the general public. At the time, I was the head of the delegation of the International Red Cross (ICRC) in Rwanda. At the end of 1994, I decided not to talk any more about the Rwandan genocide and declined all further invitations. I just wanted to go back to silence and to invisibility, as befits an ICRC delegate and my own rather shy and discreet personality.

Almost eight years [Editor's Note: now ten] have passed since the genocide was committed, and by being here I am once again talking about it. Not because I am less shy today than eight years ago, not because I need to be visible again, but because I still have some kind of debt, or rather duty, towards all those who died in Rwanda in 1994, who were given so little attention later that some people think that the Rwandan genocide can be considered as a "case study." For those who died, and especially for those who survived, the Rwandan genocide is certainly not, and never will be, a "case study." It is because of those victims that I am here today. You may kill as many people as you want, but you cannot kill their memory. Memory is the most invisible and resistant material you can find on earth. You cannot cut it like a diamond, you cannot shoot at it because you cannot see it; nevertheless, it is everywhere, all around you, in the silence, unspoken suffering, whispers, and absent looks. Sometimes you can smell it and then

*Address given at the Aegis/UK Foreign and Commonwealth Office Genocide Prevention Conference, Beth Shalom Holocaust Centre, Newark, UK, January 2002.

111

the memory clearly speaks like the whisper of silence. Sometimes the smell is still unbearable, even when things have been forgotten for decades.

Prevention, neutrality and reporting

In July 1993, two weeks before the Arusha peace agreement was signed by President Habyarimana and Alexis Kanyarengwe, then President of the Rwandan Patriotic Front (RPF), the ICRC met President Habyarimana. When we talked about the danger of anti-personnel mines on the front line, President Habyarimana told us that he was fully aware of it, but added: "The main danger is actually that the hearts and minds of the Rwandan people are mined." This was a "preventive" message.

One month later, after the Arusha peace agreement had been signed, I met Matthieu Ngirumpatse, President of the governmental party MRND, and asked his opinion about the very recent peace agreement. He told me the following: "Sir, don't believe in it too much... In Africa peace agreements are too often just scraps of paper." Just another message of "prevention."

A couple of weeks later, around fifty civilians were killed in the demilitarised zone monitored by the UN troops, led by General Roméo Dallaire. Immediately, a very aggressive campaign was launched against General Dallaire by *Radio Télévision Libre des Mille Collines* (RTLM), accusing him in a very cynical way of not being able to identify and punish those responsible for the killings. Another message of "prevention" by provoking people against the UN peacekeeping forces. The message was clearly translated into action a couple of hours after the beginning of the genocide when ten Belgian peacekeepers were slaughtered by the Rwandan army.

In January 1994, the situation in Kigali was very tense, as it was in February when one minister, Félicien Katawasi, and the President of the extremist party CDR *(Coalition pour la Défense de la République)*, Martin Bouchiana, were killed. Then the dialogue between the government and the RPF stopped. Sporadic fighting occurred in the northern part of the country.

The ICRC was visited by the Director of ECHO, Mr Santiago Gómez-Reino. I had the opportunity to have a private discussion with him, trying to convince him that the situation was very bad. Prevention again. He told me not to be so worried and pessimistic.

Just before Easter, the dean of the diplomatic corps summoned me. He advised me to be on the alert because "something bad" could happen very soon. Prevention. I asked all my people not to leave the town.

The "bad thing" happened three days later when the presidential plane was shot down, killing both the President of Rwanda and the President of Burundi. President Habyarimana had been totally correct when he told us eight months earlier that "the hearts and minds of the Rwandan people were mined." He paid the price for his own strong intuition. Useless prevention. Maybe just careful planning to start the genocide.

As Christoph Plate says: "It is not until war breaks out or famine is rife or there is a massacre that people begin to wonder what caused it. The period prior to the disaster then becomes a news item or a background story. Reports in the media can indeed influence conflicts, but they can hardly ever prevent them."[1]

The Rwandan genocide was so well covered by the media, especially by western media, that everyone could follow it on television, radio or in newspapers every day. One could say that it was "transmitted live," at least live enough to inform governments and the public about what was really happening in Rwanda.

The ICRC contributed to this media coverage in a way that it had perhaps never done before in its almost 130 years of existence. On 28 April 1994, some three weeks after the beginning of the genocide, the ICRC called on the governments concerned, including all members of the UN Security Council, to take all possible measures to put an end to the massacres. The words used – "systematic carnage," "the extermination of a significant portion of the civilian population" – left no room for doubt about what was happening.

At the same time, BBC London called us in Kigali and asked us for our estimate of the number of people killed. We said at least 250,000. One week later, they called again. We said at least 500,000. The following week, we told them: "After half a million, we stopped counting." We were never asked the same question again.

At the beginning of May, I was invited by General Roméo Dallaire to meet with the UN High Commissioner for Human Rights, Ambassador José Ayala Lasso. When we came to talking about figures, I was told I was exaggerating.

I would like to take this opportunity to pay tribute to General Dallaire's courage, actions and always helpful advice. He saved many lives, among them that of our medical coordinator who was hit by shrapnel from an RPF rocket launched on an ICRC convoy on its way from Kigali to Gitarama on 19 May. And believe me, it is not easy to work when you are sentenced to death by militiamen and, even worse, abandoned by your own organisation, as was the case of General Dallaire.

Prevention: zero. Reporting: ineffective. Maybe with one exception: on 14 April, in the presence of the Rwandan armed forces, militiamen killed six wounded civilians who were on their way to our hospital in a Red Cross ambulance. RTLM announced that the Red Cross was transporting "enemies of the Republic disguised as fake wounded." Explanations, protests. At our request, ICRC headquarters issued a strong press release which was immediately broadcast everywhere – by the BBC, *Radio France Internationale*, among others. It had a boomerang effect on the field. The Rwandan Government and media became aware of the considerable deterioration of their image. It was followed by corrections and an awareness campaign on the right of the wounded to care and the role of the Red Cross... It was a kind of test: we could have been killed for that statement, but we were not, and the Red Cross ambulances continued their work without problems. The killing of six wounded people allowed us to save thousands of others – 9,000 altogether between April and July, according to the statistics of our makeshift hospital. Speaking out is always dangerous in such situations, but exceptionally it may be effective.

Neutrality: *the* key point. Many people ask: "How can you remain neutral faced with a genocide?" Of course you cannot remain neutral. But the genocide is happening before your eyes every day. It is a fact. As a Red Cross worker, you really don't have the political – not to mention the military – means to stop it. All you can try to do is to save what can be saved, the leftovers, the wounded. And when I say wounded, I should say people not finished off by machetes or screwdrivers. This was really the case during the first weeks when we were evacuating the wounded – all of them Tutsis – to our hospital.

That is when the problems start. Humanitarian neutrality means first being on the side of the victims, *all* the victims. But when the victims belong to the same category, then their executioners start to look at you with suspicion. This must have been why, after I had given a very difficult interview to Rwandan National Radio, RTLM started to broadcast that I was without doubt a Belgian national, which was simply a death sentence. I was talking with the government authorities in Gitarama when I was informed about that. I asked them to call RTLM immediately and ask them to correct their declaration. They did so in a very efficient, but not very elegant way, by broadcasting that I "was too courageous and too clever to be a Belgian National."

A couple of days later, RTLM was targeted by the RPF. One of their most well known speakers, Noël, was badly hurt in the foot and was brought to our hospital... I felt on the safe side: our hospital had just started to have a mixed population, and this trend increased continuously in the following weeks. Wounded militiamen and members of the armed forces had nowhere else to go for medical care but our poor makeshift hospital. It became a kind of a sacred place, a strong symbol and demonstration of neutrality.

In mid-April, the new Prime Minister, Jean Kambanda, asked us to evacuate the dead bodies from the streets of Kigali. I refused, asking him to stop the killings first. Then the authorities decided to use common law prisoners to evacuate the bodies, but they had no fuel for the trucks. We gave them the fuel. I learned a couple of days later that they had evacuated 67,000 bodies from the streets of Kigali, a town with 200,000 inhabitants before 6 April.

Later on, because of the lack of chlorine and aluminum sulfate, Kigali was left without water. We provided the necessary products. And so on. These humanitarian gestures were duly appreciated.

This might explain why – at our request – the Minister of Labor and Social Welfare, Jean de Dieu Habimeza, went personally to an orphanage close to Gisenyi and, with the full support of the Rwandan armed forces, saved 300 children from certain slaughter by the militiamen. It could also explain why 35,000 people were able to survive in Kabgayi, another 8,000 in Nyarushishi camp, the only survivors from the prefecture of Cyangugu; why another 600 orphans in Butare survived. And so on. Maybe 70,000 people all together, just one millimeter of humanity out of kilometers of horrors and unspeakable suffering.

The most incredible event I witnessed personally happened at the very beginning of July, just before the RPF took over Kigali. Six heavily armed militiamen came to our hospital. They were drunk, but surprisingly not aggressive at all. They had one prisoner, a young Tutsi lady. They told me: "This woman has been with us for the past three months; she is a nurse. We are about to leave the town; we have decided not to kill her despite the fact that she is a Tutsi. As a nurse she will be more useful in your hospital than dead..."

I never received any better acknowledgment of the efficiency of neutrality.

War is destruction, negation of life. Humanitarian action works within this situation. It tries to reduce it. In the case of a genocide, it may seem a stupid gamble, since it is well known that genocidal logic is the complete negation of the humanitarian spirit and law. Whenever you can reduce this negation of life, it is a miracle. And memory never forgets miracles.

Notes
1. "Journalists' Reports Cannot Prevent Conflict," *International Review of the Red Cross*, No 839, 30 September 2000, 617-624.

8

THE CHURCH AND THE
RWANDAN TRAGEDY OF 1994

A PERSONAL VIEW

Marie Césarie Mukarwego

Introduction

Many trace the roots of genocide in Rwanda back to the era of colonization when the colonizers and missionaries divided the Rwandan people, thus creating a total rupture between two ethnic groups – Hutus and Tutsis – who previously lived in harmony. Others say Rwandan society was already divided by the power and the privileges enjoyed by some but not others. Some have noted the differences between Hutus and Tutsis in their educational practices, their social behavior, their trades, even their approach to governance. There also are other views. But all, albeit with varying degrees, charge the Church and White Europeans with having prepared the ground for the genocide.

What one must understand is that the Church is made up of human beings and thus is not shielded from the fragility and weaknesses of our humanity. Those who massacred others during the 1994 genocide were for the most part Christians killing other Christians. The killers had heard the Gospel, many times, in fact. They were quite conscious of it. Some even spoke about it. Nevertheless, they chose to put the Gospel aside. They allowed themselves be manipulated by those whose devilish project was the extermination of others.

Today in Rwanda, we are in the process of seeking reconciliation and justice through the *Gacaca* courts, where witnesses are asked to speak only about what they saw with their own eyes or heard with their own ears during the weeks and months of genocide in 1994. I shall try to do the same in this essay about the Church and the genocide in Rwanda, writing only about the experience I lived through, not about the rumors and stories I heard from others about that time.

Before the genocide of 1994: the problem of discrimination

One unfortunate fact is that in Rwanda there was discrimination against the Tutsis in the schools and public services. This discrimination was practiced by the Hutu-dominated government administrative authorities. For example, students could not freely enroll in schools, not even in Catholic schools, because enrollments were all centralized in the Ministry of Education, as they still are today. The Ministry decided who went where. We in the schools simply received lists of the pupils who were assigned to us.

What was the reaction of the Church to this practice? At one point, the Church asked the Ministry of Education if it could itself choose a certain percentage of student enrollment. We received permission to do so, but then the Ministry required us to give back to them a list of our choices, which they would either approve or disapprove according to the Ministry's own criteria. In making our selection of pupils, we nuns, brothers and priests in our associations, decided to choose poor, less privileged, but intelligent children who were likely to be overlooked by the Ministry. With these percentages, however small, the Church wanted to correct the irregularities observed in the Ministry of the Education regarding how they selected pupils. Heads of schools also wanted the right to select pupils and ask for their admission to their schools. In this way, we thought certain corrections would be possible and that an active and real protest could be made about anomalies in the system.

I remember certain meetings I attended where the subject of free admissions to the schools was discussed frankly, but then quickly eclipsed by the authorities. We did succeed, however, in having one meeting, for a whole morning, with the President of Rwanda, Juvénal Habyarimana. We told him about certain problems we felt were debilitating the country. We said to him what we wanted to say, even though later we did not see much change. We also helped to organize other actions, more directly linked to the safety of people and public peace, such as the "Marches for Peace," organized from 1990 up to January 1994. These involved many Christians and their pastors.

Another activity I participated in concerned ASUMA, the Association of Major Superiors in Rwanda. The members of ASUMA visited all the country's prisons in 1990 after arrests were made of people suspected of being accessories of *Inkotanyi*[1] (Rwandan Patriotic Army), the group which had launched an attack against Rwanda in 1990. With these visits, we tried to investigate the situation of the prisoners, tried to give them moral comfort and to submit a report supporting their release. We all knew these people were wrongfully held.

One year later, we organized visits to camps in Rwanda of displaced persons who had been unjustly deprived of their homes and were literally hostages of the parties in conflict. We took time as teams to listen to them, to be with them, and to work with them. Likewise, after the organization of an inter-African meeting of Major Superiors of Priests in Rwanda, we broadcast a radio message which denounced violence, as well as ethnic and regional discrimination. These examples, although modest, show us in support of the minorities and the innocent.

Statements of the bishops of Rwanda between 1990 and 1994

Up until 1990, the voice of the Church was neither strong nor heard very frequently. Perhaps this is understandable, as the Catholic Church of Rwanda does not have its own radio or television stations – Rwandan Television itself did not begin until 1992. The only way the leadership of the Church could address the faithful was through pastoral letters read in the Churches. Even these communications had their limitations, as they could not be re-read by people because the majority of Rwandans are illiterate. Consequently, pastoral visits of bishops to parishes around the country, or homilies and sermons given at Mass were the only means for the Catholic bishops of Rwanda to transmit their message to the people.

Between 1990 and 1994, however, the voice of the Church grew stronger in tone, audacity, and self-criticism. Various statements and pastoral letters were written in preparation for the visit of Pope John Paul II to Rwanda in September 1990. One strong letter written by the bishops was entitled, "Christ, Our Unity,"[2] and it challenged the faithful and everyone of good will to work together to build unity in the country. Several priests and brothers were upset by the comments in this letter, proof, in my view, that it was vigorous in its appeal.[3] At the time of the Pope's visit to Rwanda, the bishops again took up the topics of unity, justice, peace, and harmony and they issued additional statements which also should be read by anyone interested in the situation of the Church and what it did, tried to do, or failed to do in the years leading up to 1994, and during the genocide itself.[4]

On 7 November 1990, the bishops issued another pastoral letter, "Happy the artisans of peace, for they will be called sons of God."[5] In that letter, they challenged each section of Rwandan society:

- The authorities, whom they demanded should fight against corruption, egoism, monopolization, regionalism;
- The population, whom they invited to avoid ethnic and regionalist

opposition which was likely to lead to a dangerous civil war. Those who fomented such confrontations, they asserted, were criminals;
- Young people, to whom they entrusted the greatest part of the mission of developing the ideal of peace and harmony.

Many other letters and statements were issued between 1990 and 1994, encouraging people to work for peace and unity, urging priests to be vigilant in regard to political parties, challenging them to be the voice of those in society who did not have a voice, and admonishing parties in conflict to start direct, frank talks with each other. The bishops, through individually written pastoral letters and statements to the people in their dioceses, as well as in pastoral letters and statements issued by the Episcopal Conference of Rwanda, drew attention to problems related to the situation in the country.[6] Between 1990 and 1994, the messages multiplied and became more alarming, as deadlock developed and positions hardened between the parties in conflict.

It is also important to note the creation of the ecumenical "Committee of Contacts," formed by representatives of various Christian Churches. This committee had as its function facilitating dialogue between and among the parties in opposition, the party in power, and the armed opposition. The committee published messages and multiplied its contacts with the parties in conflict.

The messages and letters of the bishops were courageous, but they came too late. If these vigorous messages had been delivered ten years or even twenty years earlier, denouncing all injustices and discriminatory ideology, we might have avoided this genocide. But it is not enough to speak; one also needs to be heard. If the authorities of whatever persuasion, as well as the people of Rwanda, had heard and heeded these messages written by the bishops between 1990 and 1994, I believe they could have avoided the tragedy of 1994.

During the genocide

The Church, as an institution, has been put on trial for allegedly having prepared and carried out the genocide with the politicians with whom it was linked. This is both a shame and a scandal, for Rwandans and for foreigners. Did the Church betray its members, its sons and daughters?

What has been written about the Rwandan genocide by those who experienced its atrocities are expressions of their immense suffering and their wounds that are still bleeding. Revenge is the first reaction of those who have suffered so much, and the anger these atrocities provoked needs a scapegoat, one that can be heaped with violence and even with spite. The articles written by people who described the four months of the genocide said that priests had gathered people in the churches all over Rwanda in order to have them killed, and even that they had carried out the killings themselves.

People traditionally took refuge in the churches in times of trouble. Neither those who took refuge there, nor those who welcomed them, suspected what was going to happen. No one among us imagined that the killers would go into the churches and into the houses where people had found refuge. In general, the communities and pastors tried to do all that was in their power to save the people, but faced with a band of armed people, priests and brothers, whose hands were empty, who were without weapons or any means of defense, were powerless. We know that some non-violent priests and brothers were themselves killed along with those they tried to defend.

Refugees very quickly communicated their experiences as they traveled across the country. Their stories caused widespread fear. Many people, priests and nuns included, no longer dared to resist or even to welcome people into their churches and convents because the threat of death was real. We were afraid to see people die. We were also afraid to die ourselves. This was not only true for the Christians. In the strongest sense of the term, all Rwandans were paralyzed and many no longer responded to pleas for help. In some places, even soldiers themselves were afraid of the militia and would not confront them.

In regard to the accusation that the Church – priests, brothers, and nuns – handed people over, what in fact happened? The militia would arrive, demanding that everyone leave the confines of the house so the militia could check whether the occupants included any RPF accomplices. They also searched to see if there were any hidden weapons. Everyone was forced to leave the house. The *interahamwe* (Hutu militia) chose those they wanted and left the others. These scenes were repeated again and again. Today that is interpreted as a betrayal of the people who were being hidden, but few consider the psychological pressure that such a state of stress constitutes, or the fact that every day one was harassed and threatened with death.

I ask myself: Is it really fair to say that the bishops said nothing during the genocide of 1994? It is true that the Church did not speak out. We did not have the courage to assume the consequences of speaking: insecurity, imprisonment, suffering, even death. But I remember speaking to a bishop on 16 April 1994, asking him to broadcast a message to the people to stop the slaughters, and to try to persuade the Christians involved to return to reason. He answered: "I have asked permission to broadcast a message by radio, but I was refused the opportunity to do it." Even if he had been able to obtain permission, it is doubtful whether he would have been able to speak freely.

In his book, Abbé Joseph Ngomanzungu draws attention to messages during the months of April to June 1994 that the bishops tried to make on the radio, without success, however. According to Abbé Ngomanzungu, Radio Rwanda refused to allow the broadcast of an official statement prepared by the bishops of Rwanda on 9 April 1994, in which they demanded that the authorities take care of the safety of the people and their goods, that they neutralize all those who were disturbing the peace, that soldiers protect everyone without distinction of ethnic group, party or area. Everything, they said, must be done to stop the bloodshed, and they urged Rwandan Christians to welcome those who were seeking refuge from the violence and killings. Other messages also were addressed to Rwandan authorities and to the Rwandan Patriotic Front (RPF) by various bishops and by the Episcopal Conference.[7]

To the foregoing, I can add the testimony of my Assumption communities.[8] In one of them, Hutus and Tutsis were aligned against the wall to be killed. Militia men in front were ready to fire on them. A single word saved them all. A Sister recognized the head of the militia and called him by his name, saying, "You, so-and-so, you want to kill us?" He turned towards his men and shouted at them to leave the place. That is how these people were saved at the last minute. This man, head of the militia that came to that convent, is no longer alive.

In the same community, the Sisters and people who were taking refuge with them decided not to show their identity cards so as to confound the militia. It was a gesture of solidarity between the Sisters and the refugees, and among the whole group of refugees. Another group invented a ruse because they wanted to leave the country. They decided to hide their identity cards with their ethnic identity indicated and ask for certificates stating that they had lost their IDs, but still not saying what their ethnic group was. It was difficult to do, but they succeeded in leaving the country. In another community, a Hutu Sister hid Tutsi Sisters inside the convent and spent her day outside negotiating with the *interahamwe* so that they would not enter the house. She gave the militia men all the money that the community had in order to save the Sisters. They all survived; no one was killed.

There are also testimonies of lay witnesses and priests about whom little has been said. A simple night watchman, in the name of his Christian faith, refused to become part of a group of killers. He was killed immediately. Another man hid during the day so he would not be forced to join the armed groups that were hunting Tutsis. To these stories should also be added the names of Sister Félicitée, Abbé Jean Bosco, Augustin, Ananie, and others, who refused to leave their brothers and sisters in danger and died with them. These are positive examples of solidarity and also should be emphasized. Too much has been said about complicity with the militia and not enough about these acts of solidarity, which are more numerous than one thinks.

After the genocide

The Church was the first to be present among the refugees in Zaire, Burundi and Tanzania. It was the first to take steps to encourage the faithful to return to Rwanda.

In December 1994, the bishops wrote a message to the faithful, "Love your neighbor," in which they took stock of the situation after the RPF victory. "Although shaken, let us not allow ourselves to be toppled. Not all were guilty. Some people were irreproachable."[9] In the post-war and genocide period, the promotion of reconciliation and justice have been paramount for the Church.

The Church passed through difficult moments. Its priests, brothers, nuns, and bishops were criticized and condemned, but it has survived the smear campaign some people organized against it. The Church has emerged from this period a humbler, freer institution, particularly in relation to the state, and it is closer to the people of Rwanda. The proof is the *Gacaca*-synods organized in all the dioceses to encourage Christians to speak to one other, to talk to one another about the ethnic problem, to confront it, and to let themselves be challenged deeply by the events they experienced during the war and genocide in 1994. Christians, in their base communities, have spoken about their sufferings, their questions, their internal conflicts. Thanks to the support of the Church, people have confessed their part in the tragic events of our country, and some have asked for forgiveness. Some offered forgiveness in private, others in public. The Hutus, who had been soaked in the blood of genocide, asked forgiveness of the Tutsi survivors, committing themselves to restoring relations. Survivors of the genocide asked forgiveness for having sometimes accused innocent people, which resulted in their being imprisoned, and they committed themselves to visiting them. Together, these Hutus and Tutsis have committed themselves to restarting the path of reconciliation.

Because there was so much killing, there needs to be as much repentance and a determination to live the message of Christ. In such a way, we can see in action the words of Jesus, "The truth will set you free." All those who have had the courage to face the truth are internally free, healed of their wounds, or they are in the process of being healed. This process of reconciliation has been experienced by all sorts of people – by Christians of modest means, by laity engaged in the Church, by civil servants, by priests, brothers and nuns. All affirm that they have been liberated as a result of confronting the truth about themselves and the events of 1994.

A personal example is that of my own congregation. In 2000, the year of the Jubilee of the Catholic Church, the Sisters of the Assumption of Rwanda decided to record their history, beginning with their foundation in 1954 through the recent events of 1994 and to the year of jubilee. We did this within the framework of the *Gacaca*-synods. During the Church's jubilee year, all our communities were encouraged to take the step of forgiveness as a congregation, purifying our memory "of all the failures, the regrettable errors and sins which have left their traces among us." Each province lived moments of reconciliation and forgiveness in the action of grace. Our province of Rwanda-Chad joined this movement by integrating the recent history of our country. The Sisters in communities told their stories and exposed their wounds. They discussed this history and sometimes questioned the people implicated in their lives. In this step, both personally and as a community, we experienced moments of strong emotion, forgiveness, and reconciliation. As a result, we were able to celebrate together the joy of a resurrection for the province.

The process is ongoing because reconciliation is a life-long task. We are happy to carry the wounds of others and to combine the joy and the suffering of "the other" in absolute transparency and with great confidence.

We live together, Hutus and Tutsis. Our daily struggle is to accept our differences – differences of opinion about the recent history of our country, and other differences too. If there is interpersonal conflict, we agreed we would examine it, trying to reconcile ourselves without allowing resentment or bitterness to become reestablished among us.

People are getting accustomed to speaking "the truth" to one another, and they are becoming freer to ask questions which might even embarrass the authorities. They have learned how to assume responsibility for their lives and actions. It is necessary that we continue on this path without tiring.

Translated by Wendy Whitworth

Notes

1. *"Inkotanyi"* translates as 'fierce fighters'; the Rwandan Patriotic Army, formerly a battalion of the army of the King.

2. Episcopal Conference of Rwanda, *Le Christ, Notre Unité* (Letter issued in three parts: 28 February 1990, 6 May 1990, and 14 August 1990).

3. See further, Abbé Joseph Ngomanzungu, *The Church and the Rwandan Crisis of 1990-1994: Essay and Chronology* (Kigali, Rwanda: November 2000) which summarizes this letter, as well as other important statements issued by the Roman Catholic Bishops of Rwanda, other Church groups, and individuals. It is an important source for any serious scholar interested in the complexity of the Catholic Church in Rwanda before and after the 1994 genocide [Editor's note].

4. Ibid.

5. Episcopal Conference of Rwanda, *Heureux les artisans de paix, car ils seront appelés fils du Dieu*, 7 November 1990.

6. See further, C. M. Overdulve, *Rwanda, A People with a History* (Paris: l'Harmattan, 1997); also Episcopal Conference of Rwanda (CEPR), *Collection of the Letters and Messages of the Bishops of Rwanda* (Kigali, Rwanda); and Joseph Ngomanzungu, *L'Eglise et la Crise Rwandaise de 1990-1994: Essai de Chronologie* (Kigali: Pallotti Presse, 2001).

7. See further, Ngomanzungu, *L'Eglise et la Crise Rwandaise de 1990-1994: Essai de Chronologie*.

8. Sister Marie Césarie is a member of the Sisters of the Assumption in Rwanda, a Roman Catholic order of religious women with convents in different parts of the country.

9. Ngomanzungu, *L'Eglise et la Crise Rwandaise de 1990-1994: Essai de Chronologie*, 151-152.

THE
CHURCH
AND
RESPONSIBILITY

Dear People of Rwanda,

One year ago, Pope John Paul II sent me to you as his messenger of peace. Today I am with you again, with the same message, but are you still the same people of Rwanda? After all that I have seen in your land, which has become a land of mud and ashes, I do not understand, no one in the whole world can understand, nor undoubtedly can you yourselves understand, what you have become.

People of Rwanda, who are you today? I do not recognize you. Perhaps until now you have been concealing all that made your life in common difficult. However, now that you have reached the abyss of horror, you can no longer hide your misery. Therefore, I come to say to you, do not despair, convert your hearts, take advantage of this terrible lesson of your history which is probably your last chance to understand how radical your conversion must be....

It is not enough to say: I want peace. (I hear nothing else from you); peace must be made by paying the price that is very high in Rwanda. First of all, this senseless war must be stopped; it will not come to an end automatically. I implore all the political and military authorities to meet once again to declare a cease-fire and to maintain it at all costs. There can be no reason for waiting any longer. Here cease-fire means laying down your arms – machetes and the spears, for every Rwandan is called to make peace.

There have been so many "abominable massacres" (these are the Pope's words) – even inside your churches which have become slaughterhouses of the innocent. There has been so much destruction of your homes, your schools, your social centers. Even more, it is your heart that is mortally wounded....

I come to you in the name of Pope John Paul II to comfort a weakened, dispersed and decapitated Church, due to the assassinations of three Bishops, about a hundred priests, and many religious men and women. You need great fidelity to remain faithful to your Church in its weakness. But look at it carefully. She is still vibrant with the spirit of the Gospel: how very many among you have resisted evil and done heroic acts of charity! One day you will witness the truth of the saying, perennial to the Church: "the blood of martyrs is the seed of Christians."

People of Rwanda, tomorrow can no longer be as yesterday with you. You are called on by God to begin a new page of your history, written by all your brothers, glowing in mutual forgiveness. Believe it. It is possible. On it depends your honor as Christians and as human beings.

Cardinal Roger Etchegaray, Rwanda,
26 June (Gisenyi) and 28 June (Byumba) 1994

PART III

THE CHURCH AND RESPONSIBILITY

The Abyss of Horror

John K. Roth

In late June 1994, Pope John Paul II sent Cardinal Roger Etchegaray as his envoy to Rwanda. Addressing the Rwandan people after his arrival, Etchegaray spoke of "the abyss of horror" created by the mass murder that sundered them. Lest that phrase be taken merely as a rhetorical flourish, consider it in more detail.

The word *abyss* has at least three meanings. It denotes, first, a gulf or pit that is bottomless. This meaning suggests that anything or anyone entering an abyss is utterly lost. Second, *abyss* means chaos or even hell; it refers to disorder in which secure existence for anything or anyone would be impossible until order is created or restored. Third, *abyss* has not only spatial, geographical, or cosmological connotations. The term also refers to the unfathomable depths of mind and spirit that overwhelm human existence when events elude rational comprehension.

Events that elude rational comprehension are often riddled with *horror*, another term that should not be spoken or taken lightly. *Horror* refers to intense feelings of a particular kind and to the actions or conditions that cause them. The feelings, which run deep because they are intense, are those of fear, terror, shock, abhorrence, and loathing. Genocide is a primary instance of *horror* or nothing could be. An *abyss of horror*, then, would be a reality so grim, so devastating, so full of useless pain, suffering, death, and despair that it fractures the world – perhaps forever. Genocide is an *abyss of horror* or, again, nothing could be.

Every genocide has its particularities. The Armenian genocide, which took place during World War I, was not the same as the Holocaust, Nazi Germany's genocidal destruction of European Jewry during World War II.

What happened in Rwanda forty years later had distinguishing marks of its own as well. The chapters in Part III, "The Church and Responsibility," illustrate those marks, especially the essay by James M. Smith and Carol Rittner (Chapter 12), which features photos of churches as memorial sites.

Typically, the genocides committed in the twentieth century have not involved Churches in the ways that characterized the Rwandan genocide. Churches have been implicated in other genocides, and Christians have been perpetrators, victims, and bystanders in genocidal onslaughts before and after the Rwandan genocide. But rarely, if ever before, have church sanctuaries, places of worship and prayer, been the actual sites of mass murder that they became in Rwanda. In numerous places, God's houses in Rwanda became blood-drenched slaughter-benches.

If one seeks icons for an abyss of horror, one need look no further than the photographs of churches-as-memorial-sites that Smith and Rittner reproduce. One shows a crucifix with bones of the murdered in the background. Another shows an altar where a skull has replaced the communion chalice. These images show that genocide respects no haven; it disrespects what is sacred and often does so with impunity, or at least until the damage leaves justice wounded beyond healing and hope bashed hopelessly.

A genocidal abyss of horror cannot be closed. Nor can the questions that it raises be answered with confidence and finality. What can be done is to recognize that abysses of horror remain and that the questions they raise deserve to be confronted as we human beings assess and take up our responsibility for both the abysses and our responses to the questions they leave before us. The writers who contribute to Part III take up that task with passion, compassion, and insight. They do not assign responsibility in finger-pointing ways that assume moral superiority. Instead they probe assumptions, interrogate conventional wisdom, and encourage self-critical soul-searching. Such stances and responses are essential for the responsibility that is needed if the twenty-first century is to limit further abysses of horror and the genocidal impulses that always threaten to produce them.

9

GENOCIDE AND THE CHURCH IN RWANDA

AN INTERVIEW WITH TOM O'HARA, C.S.C.

Carol Rittner

Father Thomas J. O'Hara, C.S.C., a Roman Catholic priest, is a member of the Congregation of Holy Cross, a religious order of men whose members teach and minister around the world. Today he is the president of King's College, Wilkes Barre, Pennsylvania (USA), but for two years in the 1990s, O'Hara lived and taught in Uganda. In January 1996, with three other members of his order – all Westerners, no Africans – he went to Rwanda to try to find out how and where five young Tutsi Holy Cross brothers were killed during the genocide. He is haunted by the horrific stories he heard, the survivors he met, and the killing fields he visited.

In two different essays he wrote for *National Catholic Reporter*,[1] an independent American Catholic weekly newspaper, he reflected on the failures of institutional Church leadership in Rwanda during the 1994 genocide and on what he called an "extremely complicated" history of hostility between the Hutus and the Tutsis, the country's two main tribes. "The history of hostility between these two tribes," he wrote, "goes back some time. Over the years, one tribe serves as the victim and the next time the perpetrator."[2]

Before going to Rwanda, O'Hara had read some powerful statements, including pastoral letters attributed to the Rwandan Catholic bishops, that he considered prophetic and socially progressive. They seemed to be in conflict with the prevailing analysis of the Church's failures during the 1994 genocide. "They lead one to think that perhaps there was another side to this story. Perhaps the blanket criticism of the Church had been too quick and too sweeping."[3] As a political scientist, he wanted to visit Rwanda to try and find answers to the questions he had about Church leadership during the 1994 genocide, as well as to visit where the five members of his order "might have died, where they were buried in order to pay homage to their witness of faith."[4]

I interviewed Father O'Hara in August 2003.

Rittner: Tom, what took you to Africa in 1994, and why did you visit Rwanda in 1996?

O'Hara: I went to Africa in June 1994 to teach at the Philosophical Center Jinja (PCJ) in Uganda, a consortium of Roman Catholic religious communities working together to educate lay and religious men and women from various African countries for ministry in East Africa.   In September 1995, I wrote an article for the *National Catholic Reporter* decrying what I considered the silence of the Catholic bishops of Rwanda in the face of the 1994 genocide.   As you know, hundreds of thousands of Tutsis were killed during that genocide, including scores of religious and clerics who were massacred by Hutus murderously incited by the Hutu-dominated government.   Among those killed were five young Tutsis who were members of the Congregation of Holy Cross.   The remaining Holy Cross members, Hutus, fled Rwanda as the RPF (Rwandan Patriotic Front) invasion succeeded.

In January 1996, I went to Rwanda with three Holy Cross confreres to see if we could find out how and where our Rwandan Tutsi brothers had been killed during the 1994 genocide, plus we wanted to find out how Father Claude Simard, a Canadian Holy Cross priest, was killed after the genocide. The irony about Father Simard is that he stayed in Rwanda to be with the Tutsis as they faced the terrible fear of genocide, even though embassies were urging their nationals to leave the country.   He stayed to preach reconciliation after the RPF set up a new government following the defeat of the previous Hutu-dominated government, but he, too, fell victim to the terrible violence against which he was preaching.

The other reason we went to Rwanda was to visit our Holy Cross properties, because prior to the genocide, we had a novitiate and house of formation for brothers and seminarians in Butare, but afterwards the RPF government appropriated our properties. We wanted to see what shape they were in.

Rittner: Were you able to find out how and where those five Holy Cross brothers were killed?

O'Hara: When we arrived in Butare, a priest from a local parish took us to a field not far from where the CSC (Congregation of Holy Cross) novitiate had been.   He told us that a group of about fifty Tutsis were fleeing from

Butare, trying to reach Burundi, when they were caught by the militia. He was pretty certain our men had been part of the group caught by the *interahamwe*. All of the people were killed by being hacked to death with machetes. They could probably see the mountains of Burundi in the distance, but they never reached them. We visited the site of the massacre about a year and a half after the genocide had ended. Here's what I wrote in my journal about that place:

Today is January 25, 1996. I'm in Butare, 25 kilometers from the border of Burundi. I don't know if I'm going to be able to put into words all that I feel. We've just come back from the site where our Holy Cross brothers were allegedly killed, or so it seems according to the local priest. In recent months, dogs have been unearthing bodies buried in very shallow graves. It seems that some people saw a group of 50 Tutsis who were traveling to Burundi, trying to escape from Rwanda.

We took the road behind the Holy Cross novitiate to a hillside overlooking a valley. At the end of the valley was a road going up another mountain. It was the road to Burundi. You could see the hills of Burundi clearly from where we stood. The 50 apparently were caught and murdered at that point, even as they, no doubt, could see "the promised land" in the distance. Their bodies were thrown into shallow ditches about 50 yards away and covered over.

We walked to the place. I couldn't believe my eyes. We saw pieces of blood-stained clothing and bones. We walked a bit further and came upon a skull in the dirt, mouth open, teeth protruding. It was just one of the most haunting images I have ever seen in my life. It is so seared into my mind, I'll never forget it. Who knows who that person was, or how he or she may have died?

I couldn't get my mind off the CSCs who must have seen their freedom across the valley but couldn't get there. I started to cry. I find it difficult not to cry even now, as I write.

There must have been about 30 children leading us around the field, pointing out graves and bones and skeletons. At the end, the priest who was with us took us before one of the graves, and we prayed. I looked at the eyes of the children as we prayed at this grave. They seemed so sincere in their praying, yet, at the same time, this field is also their play area. They were laughing and smiling amidst all of the bones. It was just too surreal.

The valley is now called "The Valley of Death" because thousands were killed here on the way up the same road to Burundi.

To be honest, we were not certain we were praying at the grave of those five young Holy Cross brothers, but given the evidence the priest had gathered, we probably were as close as we were ever going to get to where they actually died.

Rittner: Were you afraid while you were in Rwanda?

O'Hara: Yes, I was afraid because I was a priest. Even though I was not wearing a clerical collar at the time, my passport photograph showed me dressed in a clerical shirt and from time to time I had to show my passport to various officials of the government.

Rittner: Why were you afraid? You were an American, after all, carrying an American passport. You weren't Rwandan. You weren't a Hutu or a Tutsi, so why the fear?

O'Hara: That's all true, but it was pretty clear to me that the Catholic Church in Rwanda was under a lot of suspicion. I didn't know who to trust. I heard many conflicting stories about what went on during the genocide, about what the Church did and did not do, about what individuals did and did not do, including what priests and nuns did and did not do. It was hard to know exactly where the truth lay, or who was telling the truth. There was a lot of fear in the air, so, yes, sometimes I was afraid.

I remember when I was leaving the country, for example, a guard took my passport, looked at the photo, then asked me if I was a priest. I said, "Yes, I am." He threw my passport on the floor and spit on it. I didn't know what to do, whether I should pick it up, or not. His supervisor came over and apologized for that man's behavior, then he told me that the guard had had a brother who was killed in a church during the 1994 genocide and that the man still held the Church responsible for his brother's death.

I also remember when we were making plans to go from Uganda to Rwanda, we had to go to the Rwandan Embassy in Kampala to get a visa. We had to make a strong case for why we even wanted to go to Rwanda. The Rwandans at the Embassy were not particularly eager to have any foreigners go to Rwanda, and they especially were not eager to have Western religious go there. The RPF was angry at the Church and at the United States, and here I was, an American priest, asking for permission to travel there. They weren't too happy.

Rittner: Why was the RPF so angry with the Catholic Church?

O'Hara: I think it was because during the genocide, the Roman Catholic bishops of Rwanda were generally silent, as you know. I also think they were angry at the Church because there were some Hutu priests and nuns who had encouraged Hutus to massacre Tutsis and, even worse, sometimes themselves even participated in those massacres, so the RPF government had reason to be angry.

Rittner: While you were in Rwanda, were you able to move around freely, or were your movements restricted?

O'Hara: We were able to move around freely. We visited many places, including the church of *Sainte Famille* (Holy Family church) in Kigali, where hundreds were massacred, and where Father Wenceslas Munyeshyaka had been parish priest. He's in France now, but according to what we were told, he was very comfortable with the Hutu-dominated military during President Juvénal Habyarimana's time, and he also was very friendly with the militia groups before and during the 1994 genocide. He is accused of having participated in the genocide by pointing out the Tutsis who had taken refuge in his church compound so the *interahamwe* could kill them. It's a terrible story. You can't imagine what a strange, eerie feeling it was for me to be in a church where people had been massacred and murdered during a genocide. It was a confusing, difficult place for me, and it was very hard for me to pray in such a place.

From *Sainte Famille* church, we drove on to a convent where we spent several hours talking and listening to the Sisters. It was mind-blowing. The Sisters are North Americans. One of the Sisters was from the United States. They run a place for widows and orphans. They try to give these women and children some skills so they can survive, because they don't have husbands, and in their world that is a distinct disadvantage. The Sisters also let them grow crops in their fields.

One Sister took us on a tour of the convent. Several times, as she told us what had happened there, she began to cry. Every place we went, people would tell us stories about what had happened, and then they would cry. It was very, very emotional. Their convent is very large, and in 1994, they had nearly thirty young women in the process of religious formation. During the genocide, they lost twelve young Tutsi Sisters. These young women were forced to jump into a pit latrine, and then, while they were still alive, they were killed by being covered with rocks and dirt.

They told us about how one day the *interahamwe* came, took them all to the basement, lined them up, and separated Hutus from Tutsis. We saw the corridor where the Sisters were lined up. It is L-shaped. Because they were kept at angles to each other, the Sisters couldn't see each other, although they obviously knew what was happening. Sister cried when she told us how the Hutu Sisters knelt and prayed in one corridor while the Tutsi Sisters were forced to lie face down in the adjoining corridor. At one point, two militia men put their machetes on the back of one of the Tutsi Sisters and asked her if she had anything to say. She said, "You are still my brothers." They left that day without killing anyone.

After the *interahamwe* left, thirteen Tutsi Sisters left the convent compound and tried to make their way to their own homes, but they were caught. They knew they were going to be killed, so they asked not to be killed by machete. The only other option, they were told, was to jump into the pit latrine and be buried alive, so that's what they chose. One Sister managed to escape death by standing pressed against the wall of the pit latrine as the stones and dirt came pouring down on them. She somehow survived, climbed out of the pit, and eventually made her way back and told the other Sisters what had happened.

Sister told us another incredible story about twenty-five Tutsi women and children who came to the convent looking for refuge. The Sisters took them in and hid them in a storeroom in the convent's basement. When the militia came, one of the North American Sisters met them at the door of the convent and assured them there were no Tutsis in the building, but the militia demanded to go through the house, room by room, to search for Tutsis. She led them from floor to floor, opening door after door to show them that the rooms were empty. When they went to the basement to search, she stood in front of the storeroom door behind which all the Tutsi women and children were hidden. She said the door was not quite as noticeable as the other doors in the hallway. Brazenly, she pointed to the hallway and said, "There they are, you can see all the rooms. See for yourselves. There is no one here except us." Miraculously, the Hutu militia believed her, and the Tutsis hidden behind the door in front of which she was standing were saved.

That courageous nun told us other stories about how other people also protected their neighbors. She also told us a story about sixty Hutus who were killed at a Catholic parish because they tried to protect their Tutsi neighbors and friends.

Rittner: When you were in Rwanda, were there still signs of the civil war and the genocide in evidence, or had it all been pretty well cleared up and cleaned up?

O'Hara: Even in January 1996, we still saw lots of signs of the 1994 war all around us. On the veranda of the convent, for example, there were two huge indentations from mortar attacks in the middle rail, and in the chapel, right next to the crucifix, was a big bullet hole that had still not been repaired. The Sisters wanted to leave the wall as it was, unrepaired, the bullet hole there, next to the cross, a constant reminder to them of the pain people experienced during the 1994 genocide – and were still experiencing in the aftermath of the genocide.

I asked one of the Sisters if the men who came and threatened them were Catholic, and she said, "Of course, they were Catholic, but their Catholicism was a very shallow Catholicism." I also asked her how the government was responding to the Church in 1996. She said, "The government tolerates us now."

As far as I could tell, the Church also was extremely cautious in dealing with the government, perhaps because the Church hierarchy and even some religious apparently *were* part of the problem. It's clear also, however, that there are many stories of heroism, stories about Church people and other committed Christians who tried to save people during the genocide. The complication and confusion results, I think, because *all* Church people are being lumped together and condemned as one because the bishops were basically silent during the 1994 genocide, and because some priests and nuns in Rwanda are identified with the *genocidaires* and have even been convicted of the crime of genocide.

Rittner: You met a lot of people while you were in Rwanda, both clergy and non-clergy, nuns and lay people, villagers, city folks, and survivors. Did you meet any killers?

O'Hara: To be honest, I don't know. Hundreds of thousands of people were massacred in a very short time, and you need a lot of people to carry out such a project, but whether or not I met any killers, I just can't say. What I can say is that in January 1996, there seemed to be a lot of people in Rwandan jails. In fact, the jails were overflowing, literally bursting at the seams. Again, based on what I was told, there were some people in these jails because someone else had identified them as being part of the *interahamwe*, the people who were incited by the Hutu-dominated government actually to do the killing in 1994. Some people I met seemed afraid that they too might be pointed out as *genocidaires*, not because they were involved in the 1994 genocide, but because someone might have a grudge against them and want to get even, so people were fearful and suspicious.

Rittner: From what you could observe while you were in Rwanda, has the Church tried to make any response to the 1994 genocide?

O'Hara: I don't mean to be hopelessly romantic or idealistic, but we have to remember that "the Church" is the people. We often limit "the Church" to the bishops, which is a very incomplete notion of Church.

I think it's absolutely clear that during the months of the genocide, April to July 1994, the Rwandan bishops failed to live up to their Christian convictions, failed to give moral leadership in a time of evil, and failed to condemn the genocide. But they're not the whole "Church," they are only part of "the Church." We have to remember that there were Hutu Catholics who lived up to the highest ideals of the Gospel by risking their lives trying to save Tutsis – they're also part of "the Church" because "the Church" is the people of God. We mustn't forget that. I don't know all that the Church in Rwanda tried to do after the genocide, but whatever it was or is, I'm sure it's not enough.

I do know that some priests organized a meeting after the genocide ended to try to begin the process of healing within "the Church" and within the country. While I didn't meet any Rwandan bishops, I did meet some of the priests who organized that conference, and I found them absolutely determined to face up to and deal honestly with the failures of "the Church," both the failures of the hierarchy, the failures of the clergy and religious, and the failures of so-called "ordinary" Catholic Christians during the 1994 genocide.

Rittner: What about your own Holy Cross Congregation, in Rwanda and beyond, how has it responded to the genocide and its ramifications?

O'Hara: We've been in East Africa for more than fifty years, but, prior to the 1994 genocide, in Rwanda itself only for about twenty years. French Canadian brothers started a trade school there for young men. After a while, both Tutsis and Hutus asked to join the Holy Cross community. A candidacy program and a novitiate were established, and, as I said, five of our men were killed during the 1994 genocide, and later our property was appropriated by the RPF government. There is considerable discussion now about when it might be appropriate for us to go back to Rwanda, but it's a delicate issue.

Not long ago, and for the first time, a Rwandese Tutsi, Father James Burassa, was elected Holy Cross district superior. He lost his family in the 1994 genocide. While I was in Uganda, Father Burassa made his final vows. I went to his final profession ceremony and Mass. I remember after he made his vows, he began to dance in thanksgiving. Another Tutsi brother got up and joined him and some Tutsi nuns also started to dance. Then, some Hutu brothers got up, tentatively at first and also started to dance. It was a very, very emotional experience for everyone, because ethnic tensions were still so high.

Unfortunately, the scars of the genocide are still fresh in the minds of our African CSCs. We have to come to come to grips with this and try to do something about it, but the question is *how* to do so because tribalism in Africa seems to be much more powerful than religion is. It's an issue we have to face, but also one that the Church in Africa has to face and come to terms with. It's not easy.

Rittner: I don't remember exactly who wrote this – maybe it was the late Peter Hebblethwaite at the time of the 1994 genocide in Rwanda – but what I remember is the comment that tribalism in Africa is more powerful than the waters of baptism. That really struck me. I also remember reading that what the Church did in Africa – and probably in other parts of the world as well – was "sacramentalize," but it did not "evangelize." Do you think there's any validity to those comments?

O'Hara: I think it's true that tribalism is an overwhelmingly defining factor in Africa, and I also think it's no exaggeration to say that tribalism in Africa was, probably still is, more powerful than baptism, even today. As for sacramentalizing versus evangelizing, it's hard for me to understand how people who have apparently accepted the Gospel, who go to church on Sundays and holy days, perhaps even go to church daily, could hack people to death with machetes just because they are different from themselves. But then it's also hard for me to understand how American Christians can sometimes do what they do in the name of American foreign policy. I don't want to categorize the faith of Africans as shallow, because I don't see the faith of American Catholics as so strong, or different from what I experienced in Africa.

Rittner: It's now a decade after the genocide in Rwanda. What are your thoughts and feelings today about what you experienced in Rwanda, short as your visit there may have been? What questions are you left with about the Church, about the leadership of bishops, about priests, and nuns, and the laity?

O'Hara: I re-read parts of my journal last night. I was very emotional, because this stuff is hard for me to read, even more than seven years later. I have questions about the degree to which governments and organized religion will "go along" simply to "get along." I am haunted by questions about the kind of pervasive evil that can overcome the Gospel. Rwanda was a very, very dark page of the Church in Africa, which is not to say that there were not, and are not, good churchmen and women who continue to risk their lives in service to others in Africa and elsewhere, that there aren't good men and women, religious and clergy, including bishops, who continue to work for justice, peace, and reconciliation in Rwanda. We can't ignore those people, even though we have to face the failures at the heart of the Church there and elsewhere, but we have to recognize that words aren't enough. It's not enough to issue pastoral statements, even if the words are so-called "prophetic." What's needed is to turn prophetic words into prophetic actions. The reality is that you can promulgate all you want, but it's actions that are going to make the impact on people's lives and in society.

The issue of the 1994 genocide in Rwanda and the Church – the whole Church, not just the institutional leadership of the Church, important as that was, and is – is extremely complicated. I think it does not help anyone to just look for the "good guys" and the "bad guys" and then to make blanket statements. Evil was perpetrated; evil occurred. The hierarchy of the Church in Rwanda is not without fault and blame for what happened; the United Nations is not without blame, and neither is the American government and the larger international community. There are no saviors in the sad story of Rwanda. I don't think all the evil was rooted out or that goodness overcame the evil. No one in Rwanda has escaped the pain and suffering or the aftermath of the genocide. I think Rwanda is still in a very difficult situation, but it is not a land without hope. Courageous Christians are there, willing to start again, to try to really be what all of us who are called to be disciples of Christ are called to be. They deserve the support of the universal Church.

Rittner: Thank you for taking the time to speak with me about your experiences and insights.

Notes

1. Thomas J. O'Hara, "Rwandan Bishops Faltered in the Face of Crisis," *National Catholic Reporter*, 29 September 1995, 16-17; Thomas J. O'Hara, "Amid Graves, Some Rwandans Reconcile," *National Catholic Reporter*, 23 February 1996, 10-11.

2. O'Hara, "Amid Graves, Some Rwandans Reconcile," *National Catholic Reporter*, 11.

3. Ibid.

4. Ibid.

10

THE CHRISTIAN CHURCHES AND THE CONSTRUCTION OF A GENOCIDAL MENTALITY IN RWANDA

Matthias Bjørnlund, Eric Markusen, Peter Steenberg, Rafiki Ubaldo

Introduction

In just over 100 days in 1994, the tiny, densely-populated nation of Rwanda erupted into one of the most savage and lethal genocides of the 20th century. In that short span of time, seventy-five percent of the Tutsis in Rwanda – as many as 800,000 – were exterminated alongside thousands of pro-democracy Hutus. Hundreds of thousands of killers and accomplices were responsible for the slaughter. Among the *genocidaires*, there were many poorly-educated young men recruited by the government for the express purpose of slaughtering Tutsis, but there were also many educated people.

The Rwandan genocide had a number of peculiarly Christian aspects or dimensions. Rwanda was the most Christian nation of Africa, with as many as ninety percent of the population identified as Christians, sixty percent of whom were Roman Catholic.[1] Moreover, as we discuss below, the Christian Churches in Rwanda – and the Catholic Church in particular, which was the first to establish missions around the year 1900 – exercised considerable power in Rwandan society, both during the colonial period and after independence.

Also, unlike most other genocides in which members of one religious group attempt to eliminate members of a different religious group, in Rwanda both the killers and their victims were Christian, often fellow Catholics, Anglicans, or Seventh Day Adventists. The Organization of African Unity, in its report on the genocide, noted that "many priests and pastors

committed heinous acts of betrayal, some under coercion, others not.
Significant numbers of prominent Christians were involved in the
killings...”[2]

For example, on 19 February 2003, the International Criminal Tribunal
for Rwanda found Pastor Elizaphan Ntakirutimana (and his physician son)
guilty of genocide for their roles in several massacres of Tutsi Christians who
had sought refuge in buildings in the Seventh Day Adventist complex
headed by Ntakirutimana.[3] Catholic, Anglican, and other churches and
church-school-hospital complexes became, according to the Organization of
African Unity Report, “...primary killing sites. Many churches became
graveyards.”[4]

The question then naturally arises: what made so many thousands of
ordinary Hutus turn against friends, family members and members of their
own congregations?[5] Since we believe that, as Bill Berkeley puts it, “Hate
mongering in Africa, no less than elsewhere in the world, is an acquired
skill,”[6] it makes sense to explore how such a “skill” was acquired in Rwanda.
To try to answer this question, we attempt an exploratory, preliminary
application of a concept from the field of genocide studies, the so-called
“genocidal mentality,” to the case of the Rwandan genocide, and in particular
to the role of the most influential Church in Rwandan society, the Roman
Catholic Church.

After discussing the concept of genocidal mentality in the following
section, we will then examine how the Roman Catholic Church, as a powerful
institution in Rwandan society both during and after colonialization, may
have helped to create what eventually became a pervasive genocidal
mentality, in which members of the elite and masses came to believe that
they should and must exterminate their Tutsi neighbors.

We intend to explore how the Roman Catholic Church and its
missionaries during the colonial period helped define and then supported
the Tutsi minority – and then, as Rwanda became independent and had
national elections, abruptly reversed course and supported the Hutu-
dominated government and promoted Hutus in Church-supported religious
and educational programs. There is general agreement among scholars that
the Churches in this way contributed to the perpetuation of fear and hatred
between Tutsis and Hutus, and therefore can be counted among Christian
Churches from all over the world that, as Omer Bartov and Phyllis Mack
write, have been “...involved on several levels in preparing the theological,
moral, political, and mythical groundwork for genocide in this century.”[7]

We reiterate that this is a preliminary, exploratory study. We do not presume to have firm conclusions, and much more work needs to be done on matters we do discuss. However, our goal is to try and shed some light on how such a tragedy came about.

The concept of genocidal mentality

In 1990, Robert Jay Lifton and Eric Markusen published the book *The Genocidal Mentality: Nazi Holocaust and Nuclear Threat*, in which they examined the analogies (and "dis-analogies") between the mindsets of perpetrators of the Holocaust and nuclear strategists. One of the fundamental ideas behind the concept of a genocidal mentality is that the ideological and mental processes that facilitated the Holocaust resemble and can be compared to processes leading to other cases of genocidal violence. Even though each case takes place in specific historical circumstances, many of the mechanisms that are used to prepare for and justify destruction of a targeted group are similar. In the nuclear context, Lifton and Markusen defined genocidal mentality as "a mindset that includes individual and collective willingness to produce, deploy, and, according to certain standards of necessity, use weapons known to destroy entire human populations – millions, or tens or hundreds of millions of people."[8] In 1999, in a short entry in the *Encyclopedia of Genocide*, Markusen and Lifton expanded the concept to include "the willingness of governments, and their citizens, to engage in the mass killing of innocent people."[9]

Preconditions for a genocidal mentality

Preconditions for a pervasive genocidal mentality in both elite and general population include distrust, fear and hate, generated by real or perceived historic injustices committed by one group against another, by economic crisis, and by major societal upheaval, particularly war. Then, in order for actual genocide to take place, a sufficient number of individuals within the genocidal regime must be willing to engage directly in, or support, the killing and other forms of destruction of large numbers of human beings.[10]

In describing the situation in Europe after World War I, Omer Bartov exemplifies these preconditions when he emphasizes "...the links between the trauma of war and the new destructive urge of European society, between fear of personal and collective annihilation and the evolution of a genocidal mentality, all within the context of this new and devastating event of industrial killing."[11] This is reiterated by Lifton who writes that when a society is exposed to "...extremes of social, political, and cultural collapse," the people can experience "...psychohistorical dislocation, a breakdown of the social and institutional arrangements that ordinarily anchor human lives,"[12] and by Ervin Staub, who states that, "One frequent starting point for group violence is represented by difficult conditions of life in a society, such as severe economic problems, intense political conflict, or rapid and substantial social change."[13]

According to Leo Kuper, the risk that such "difficult conditions of life" will lead to organized mass violence like genocide is generally heightened in what he calls "plural societies." Plural societies, in Kuper's definition, are societies with substantial cleavages between ethnic and/or religious groups, and this is often a precondition for domestic (as opposed to e.g. "utilitarian" or colonial) genocide. In such societies, "There is often a history of conflict, which is expressed in the crystallization of historic memories and in hostile and dehumanizing perceptions of other groups... The effect is to create a general status, a total identity, based on race, nationality, ethnicity, or religion."[14]

From preconditions to a genocidal mentality

As a consequence of the above-mentioned preconditions: 1) Individuals or groups imbued by an elitist and rudimentary genocidal mentality (and/or driven by desire for personal and political gain) may begin to blame one or more groups – ethnic, racial, religious, political, or other – for the real or perceived societal ills and historical injustices. If these individuals and groups create or join what would usually be a totalitarian party or other exclusivist and undemocratic political platform, this may then lead to the development of an actual genocidal ideology that not only identifies one or more groups as the root cause of problems, but also proposes their removal as a necessary and legitimate means to solving these problems.[15]

A well-known case in point to illustrate this development is the story of Adolf Hitler, who, as Ian Kershaw states, "traumatised by defeat and revolution, and looking for those to blame... converted his existing, until now probably relatively conventional, antisemitism into a full-blown political ideology aimed at expunging the 'disgrace' as he saw it."[16] According to Lifton, the basic genocidal dynamic in such a genocidal ideology can be explained by a perception of collective illness and a vision of a cure.[17] The first step toward a cure is then the construction of an ideology "that explains the malaise and promises to restore the sense of integrity and security that was destroyed or threatened by the dislocating 'illness'."[18]

2) If the totalitarian group with genocidal inclinations or desires gains power, the next steps include an escalating campaign of discrimination and marginalization, as expressed by Barbara Harff: "...the early stages of genocidal policies are likely to include campaigns of hate propaganda and the issuance of directives and laws that provide justifications and instructions for acting against target groups."[19] Ultimately, this process will result in mass violence against such groups. If a regime succeeds in creating a broad popular basis for such an atmosphere, and also succeeds in encouraging and staging such acts, a genocidal mentality has been created.

Elements of the genocidal mentality

For the present purposes, we will focus on three elements of the genocidal mentality: "legitimation," "the healing-killing paradox," and "dehumanization." These components are used by perpetrators and accomplices on different levels of society to justify, both politically and psychologically, the actual implementation of genocide.[20]

Legitimation

"Legitimation" has been used as a top-down approach to turn ordinary people into perpetrators of, or accomplices in, genocide, throughout the twentieth century. As Roger W. Smith writes: "Genocide must be legitimated by tradition, culture, or ideology; sanctions for mass murder must be given by those in authority; the forces of destruction have to be mobilized and directed; and the whole process has to be rationalized so that it makes sense to the perpetrators and their accomplices."[21]

The notion of "legitimation" is a crucial part of any ideology – "ideology" understood as a system of beliefs supporting a political agenda – even in dictatorships like Nazi Germany. The argument in such systems is often that, "If ideological claims are considered absolutely true, then their consequences must be viewed as equally absolutely legitimate."[22] This means that even racist and murderous ideologies need to be legitimated in the eyes of the regime itself, its followers, and the outside world. Furthermore, legitimation is important in creating a genocidal mentality, since it can function as direct or indirect authorization of transgressions via the dissemination of a genocidal ideology. A definition of legitimation given by Terry Eagleton illustrates this: "Legitimation refers to the process by which a ruling power comes to secure from its subjects an at least tacit consent to its authority... It can have something of a pejorative smack about it, suggesting the need to make respectable otherwise illicit interests."[23]

The detection in a society of the practice of legitimation of, for instance, persecution, is in itself not sufficient to predict or detect a genocidal mentality: that leaders decide to legitimate the overall societal marginalization or scapegoating of an out-group does not necessarily mean that a genocide has been planned or that it will take place. But, together with societal disruption, cleavages and with other elements of the genocidal mentality, legitimation is an essential precondition for genocide.[24]

The healing-killing paradox

The "healing-killing paradox," where killing becomes a prerequisite for healing, is another important element of a genocidal mentality.[25] It is a mirror image of (and is legitimated by) the illness/cure-component of a genocidal ideology, but the healing-killing paradox is directed towards justifying the actual killings by a perpetrator. By destroying (members of) a group that is viewed as being responsible for the societal "illness," the perpetrator group and its members are then saved or cured. Because the targeted group is perceived as a threat, moral and ethical transgressions in the course of destroying this group are generally viewed as ugly, but necessary, patriotic and legitimate acts.[26]

As with most other elements of the genocidal mentality, this "paradox" is usually part of a deliberate strategy initiated by the societal elite: propaganda, euphemisms, threats and indoctrination are used on a collective level to create what Lifton calls an "institutionalized schizophrenic mindset." Lifton states that for the individual "healer," in this case any Nazi doctor in the death camps, this mindset meant that he became a killer "...in connection with the larger biomedical vision (curing the Nordic race by ridding it of its Jewish infection), whatever the degree of intensity or amorphousness of his involvement in that vision."[27]

Dehumanization

The healing-killing paradox is connected to another common element in the ideological creation of a genocidal mentality, the dehumanization of victims. Dehumanizing images of the perceived enemy are often systematically spread by using various forms of state-sponsored propaganda, legitimated by people with the power to decisively influence hearts and minds: politicians, priests, teachers, etc. Then, on an individual level, destroying the group becomes easier: by regarding members of a targeted group as vermin, subhuman, or less-than-human, the victims no longer merit empathy or mercy.[28] As Gregory H. Stanton puts it: "One group denies the humanity of another group. Members of it are equated with animals, vermin, insects or diseases. Dehumanization overcomes the normal human revulsion against murder. At this stage, hate propaganda in print and on hate radios is used to vilify the victim group."[29]

Other discussions of the genocidal mentality

Other scholars have used or been inspired by the notion of a genocidal mentality, although they have not attempted to give an exact definition.[30] The renowned historian Ian Kershaw, in a 2003 paper titled "Genocidal Mentalities," stressed that in order to understand how and why genocide occurs, it is necessary to comprehend both "...the circumstances which draw individuals into perpetrating mass murder, *and* the mindset of, especially, the leadership groups where a strong ideological predisposition to actions which could turn into genocide prevails."[31]

Although Kershaw's notion of "genocidal mentalities" seems to have been developed independently of Lifton and Markusen's notion, there are important similarities. As a common element of and precondition for creating and sustaining a genocidal mentality, Kershaw implicitly recognizes the principle of the healing-killing paradox when he describes Nazi ideology as amounting to "a utopian vision of national salvation, to be attained by internal 'cleansing' of 'impure elements.'"[32] He also explicitly notes the importance of dehumanizing the enemy, and the role of state propaganda in this process.[33] Regarding individual psychological factors, Kershaw recognizes how war and propaganda brutalize attitudes, "both towards the military enemy and towards the stereotyped 'enemies within.'"[34]

The psychologist Dan Bar-On partly builds his notion of the genocidal mentality on Lifton's 1986 book, *The Nazi Doctors: Medical Killing and the Psychology of Genocide*, and focuses on the socialization of genocidal killers in his paper, "Genocidal Mentalities Have To Be Developed."[35] Bar-On's notion of the concept generally follows the same lines as Lifton and Markusen, as he recognizes the importance of a context of severe societal crisis, and of key elements such as the healing-killing paradox (implicitly), and dehumanization (explicitly). This is shown when he states that the rationale for committing genocide "must include a 'moral' or 'positive' goal to be achieved by the genocide (e.g., 'purity of the race,' 'eliminating the cancer of our nation'), combined with monolithic dehumanization and devaluation of the target population..."[36]

One result of such an ideologically-driven genocidal process is that the perpetrators, as noted also by Lifton and Markusen, perceive themselves as "moral people": they were on a mission.[37] Also, Bar-On notes how perpetrators are often systematically desensitized by training process. This process is created by the "architects of genocide," the political and military leaders. Propaganda and socialization of killers is necessary since perpetrators are usually "normal" people: they are not born with genocidal mentalities.

In sum, there is consensus among those who have dealt with the concept of "genocidal mentality." For genocide to occur, first a genocidal mentality, building on past myths and ideologies, has to be developed in the societal elite or in totalitarian groups aspiring for power. This takes place in periods of chaos, cleavages and social trauma, and the genocidal mentality then becomes the basis of a genocidal ideology which claims to cure the societal "illness" by eliminating one or more groups. The genocidal ideology is in turn used to disseminate the genocidal mentality in society. Key elements of the genocidal mentality are legitimation, the healing-killing paradox and dehumanization.

The Catholic Church in Rwanda and the Hamitic Myth: preconditions for a genocidal mentality?

Steve Utterwulghe has stated that "The prevalence of... an anti-Tutsi atmosphere was indubitably inflamed by extreme propaganda and a burdensome socio-economic situation, but the genocidal mentality was a product of a longer and much more complex process."[38] In light of the preconditions for a genocidal mentality that we have identified, we will focus on an examination of the role that some of the "healers" of Rwandan society – the organisation of the Roman Catholic Church and its members – might have played in facilitating such a mentality, with particular emphasis on their significant role in the creation, legitimation and institutionalization of the so-called "Hamitic Myth."

The Hamitic Myth

When studying literature on the colonial period in Rwanda, it soon becomes clear that a wide variety of scholars agree that missionaries and Churches in Rwanda helped create and legitimate what eventually became what Kuper calls a "plural society" – a society with ethnic cleavages and fatal political and economic divisions that potentially can be "cured" by ethnic or racial "homogenization" by groups in power.[39] In Rwandan society, a very important historical precondition for the creation of cleavages was the fear and distrust created by imposed and unjust ethnic divisions that stemmed in large part from the colonial period.

From the beginning of the German colonialization of Rwanda in the 1890s, Rwandan society simultaneously experienced the disintegration of political and social structures, and the construction of rigid identities – Tutsi, Hutu and Twa – which transformed Rwandan society socially, economically and politically. Throughout a nationwide network of Catholic missions and through Church-dominated activities like education, Tutsis were designated as "Hamites," literally descendants of Noah's youngest son Ham, arguing that at some point in the distant past the Tutsis must have been exposed to Biblical influence, thus explaining the disposition to embrace Christianity that gave the Tutsis a privileged place in Christian evangelism.[40] As Timothy Longman explains:

> In Rwanda, missionaries played a primary role in creating ethnic myths and interpreting Rwandan social organization – not only for colonial administrators, but ultimately for the Rwandan population itself. The concepts of ethnicity developed by the missionaries served as a basis for the German and Belgian colonial policies of indirect rule which helped to transform relatively flexible pre-colonial social categories into clearly defined ethnic groups. Following independence, leaders who were trained in church schools relied extensively on ethnic ideologies to gain support, thus helping to intensify and solidify ethnic divisions.[41]

This was not an unusual colonial practice. As Bill Berkeley states: "...the gathering of Africans into identifiable 'tribes' was... a convenient administrative tool.... Tribalism solved the colonial dilemma of how to dominate and exploit vast numbers of indigenous inhabitants with a limited number of colonial agents, by mobilizing groups on the basis of linguistic and cultural similarities that formerly had been irrelevant."[42]

From the beginning of the colonial period, this was accomplished by European missionaries (especially the so-called "White Fathers," Roman Catholic missionaries from the order of "The Society of Missionaries of Our

Lady of Africa"), by colonizers, and by anthropologists inspired by Darwinist ideas of ethnic and racial hierarchy. Religious, political, and pseudo-scientific ideas and practices were instrumental in dividing the Rwandans into three distinct races: the "pygmoid" Twa who were the indigenous, primitive inhabitants of Rwanda; the "Bantuic" or "Negroid" Hutu, who were farmers that at some point drove the Twa hunters and gatherers from the soil; and the pastoral "Hamitic" (and/or "half-European," "*nègres aristocratiques*," "Semitic," etc.) Tutsi, who arrived as the last group. Then, as Christian Scherrer describes it, "The German colonial rulers, the Catholic missionaries, and later also the Belgians lent this classification pseudo-scientific weight by citing human measurements [...] and degrees of skin pigmentation."[43]

Missionaries and colonizers generally ignored the fact that in the pre-colonial period, there was both a degree of social mobility and frequent intermarriage among these groups, making the system less based on ethnicity than on what we could call "class"[44] or "clans."[45] Also, the Hutu, Tutsi and Twa "ethnic groups" do not correspond with what Nigel Eltringham has called the "...'conventional' definition of such entities: they do not speak different languages, practice different religions, eat different food, reside in different territories."[46] Even more problematic, ethnic divisions were systematically racialized, making the already inflexible cultural and political notions of ethnicity a matter of biology. Thus, in the colonial period, it was to become official history that Tutsis, by means of their "half-European" mental and physical features, since at least around the 17th century had dominated and exploited the Hutu and Twa "races," and that the European colonizers simply were a natural extension of this rigid, hierarchical system.

As stated in the section discussing the genocidal mentality, legitimating ethnic and racial stereotyping is not necessarily the same thing as legitimating genocide by creating a genocidal mentality, but, as the anthropologist Alexander Laban Hinton explains it, "The very act of categorizing entails essentialization, as certain naturalized traits are attributed to given groups. Nationalist ideologies thrive on such categorizations, since they construct unmarked categories of normalcy that privilege, and often legitimate, domination by one type of person over another (marked, subordinate, binary opposite, dehumanized) one."[47]

The institutionalization of the Hamitic Myth

The Churches and missionaries in colonial Rwanda sometimes protested against what Christophe Kougniazondé has called "...the ruthless iron fist of the Belgian colonial state,"[48] for example, the arbitrary punishment and forced labor that was imposed on especially Hutus. However, he continues, "...religious influence, on the other hand, constituted the superstructural rampart without which colonial brutality against, and de-humanization of, the Rwandese people could not have reached its goal without any major social explosions against the Belgian colonial regime."[49] In working closely with, and thereby legitimating, the colonial administration, the Churches, and the Roman Catholic Church in particular, were also instrumental in institutionalizing the racist Hamitic Myth and the ethnic divisions.

The impact of the Christian Churches in Rwanda was strengthened by the fact that they were the nation's second largest employers, only surpassed by the government, thereby making them a major material as well as spiritual influence on the general population.[50] On a practical level, missionaries helped the process of institutionalizing racism by teaching this fabricated version of Rwandan history in the country's primarily Catholic schools, and by selecting Tutsis "... to promote 'western civilization founded on Christianity.' The other groups, the Bahutu and Batwa, constituted a mass of [commoners] relegated to the status of second-class citizens."[51]

But even though the myth was created that all Tutsis thereby were made rulers, in fact only around ten percent of this group had any actual influence or wealth; most Tutsis had little material benefit from this "caste system."[52] As Timothy Longman writes, "The inaccurate idea promulgated by the missionaries that Tutsi had grossly exploited the Hutu for centuries continues to shape Hutu understanding of Rwandan history and eventually became a primary ideological justification for genocide."[53] In colonial Rwanda, discrimination and the creation and institutionalization of racial cleavages – features that historically have served as important preconditions for a genocidal mentality – were wholeheartedly supported and legitimated by both individual clergy and by the Churches as institutions – especially the Catholic Church.[54]

Post-colonial Rwanda: religion, the Hamitic Myth and the genocidal mentality
In the so-called "Hutu social revolution" of the late 1950s that culminated in independence in 1962, the tables turned: now the Hutu majority controlled Rwanda, and around 150,000 Tutsis had to flee from massacres and persecution to neighboring countries like Congo, Uganda and Burundi. There, groups of guerillas that later became a military insurgence were organized among the refugees.[55]

MATTHIAS BJØRNLUND, ERIC MARKUSEN, PETER STEENBERG,
RAFIKI UBALDO

The Belgian colonial authorities, backed by the Catholic Church, had in the 1950s concluded that even though there were rising nationalist aspirations among both Tutsis and Hutus, Tutsi nationalists were considered a greater threat because of alleged leftist leanings. The way to avoid Communism in Rwanda would therefore be to support Hutu nationalists, especially in the all-Hutu PARMEHUTU (*Parti du Mouvement de L'Emancipation Hutu*), against the Tutsis.[56]

During this period of political upheaval, a new generation of Belgian missionaries and civil servants reacted against the injustice suffered by the Hutu majority and started supporting their emancipation, ignoring the fact that the vast majority of Tutsis were equally poor and oppressed. Opportunism and idealism resulted in a complete reversal of support and sympathies from the small Tutsi elite that the colonialists and Churches had placed in their dominant positions, to the Hutu majority.[57]

The Bahutu Manifesto, March 1957

That racial divisiveness was on the agenda of the PARMEHUTU soon became clear. The racialization in the colonial period of both real and perceived differences between Hutus and Tutsis was intensified and radicalized, and the Catholic Church as an institution played a significant role in this process. According to Mahmood Mamdani, "It is from the ranks of the Church-connected movement that the leadership of the 1959 Revolution was drawn. On the morrow of the revolution, that same leadership used the power of the state to establish control over Church education, both in terms of its content and its personnel. The fusion of the Church and the state, both in personnel and in vision, was symbolized by the fact that the archbishop of Rwanda sat as a formal member of the Central Committee of the ruling party until he was forced to resign in the early 1990s, on the eve of the Pope's visit to Rwanda."[58]

An important example of Church involvement was that the pre-independence "Bahutu Manifesto" of March 1957 was supported by significant members of the Catholic Church in Rwanda. The manifesto was written in part by PARMEHUTU leader, former editor of the Catholic paper *Kinyamateka*, and later president Grégoire Kayibanda, among others. In a 1991 semi-official Rwandan academic publication, it is stated that "The sketch of the manifesto was reviewed and commented on by [the cleric Chanoine Ernote and other clerics] before being published,"[59] while Jean-Pierre Chrétien writes that "the manifesto was made popular among Hutus through Catholic structures" with the help of the printing house of the Diocese of Kabgayi, and of Fathers like Arthur Dejemeppe.[60] This was the case even though the manifesto explicitly both continued and radicalized colonial ethnic divisions by designating Tutsis as not only an oppressive Rwandan ethnic elite that should give up power, but as a foreign race that did not belong in Rwanda. According to Mamdani, "[The manifesto] claimed that 'the conflict between Hutu and Hamites – i.e., foreign-Tutsi' was the heart of the Rwandan problem..."[61]

The radicalization and racialization of ethnicity that took place during the rule of subsequent Hutu regimes was not only based on this accumulated sense of injustice and anger towards Tutsis, but also on the more pragmatic idea that marginalization of Tutsis would be economically and politically advantageous for Hutus. Thereby the ruling (and from 1966 only legal) party PARMEHUTU secured complete control.

Even though the name of the ruling Hutu party changed to MRND (*Mouvement Révolutionnaire National pour le Développement*) in 1975, the racist ideology stayed largely the same. In the years leading up to the 1994 genocide there was a continuing pattern of Hutus discriminating against and, after the RPF (*Rwandan Patriotic Front*) invasion in 1990, massacring civilian Tutsis,[62] of impunity for such crimes, of fights between the Rwandan army and Tutsi guerillas, and of Tutsis fleeing the country. This was accompanied by an increasingly dehumanizing rhetoric against Tutsis that had as an important part of its basis the Hamitic Myth.

For example, in a public speech in Butare in September 1959, the future President Grégoire Kayibanda expressed this kind of rhetoric when he said that "Our movement focuses on the Hutu group: outraged, humiliated, despised by the Tutsi invader... We have to enlighten the population, we are here to give the country to its rightful owners: It is the country of Bahutu."[63] But Kayibanda did not stop at what could be interpreted as "mere" legitimation of ethnic divisions. In the context of continuing attacks from "*inyenzi*," ["cockroaches," i. e., Tutsi guerillas], in thinly-veiled phrases he threatened the whole Tutsi "race" with genocide. In March 1964, in an editorial in the Rwandan magazine *La Croix*, No. 31, addressed to "*Rwandais Emigrés ou Réfugiés à l'Etranger*" (i.e. exiled Tutsis), the now president Kayibanda wrote that "...suppose that you [Tutsi invaders] against all odds overtook Kigali by attack. How do you imagine the chaos of which you would be the first victim? Obviously: you guess it, otherwise you would not act like... desperados! You would say among yourselves: 'It would be the total and hasty end of the Tutsi race.' Who is genocidal? [*Qui est genocide?*]"

Significantly, our source for this Kayibanda editorial is an issue of the Rwandan magazine *Dialogue*, No. 146, May-June 1991. In this influential magazine for the Rwandan elite, under the heading "Society and Development," Kayibanda's speech is introduced by the editors as follows: "27 years later, this message by President Kayibanda remains of remarkable actuality. It definitely shows that the October war [i.e., the 1990 RPF invasion] is the consequence of the denial and conservatism of a party of Rwandan refugees who have never accepted their defeat." Even more significantly for the purpose of this article, *Dialogue* had strong ties with the Rwandan Catholic Church: "The magazine *Dialogue*, without being an organ of the Church, is however more than just inspired by Christianity. It is founded by a cleric (the Abbot Massion). Priests (G. Musy, Y. Pomerleau, G. Theunis) are the pillars of this magazine."[64]

The editors of *Dialogue* clearly saw important parallels between earlier Tutsi attacks on Rwanda, and suggested a solution similar to the one Kayibanda threatened to use in 1964: genocide. Only this time, it was in the context of an actual civil war, and actual genocide was committed only three years later. The re-printing of the Kayibanda editorial is a clear sign of an emerging genocidal ideology. In the 1991 context of ethnic cleavages and social trauma, it is also a sign of how a genocidal mentality had developed since independence: influential parts of Rwandan society, including Catholic clergy, proposed or helped propose genocide as a solution to real or perceived societal problems. And the Catholic Church as an institution did not protest. In the highly Christianized Rwandan society, the combination of Church clergy cooperating with genocidal elements and lack of protest from the Church as an institution would be seen by many as legitimation and tacit agreement. As Hugh McCullum states: "Church pulpits could have provided an opportunity for almost the entire population to hear a strong message that could have prevented the genocide. Instead the leaders remained silent."[65]

After this brief review of events during and after Rwandan independence, we tentatively conclude that during this period, preconditions for a genocidal mentality in Rwanda (historically exemplified by the Hamitic Myth and the institutionalization of ethnic divisions that had been aggravated by social disruption, i.e., revolution, massacres, guerila attacks, etc.) led to the development of a genocidal mentality in the Hutu elite (especially in PARMEHUTU, the ruling, totalitarian party of the new Republic), which then led to the creation of an anti-Tutsi ideology that had increasingly strong genocidal elements. As the Burundian scholar, Father Adrien Ntabona, states, "The genocidal ideology is the consequence of totalitarian ethnocentrism. First one imposes a totality of ideas and afterwards one massacres those who do not agree, especially those of the other race. That genocidal wish in our region was born with the Rwandese revolution in 1959."[66]

Racism, the Hamitic Myth and Christian imagery

As the following statement made by a Twa man in Kigali in 1993 indicates, the Hamitic Myth had been thoroughly internalized in Rwandan society on the eve of genocide: "Our ancestors were the first to occupy this territory when it was totally forested... Their happiness and pleasure in their way of life and the adequacy of resources in their environment were disrupted by the land tillers (Hutu) who came second... They overran the forests and our ancestors were forced to shift from time to time further away from the machete and hoe. By the time the Hamites (Ba-Tutsi) arrived along with their herds of cattle the forest had nearly vanished and the country was becoming semi-arid."[67]

This racist myth was not completely uncontested, though. In the years leading up to the 1994 genocide, there was, for instance, some awareness in the Rwandan Catholic Church of the problems created by Church involvement in the institutionalization of the Hamitic Myth and of the subsequent discrimination against Tutsis in Rwandan society, including Church-run schools. In a letter of 8 May 1989, P. Augustin Ntagara, Professor and Dean at the *Grand Séminaire* of Nyakibanda, wrote about these problems to Joseph Ruzindana, Bishop of the Byumba Diocese and President of the Episcopal Conference: "...I have to inform you about the 'virus' that for the last 15 years has been eating away our Catholic Church of Rwanda in general... that virus is racism – it is a matter of fact. The last 15 years our Church has adopted a policy of apartheid, disguised behind slogans of unity and peace..."[68]

But the official political use of the Hamitic Myth – and thereby the legitimation of a society divided along "racial" lines – was still generally supported by the Churches of Rwanda and its now mainly Hutu clergy.[69] The new priesthood simply maintained the practices of their European predecessors. And as indicated by the 1991 reprint of Kayibanda's 1964 speech in the magazine *Dialogue*, genocide was even considered by influential, Church-affiliated segments of Rwandan society to be an option for "solving" problems of ethnic cleavages and social disruption. The political and economic context of this growing genocidal mentality had all the marks of what Staub calls "difficult conditions of life": the RPF invasion of October 1990 spread fear and further radicalized the political climate in Rwanda,[70] and the country was in a severe economic crisis. Newbury and Newbury write that "...Rwanda of the late 1980s and early 1990s was characterized by growing regional differentiation in political access, social polarization between rich and poor, and a strong awareness of increasing marginalization among urban poor and the majority of rural dwellers."[71]

In this context, Christian images were used by President Habyarimana's Hutu government and its propagandists to convey messages of Hutu unity against not just the Tutsis in the RPF, but against Tutsis in general. For instance, on the front page of a 1991 issue of *Kangura*, "...a weekly newspaper with a relatively small circulation but which had the support of powerful government and military figures,"[72] there is a manipulated picture of President Habyarimana where he is made to look like he is wearing the vestiture of a Catholic Bishop. In his hand he holds a book with the word "*Ubumwe*," meaning "unity," on it, and a caption next to the picture reads: "My Christianity is the reason why Rwandans consider me a priest. Therefore, the malcontents have to realize that if I take off the robe, Hutu can take decisions."[73] As with the article in *Dialogue*, such use of powerful religious imagery probably had the desired effect that many readers of *Kangura* saw it as the Roman Catholic Church legitimating the government and its thinly-veiled threats of violence against "malcontents," i.e., Tutsis – especially since the Church as an institution generally did not react against or comment on such use.

The crystallization of a genocidal mentality: dehumanization, the healing-killing paradox and the Hamitic Myth

The marginalizing and stigmatizing anti-Tutsi propaganda that was systematically spread before and during the genocide can be seen as promoting the development of both the healing-killing complex and dehumanization. By placing the Tutsis "outside the universe of obligation" of the majority Hutus, persecution and finally genocide was both legitimated by the elite as well as made relatively easy for the individual perpetrator on a psychological level.[74] Dehumanization was facilitated by the Hamitic Myth, which designated Tutsis as "foreign invaders" who would bring back feudalism.[75] According to the propaganda in the media, especially on the hate radio RTLM (*Radio-Télévision Libre des Mille Collines*) it was either kill or be killed.[76] A worldview had already been established of "us" vs. "them," and fear and hatred in the context of war and poverty intensified intergroup hostility. As Scott Peterson states, in the mind of many Hutus, "There was no question about it: the loser was to be annihilated."[77] Dehumanization was exacerbated by the widespread use of anti-Tutsi derogatory terms like "cockroach," "hyena," "eaters of our sweat," "weeds," and "weight upon our back."[78] Also, the both euphemistic and literally dehumanizing term "tall trees" – referring to the physiognomic stereotype of Tutsi height – was used during the genocide when Hutus were instructed to cut such "trees" down to size.[79]

A fundamental example of the healing-killing paradox, which is also closely linked to the Hamitic Myth, is given by Alexander Hinton: "...unity was imagined by the Hutu extremist elite [as] a purified nation with a purified, reified 'Hutu culture' expunged of all elements of 'Tutsi culture' and rid of all who would resist the encompassing powers of the state."[80] As a concrete example of the link between the healing-killing paradox and the Hamitic Myth in Rwandan context, Philip Gourevitch mentions the Rwandan Hutu extremist and leading race theorist Hassan Ngeze, "...the original high-profile archetype of the Rwandan Hutu *genocidaire*" whose "imitators and disciples were soon legion."[81]

In December 1990, shortly after the RPF invasion, Ngeze published the infamous "Hutu Ten Commandments" in *Kangura*, of which he himself was the editor. As Gourevitch states, with the publishing of "The Hutu Ten Commandments," Ngeze "...in a few, swift strokes... revived, revised, and reconciled the Hamitic myth and the rhetoric of the Hutu revolution to articulate a doctrine of militant Hutu purity." Using strong Biblical imagery, these "...widely circulated and immensely popular" Commandments among other things condemned "interracial" marriages, claimed that all Tutsi women were Tutsi agents, and that Hutus should have "unity and solidarity" against their "common Tutsi enemy" – not just the RPF, but Tutsis in general.[82] And, as Gourevitch writes,

President Habyarimana championed their publication as proof of Rwanda's "freedom of the press." Community leaders across Rwanda regarded them as tantamount to law, and read them aloud at public meetings. The message was hardly unfamiliar, but with its whiff of holy war and its unforgiving warnings to the lapsed Hutus, even

Rwanda's most unsophisticated peasantry could not fail to grasp that it had hit an altogether new pitch of alarm. The eighth and most often quoted commandment said: "Hutus must stop having mercy on the Tutsis."[83]

Although we are not aware of any evidence of direct involvement of the Catholic Church as an institution or of individual clergy in the making or distribution of "The Hutu Ten Commandments," a picture emerges of 1) a widely popular call by a known racist and Hutu extremist for racial segregation and mercilessness against the Tutsi minority – for dehumanization and healing by getting rid of the Tutsi "sickness,"[84] 2) a government that openly hails this as an expression of "freedom of the press," 3) a Catholic Church that, as we have shown, supported and to some extent was part of the government, that had helped create and institutionalize the Hamitic Myth that once again was used by Hutu extremists, and that did not protest, not even against the way Ngeze's message was conveyed through and legitimated by strong Christian imagery – the Ten Commandments, i.e., Christian basic law.

Conclusion

Did the Roman Catholic Church in Rwanda have a genocidal mentality? That, of course, first of all depends on how one defines "the Church" as an institution. But as Timothy Longman states, in Central African context "...different individuals and organizations within the same church use church resources and influence for a wide variety of purposes, some of which are contradictory. The churches are thus contested terrain, sites in which political alliances compete for support. Simultaneously serving the interests of the powerful and undermining their power, the churches appear Janus-faced."[85] This is perhaps one of the reasons why in the secondary sources we have consulted on the 1994 genocide and the Churches in Rwanda there are no real attempts made to define "the Church" or "the Churches" as institutions.

Churches, as Longman continues to explain, especially in a strongly Christian nation like Rwanda, are "centers of power" as well as "institutions with a moral agenda."[86] But if a definition of "the Church" as an "institution" is that it is a societal unit with a relatively clear and explicit purpose or agenda, then it appears that the Rwandan Roman Catholic Church did not fit even this very loose definition: as an institution it did not have a clearly defined agenda, mentality, or policy, genocidal or otherwise – other than perhaps becoming (and staying) powerful, and Christianizing the country. That the Catholic Church in Rwanda does not fit the above definition does not mean, of course, that it was not an institution – it means that it did not have one authoritative, uncontested "voice" to speak with, and that it was often used for contradictory purposes.

But it remained generally uncontested among Church clergy – from the beginning of colonization to the genocide – that the Church should become and remain powerful, just as the country should become and remain Christian. And this is probably exactly how the Catholic Church as an institution contributed the most to the creation of a genocidal mentality. In its struggle to Christianize Rwanda, it allied itself firstly with the colonial powers and, through the creation and institutionalization of the racist and oppressive Hamitic Myth, with the Tutsis. This, together with social disruption, laid the foundations – the preconditions – for a genocidal mentality. Then, when the colonizers and the Tutsis were losing power, the Catholic Church allied itself with the majority Hutus while continuing to help create and support "racial" cleavages, dehumanization and the healing-killing paradox through the Hamitic Myth, as it was used, for example, in the Bahutu Manifesto and in "The Hutu Ten Commandments."

Even at this late point, shortly after the RPF invasion in October 1990, it seems that few people within the Church probably had a genuinely developed genocidal mentality in the sense that they explicitly desired, and participated in the planning of, the destruction of the Tutsi "race." So, although we recommend further research on the subject, we tentatively conclude that with our present (lack of) knowledge, it is not possible to conclude that the Catholic Church in Rwanda as an institution had a genocidal mentality.

But it seems possible to conclude that the Catholic Church was instrumental in the creation of important preconditions for a genocidal mentality. Also, the Church had – as a powerful institution, in the whole period covered in this chapter, and during the genocide – the opportunity to speak against widespread racism, systematic oppression, and frequent massacres. The Church generally failed to do so, perhaps partly out of opportunism. But no matter what the reason(s) were, they were thereby legitimating these crimes, abandoning the victims, and even acting as an accomplice in genocide. As Charles de Lespinay writes,

MATTHIAS BJØRNLUND, ERIC MARKUSEN, PETER STEENBERG,
RAFIKI UBALDO

One should not overlook the courageous deeds of both clergymen (many of whom were killed) and parishioners during and after the massacres. Research by various specialists..., however, has highlighted the church missionaries' *principal* contribution to the official recognition and teaching of biblically based racial myths. This institutionalized practice began in the early colonial era and has persisted after independence, quite apart from the more direct involvement of some priests in genocidal acts. While it may not be fair to hold religious institutions equally responsible as political authorities in mass killings and genocide, it still appears, at first blush, that religious officials, backed by their respective churches, were directly involved, either through complicity or incompetence, in the promotion of criminal ideologies.[87]

Notes

1. For "ninety percent," see Charles de Lespinay in O. Bartov and P. Mack, eds., *In God's Name – Genocide and Religion in the Twentieth Century* (New York/Oxford: Berghahn Books, 2001), 162; on "sixty percent Catholic," see Organization for African Unity (OAU) report on www.internetdiscovery.org/forthetruth/Rwanda-e/EN-14-CH.htm, para 14.70.

2. *OAU Report*, para 14.68.

3. Prosecutor v. Elizaphan Ntakirutimana and Gerard Ntakirutimana, Judgement, Case No. ICTR-96-T & ICTR-96-17-T, 19 February 2003.

4. *OAU Report*, para 14.65.

5. On the number of perpetrators in Rwanda, see e.g. Mahmood Mamdani, *When Victims Become Killers – Colonialism, Nativism, and the Genocide in Rwanda* (Princeton: Princeton University Press, 2001), 185: "...Rwanda has perpetrators at least in the hundreds of thousands..."

6. Bill Berkeley, *The Graves Are Not Yet Full – Race, Tribe and Power in the Heart of Africa* (New York: Basic Books, 2001), 13.

7. Omer Bartov and Phyllis Mack, eds., *In God's Name – Genocide and Religion in the Twentieth Century* (New York/Oxford: Berghahn Books, 2001), 3.

8. R.J. Lifton and E. Markusen, *The Genocidal Mentality: Nazi Holocaust and Nuclear Threat*, (New York: Basic Books, 1990), 3. To our knowledge, the earliest uses of the term "genocidal mentality" originate in the mid-1980s. In 1984, Gerard Vanderhaar wrote a short paper, "Genocidal Mentality: Nuclear Weapons on Civilian Populations," included in an anthology edited by Israel W. Charny, *Toward the Understanding and Prevention of Genocide* (Boulder, Colorado: Westview Press, 1984). In his paper, Vanderhaar pointed out on p. 175 "the striking similarities between the mentality of those who are prepared to use nuclear

weapons on civilian populations today, and the mentality of those who perpetrated the Nazi Holocaust 40 years ago." In determining how clinically normal human beings can plan and execute indiscriminate mass killing, he emphazised two key elements: dehumanization of the victims, defined as "the tendency to view those who are to be killed as though they do not quite belong to the human race," and desensitization of the self of the perpetrator, defined as the emotional blocking of feelings of compassion and guilt "that would normally arise when inflicting suffering on other human beings." And in 1985, in the article "The Genocidal Mentality: Phillip II of Spain and Sultan Abdul Hamid II," in *Omega: The Journal of Death and Dying* (Vol.16, No.1) Robert Kuttner used the term "genocidal mentality" in a comparison of the two leaders named in the title with Adolf Hitler, in order to discern personality characteristics that may dispose an individual to desire or support genocide. The author found bureaucracy and a belief in a Messianic destiny to be contributors to the formation of a genocidal mentality.

9. In Israel W. Charny, ed., *Encyclopedia of Genocide*, Vol. 1 (Santa Barbara, California: ABC-CLIO, 1999), 250-51.

10. Eric Markusen in Carol Rittner, John K. Roth, James M. Smith, eds., *Will Genocide Ever End?* (St Paul, Minnesota: Paragon House, 2002). That a genocidal mentality has to be actually created in the minds of all perpetrators is disputed. Leo Kuper, *The Prevention of Genocide* (New Haven: Yale University Press, 1985), 196, writes that scholars should "...re-examine the liberal assumption that the inhibitions against killing members of our own species are of such strength as to require the ideological dehumanization of the victims as a precondition for massacre." Unfortunately, this is undoubtedly right in some, perhaps even many, cases. But as we attempt to show in this section, there is also evidence that especially 20th-century history has been marked by systematic and successful "ideological dehumanization" that has led to massacre and genocide.

11. Paper on www.muweb.millersville.edu/holo-con/bartov.html.

12. Lifton, *Destroying the World to Save It – Aum Shinrikyo, Apocalyptic Violence, and the New Global Terrorism* (New York: Metropolitan Books, 1999), 236-37.

13. In Summers and Markusen, eds., *Collective Violence: Harmful Behavior in Groups and Governments*, (Lanham, MD: Rowman and Littlefield), 195. See also Helen Fein in *Human Rights Review*, April-June 2000, Vol. 1, No. 3, 49: "Genocide virtually always occurs within a context of war, and sometimes triggers war or the renewal of war." That social disruption has been a necessary precondition in all modern genocides is convincingly disputed by Roger W. Smith who writes that in some of what we would call "utilitarian genocides," "...crisis has not always existed: the Indians of Paraguay, Brazil, and Peru, for example, have been destroyed out of cold calculation of gain (and in some cases, sadistic pleasure) rather than as the result of economic crisis." In Isidor Wallimann and Michael N. Dobkowski, eds., *Genocide and the Modern Age – Etiology and Case Studies of Mass Death*, (New York: Greenwood Press, 1987), 23.

14. Kuper, *The Prevention of Genocide*, 200-201.

15. Markusen, in Rittner, Roth, Smith, eds., *Will Genocide Ever End?*

16. *The Aegis Review on Genocide* (Vol. 1, No. 1, Spring 2003), 6-7.

17. R.J. Lifton, *The Nazi Doctors – Medical Killing and the Psychology of Genocide* (New York: Basic Books, 1986), 467. Eric D. Weitz writes that 20th-century revolutionary and genocidal regimes like Nazi Germany, Stalin's Soviet Union, and Pol Pot's Cambodia invariably deployed "...the powerful metaphors of 'cleanliness' and 'purity'" and aimed at creating "...healthy new social organisms and dispensing with the diseased and degenerate aspects of the old." Weitz in Robert Gellately and Ben Kiernan, eds., *The Specter of Genocide – Mass Murder in Historical Perspective* (Cambridge: Cambridge University Press, 2003), 59.

18. Markusen and Mirkovic in Tatz, Arnold and Tatz, eds., *Genocide Perspectives II – Essays on Holocaust and Genocide* (Sydney: Brandl & Schlesinger, 2003), 198.

19. See also Barbara Harff, in Helen Fein, ed., *Genocide Watch* (New Haven: Yale University Press, 1992), 38.

20. We have in this article chosen to focus on the elements of a genocidal mentality that are more directly initiated by or connected to political and ideological institutions like state and church. On a more individual level, there are a number of other psychological factors that facilitate participation in genocide and help create a genocidal mentality, since it is one thing to ideologically justify mass killing of defenseless men, women, and children, but quite another to engage in killing without being tormented by empathy for the victims. Assuming that the individual perpetrator is a "normal" person, psychological defense mechanisms are crucial in creating a state of mind in which the perpetrator can preserve a positive self-image, while still carrying out genocidal acts. One such mechanism is "desensitization," the gradual erosion of the perpetrator's moral inhibitions caused by participation in brutal and brutalizing acts: the first killing is the hardest, then, gradually, it becomes routinized. Desensitization can be a result of deliberate policies created by the genocidal elite, as well as a function of extreme situations like war. See Lifton and Markusen, *The Genocidal Mentality*.

21. Smith in Wallimann and Dobkowski, eds., *Genocide and the Modern Age*, 22.

22. Lifton and Markusen, *The Genocidal Mentality*, 94.

23. Eagleton, *Ideology: An Introduction* (London: Verso, 1991), 54.

24. We acknowledge that it generally is a simplification to call legitimation of behavior a top-down approach. As Weitz, in R. Gellately and B. Kiernan, eds., *The Specter of Genocide*, 61, writes: "The exercise of power is never solely a matter of command. It is an ongoing process of negotiation, one that is marked by conformity, compliance, distance, and withdrawal, a process of fluid movement between inner and outer faces."

25. The term "healing-killing paradox" was originally suggested by Lifton in his 1986 book, *The Nazi Doctors: Medical Killing and the Psychology of Genocide*, especially pp. 430-433.

26. See Markusen in *Aegis Review on Genocide*, Spring 2003, 12.

27. Lifton, *The Nazi Doctors*, 150. See also Lifton, *Destroying the World to Save It – Aum Shinrikyo, Apocalyptic Violence, and the New Global Terrorism*, 136-163, 208.

28. Dehumanization, like legitimation, is of course not exclusively the result of a genocidal ideology spread deliberately by the societal elite. Basic psychological mechanisms complement and reinforce such efforts: "By devaluing and scapegoating others, people defend their identities and views of themselves and

escape feelings of responsibility for their own and their group's inability to protect them and their families. They adopt ideologies, that is, conceptions of how to live life, that provide a new understanding of reality and hope for the future. Unfortunately, they usually also designate enemies who stand in the way of the ideology's fulfillment." Staub in Summers and Markusen, eds., *Collective Violence: Harmful Behavior in Groups and Governments*, 196.

29. Stanton on www.helpgsi.org/genocide.shtml. For a discussion of dehumanization as a function of modern bureaucracy, see Zygmunt Bauman, *Modernity and the Holocaust* (Ithaca, New York: Cornell University Press, 1989), 102ff.

30. Other scholars include Ashis Nandy, "The Epidemic of Nuclearism: A Clinical Profile of the Genocidal Mentality," on www.transnational.org/forum/meet/nandy_nuclearism.html. See also Robert Gellately, in Gellately and Kiernan, eds., *The Specter of Genocide*. Gellately on pp. 254-255 describes how a "genocidal mentality" was created in large parts of the German elite before and during World War II, and how that mentality "...partly filtered down to the millions in the armed forces." This mentality meant that "...organized and even serial genocides, the wholesale transfer of populations, and the use of mass starvation as 'rational' policy... came to be seen as thinkable and practicable," 262. In some instances, the notion of genocidal mentality has been stretched a good deal, like in New York in the late 1980s, when the opposition of officials to provide drug users with sterile needles to combat HIV/AIDS was attributed by some to a genocidal mentality. See article by Amy L. Fairchild and Ronald Bayer on www.sciencemag.org/cgi/content/full/284/5416/919.

31. Kershaw in *Aegis Review on Genocide*, Spring 2003, 4. Italics in original.

32. Ibid., 6.

33. Ibid., 8-9.

34. Ibid., 6. Kershaw seems to disagree with Lifton and Markusen on some points, e.g., whether or not genocidal killers are "normal"; that is, whether we can truly understand, and find the rationale, in their behavior. Kershaw writes that it is important to try to understand "the deeply inhumane and utterly alien mentalities that are likely to produce genocidal atrocities in times to come..." p. 10. Also, Kershaw believes that in liberal societies, "genocidal mentalities scarcely exist." This is in contrast with Lifton and Markusen, *The Genocidal Mentality*, who, as noted, believe that the willingness of e.g., the United States to use its vast arsenal of nuclear weapons is a clear indication of the genocidal mentality.

35. Dan Bar-On in *Aegis Review on Genocide*, Spring 2003.

36. Ibid., 16.

37. Ibid., 17.

38. Utterwulghe, "Rwanda's Protracted Social Conflict: Considering the Subjective Perspective in Conflict Resolution Strategies," essay in *The Online Journal of Peace and Conflict Resolution* (Issue 2.3, August 1999), www.trinstitute.org/ojpcr/2_3utter.htm

39. See e.g., Linda Melvern, *A People Betrayed – The Role of the West in Rwanda's Genocide* (London, New York: Zed Books, 2000), 8, 10-11, 20; Mamdani, *When Victims Become Killers*, 232; Scott Peterson, *Me Against My Brother – At War in Somalia, Sudan and Rwanda*, (New York: Routledge, 2000, 274; Joan Kakwenzire and Dixon Kamukama in Adelman and Suhrke, eds., *The Path of a Genocide – The*

Rwanda Crisis from Uganda to Zaire, (New Brunswick, NJ: Transaction Publishers, 1999), 85; Tharcisse Gatwa, "Resisting Democracy in Rwanda – Genocide and Reconciliation," in *Reformed World*, (Vol. 48, No. 4, December 1998), on www.warc.ch/dcw/rw984/04.html; Charles de Lespinay in Bartov and Mack, eds., *In God's Name – Genocide and Religion in the Twentieth Century*, 162-163; Christophe C. Kougniazondé, "Peace by Non-Lethal Means: A Transcultural Approach to Healing Genocidal Wounds in Rwanda," paper on www.nd.edu/~krocinst/ocpapers/op_13_1.html, 1997, 5; Lucy Carr, "Understanding and Responding to Genocide in Rwanda: The Approaches of Christianity and African Traditional Religions," paper on http://129.194.252.80/catfiles.0007.pdf, 1994, 8; Christopher C. Taylor, *Sacrifice As Terror – The Rwandan Genocide of 1994* (Oxford: Berg, 1999), 60; Hugh McCullum, *The Angels Have Left Us – The Rwanda Tragedy and the Churches* (Geneva: WCC Publications, 1995), 4.

40. Or as Ian Linden explains in *Church and Revolution in Rwanda* (Manchester: Manchester University Press, 1977), 165: "...it seemed to the missionaries that Hamitic history had involved the progressive dilution of some religious essence preordained to flower into the fullness of Christianity."

41. Longman, in Bartov and Mack, eds., *In God's Name – Genocide and Religion in the Twentieth Century*, 144-145.

42. Berkeley, *The Graves Are Not Yet Full*, 12.

43. Scherrer, *Genocide and Crisis in Central Africa*, (Westport, Connecticut: Praeger, 2002), 21.

44. Catherine Watson, "Exile From Rwanda: Background to an Invasion," The US Committee for Refugees, Issue Paper, February 1991, 3.

45. Nigel Eltringham, "Rwanda: Grappling with Definitions of Ethnicity," paper presented at IAGS (International Association of Genocide Scholars) Conference in Galway, June 2003, 8.

46. Ibid., 2.

47. Hinton in Hinton, ed., *Annihilating Difference – The Anthropology of Genocide* (Berkeley: University of California Press, 2002), 28.

48. Kougniazondé, "Peace by Non-Lethal Means," 5.

49. Ibid., 5-6. On the generally dehumanizing effect of colonialism, see Frantz Fanon, *The Wretched of the Earth* (New York: Grove Press, 1968), 250.

50. See e.g., Longman, "Empowering the Weak and Protecting the Powerful: The Contradictory Nature of Christian Churches in Rwanda, Burundi, and the Democratic Republic of Congo," paper on http://faculty.vasser.edu/tilongma/ASR97-Churches.htlm, 1998, 2.

51. Tharcisse Gatwa, "Resisting Democracy in Rwanda – Genocide and Reconciliation," 2. Roger Bowen, in "Genocide in Rwanda 1994 – an Anglican perspective," p. 6, paper delivered at the 2003 London conference, "The Church and Genocide: Rwanda 1994," writes that "In Rwanda, the Churches' authoritarian teaching style which encouraged little reflection, avoided the crucial issues troubling the society" and "...inculcated uncritical obedience to Government authorities." See also Longman in Bartov and Mack, eds., *In God's Name – Genocide and Religion in the Twentieth Century*, 142.

52. Watson, "Exile From Rwanda: Background to an Invasion," 2-3.

53. Longman in Bartov and Mack, eds., *In God's Name – Genocide and Religion in the Twentieth Century*, 147.

54. See also Longman, "Empowering the Weak and Protecting the Powerful," p. 4, who writes that "Churches helped to provide symbolic legitimacy to the state, while the state facilitated church activities. States rewarded the most cooperative churches with privileged access to the population and actively hindered the operations of uncooperative churches."

55. Johan Pottier, *Re-Imagining Rwanda – Conflict, Survival and Disinformation in the Late Twentieth Century* (Cambridge: Cambridge University Press, 2002), 209; Watson, "Exile From Rwanda: Background to an Invasion," 4.

56. See e.g., Mamdani, *When Victims Become Killers*, 120. Longman, "Empowering the Weak and Protecting the Powerful," p. 7, writes that "Both Hutu and Tutsi in Rwanda credit the Catholic church as a major force behind the 1959 peasant revolt that resulted in a transfer of political power from Tutsi to Hutu."

57. See e.g., Rev. Dr. Antoine Kambanda, "The Church and Genocide: Rwanda 1994," p. 5, paper delivered at the 2003 London conference of the same title. On the "Hutu social revolution" in general, Kuper, in Leo Kuper and M. G. Smith, eds., *Pluralism in Africa* (Berkeley: University of California Press, 1969), 153, commented that "The process of political change in plural societies often takes the form of violent conflict, as in Algeria, Zanzibar, and Rwanda..."

58. Mamdani, *When Victims Become Killers*, 232.

59. Jean Gualbert Rumiya et al., *Les Relations Interethniques au Rwanda à la Lumière de l'Aggression d'Octobre 1990* (Ruhengeri: Editions Universitaires du Rwanda, 1991), 151.

60. *L'Afrique des Grands Lacs – Deux Mille Ans d'Histoire* (Paris: Aubier, 2000), 264-265.

61. Mamdani, *When Victims Become Killers*, 103; see also Lespinay, in Bartov and Mack, eds., *In God's Name – Genocide and Religion in the Twentieth Century*, 167. The view that the Tutsis were a "foreign race" was shared by many western academics around the time of the "Hutu Revolution." See e. g., George H. T. Kimble, *Tropical Africa*, Vol. I-II (New York: The Twentieth Century Fund, 1960), Vol. I, 105, who states that Rwanda had for a long period been "...ruled by a caste of alien Hamitic warriors..." Also C. G. Seligman, *Races of Africa* (London: Oxford University Press, 1961), 193; John Gunther, *Inside Africa* (London: Hamish Hamilton, 1955), 225, 673-677.

62. Mamdani, *When Victims Become Killers*, 192.

63. Quoted in *"Un Groupe de Prêtres de Kigali,"* i.e., the progressive theologian Bernardin Muzungu et al., *Des Prêtres Rwandais S'interrogent* (Bujumbara: Lavigerie, 1995), 23.

64. Ibid., 90. Italics in original text. Gérard Prunier, *The Rwanda Crisis 1959-1994 – History of a Genocide* (London: Hurst & Co., 1995), 81, calls *Dialogue* a "...quality Catholic-sponsored review..." that was one of the organs through which the Catholic church in Rwanda rationalized why they first "...had admired the Tutsi and helped them rule, but now [around the time of independence] admired the Hutu and helped them rule. In both cases, this was perceived (and abundantly

explained) as being the work of divine providence and a great step forward in the building of a Christian society in Rwanda." Mamdani, *When Victims Become Killers*, p. 125, shows that the use of European clergy to support Hutu power was not unusual: "The European clergy came to function more or less as a backup force for the Hutu counterelite, providing them with everything from ghostwriters for manifestos and UN petitions to external contact."

65. McCullum, *The Angels Have Left Us*, 68.

66. Interview in *Wajibu – A Journal of Social and Religious Concern* (Vol. 16, No. 1, 2001), on www.peacelink.it/wajibu/13_issue/p1.html. Ntabona also emphasizes that "[The Catholic church as well as the other churches in the region] are being eroded by totalitarian ethnocentrism, by the murderous ideology."

67. Quoted in Jerome Lewis and Judy Knight, *The Twa of Rwanda*, IWGIA (International Work Group for Indigenous Affairs) Document No. 78, 1995, 22.

68. Document collected by Rafiki Ubaldo in Rwanda in 1999.

69. Longman, in Bartov and Mack, eds., *In God's Name – Genocide and Religion in the Twentieth Century*, 154, writes that "Some individuals and agencies within the churches did, in fact, contest the scapegoating of Tutsi.... On the whole, however, the churches did little to halt the build-up to genocide. Many church leaders had profited substantially from the status quo and had a vested interest in preserving configurations of power."

70. Catherine Newbury and David Newbury, in "Identity, Genocide, and Reconstruction in Rwanda," paper prepared for the Brussels Conference on *Les Racines de la Violence dans la Région des Grands-Lacs*, 1995, p. 8, write that "It was only after the attack of the RPF at the beginning of October in 1990 that the Habyarimana regime made particular targets of the Tutsi within the country."

71. Ibid., 10.

72. Melvern, *A People Betrayed*, 71-72.

73. *Kangura*, No. 25, November 1991.

74. The term "[placing a group or groups outside the] universe of obligation," a term that denotes systematic marginalization and dehumanization, was coined by Helen Fein; see e.g., Fein, *Accounting for Genocide – National Responses and Jewish Victimization during the Holocaust*, (New York: The Free Press, 1979), 4, 8-9.

75. Berkeley, *The Graves Are Not Yet Full*, 270-271.

76. Peterson, *Me Against My Brother*, 256.

77. Ibid., 260.

78. Ibid., p. 270; Taylor in Hinton, ed., *Annihilating Difference*, 159, 168-69; Berkeley, *The Graves Are Not Yet Full*, 2.

79. Taylor in Hinton, ed., *Annihilating Difference*, 169.

80. Paraphrasing Taylor in Hinton, ed., *Annihilating Difference*, 20.

81. Philip Gourevitch, *We Wish To Inform You That Tomorrow We Will be Killed With Our Families – Stories from Rwanda*, (New York: Farrar Straus and Giroux, 1998), 87.

82. Ibid., 88. See also Melvern, *A People Betrayed*, 72, on the "Hutu Ten Commandments" which "...were instructions to mistreat and discriminate against Tutsi."

83. Gourevitch, *We Wish To Inform You That Tomorrow We Will be Killed With Our Families*, 88.

84. Gourevitch, *We Wish To Inform You That Tomorrow We Will be Killed With Our Families*, 87, mentions that "When another paper ran a cartoon depicting Ngeze on a couch, being psychoanalyzed by 'the democratic press' – Ngeze: I'm sick doctor!! Doctor: Your sickness?! Ngeze: The Tutsis...Tutsis...Tutsis!!!!!!! – Ngeze picked it up and ran it in *Kangura*."

85. Longman, "Empowering the Weak and Protecting the Powerful," 4.

86. Ibid., 7.

87. Lespinay, in Bartov and Mack, eds., *In God's Name – Genocide and Religion in the Twentieth Century*, 162. Italics in original.

11
THE RWANDAN GENOCIDE AND THE BRITISH RELIGIOUS PRESS – ROMAN CATHOLIC, ANGLICAN AND BAPTIST

Margaret Brearley

Rwanda is a strongly Christian country. "The second largest employer after the state, was the Church. Around the churches there grew schools, health clinics and printing presses for religious tracts. Church attendance was high... Not less than 90% of the population was Christian, and more than half of those were Catholic."[1]

The genocide between April and July 1994 was a Christian genocide. The Churches were multi-ethnic, and Christians killed other Christians within the same denomination. Moreover, the Church itself "was implicated in the genocide in numerous ways... According to some estimates more people were killed in church buildings than anywhere else." There were "numerous examples of clergy who turned people over to be killed" and even "clergy who participated in death squads... In response to the massacres, the church hierarchies remained mostly silent. Catholic and Protestant leaders signed a joint letter in May that called for an end to massacres yet failed to condemn them or to characterize the violence as genocide. Church leaders otherwise failed to speak out, portraying the genocide as a justified defensive action within the context of a civil war... The result of the participation by clergy and the silence of the official church is clear. Many Christians clearly believed that in participating in the massacre of Tutsi, they were doing the will of the church."[2]

Since the national Churches in Rwanda were both complicit and silent, the response of the international Church was likely to be ambiguous at best, and so it proved. During the genocide, the Pope made numerous strong statements. He called for an end to "catastrophic violence" and "urged

169

Catholics in Rwanda and Burundi to implement 'the commandment of fraternal love' in the days following the killings" (*Catholic Herald*, 15 April).[3] The Pope expressed intense sympathy with suffering Rwandans: the news from Rwanda had "provoked great suffering among us all" (*The Universe*, 17 April); "I am close to these people in their agony" (*The Universe*, 22 May); "Who can remain indifferent?" (*Catholic Herald*, 29 July). Yet papal language presenting the massacres initially as "an unspeakable drama" and "fratricidal massacre," and pleas to international leaders to help "to curb this destruction and death" (*The Tablet*, 16 April), implied that there was equal violence on both sides of the ethnic divide. There was no specificity in calls to the Rwandan people to stop a "catastrophic wave" of ethnic and political violence (*The Universe*, 10 April), no overt plea to Rwandan Church leaders to use their authority.

Similarly, the International Affairs Department of Catholic Bishops in England and Wales "registered its shock and horror at the awful violence which has erupted in Rwanda," deplored "this mindless violence" and called only in general terms "for a cessation of this violence" (*The Universe*, 10 April).

The Rome Synod of African bishops was held from 10 April until 4 May. It was announced beforehand that the Synod would demonstrate that the Catholic Church "was putting Africa at the centre of attention." The Pope expressed a hope that the Synod would awaken a new awareness of "the duty of solidarity" towards Africa and "underline the interest and commitment of the entire Church to this continent" (*The Tablet*, 5 March). While the African Synod was taking place in Rome, at least half a million Tutsis were slaughtered. Yet the Synod itself, in which inculturation was "the dominant theme" (*The Tablet*, 23 April) and which debated at length such issues as second wives, drumming in church, and liturgical vestments, failed to address the ongoing genocide in any meaningful way, thus highlighting the gulf between fine oratory and true sympathy.

There were many ironies at the African Synod. Noting the juxtaposition of the exuberant opening with dancing and drums with the absence of the Rwandan bishops, remaining with their people "in the midst of a terrible tragedy," *The Tablet* (16 April) predicted "that stark and dramatic contrast, between the joyful celebration of life and the terrifying reality of fratricidal conflict and death, may indeed be a leitmotiv for this historic month-long Synod." It was not. The Rwandan genocide was scarcely mentioned. Only on the final day of speech-making was Rwanda mentioned powerfully by Bishop Ntamwana of Bujumbura, Burundi. Speaking of Rwanda, where "unfortunately, the political situation... is not getting better" and Burundi, Ntamwana asked rhetorically: "These countries are among the most evangelised of Africa. Therefore, how can one explain such killings, violence on such a scale?" (*The Tablet*, 30 April). At the very end of the Synod Rwanda was mentioned as just one African concern among many: "The cries of the people of Rwanda, Sudan, Angola, Liberia, Sierra Leone, Somalia and parts of Central Africa rend our hearts, said the bishops" (*The Universe*, 15 May).

At the Synod, describing Africa as "in a way, the second homeland of Jesus," the Pope praised Africans' love of life, despite "old tensions and bloody wars." He stressed the vital role of the Church, which "must promote an urgent and radical work of reconciliation" (*The Tablet*, 16 April). Yet the Pope's own words directed specifically to Rwandan Catholics, urging them "not to give way to feelings of hatred and reprisal," could have been misinterpreted by those engaging in genocide as implying some kind of justification for their deeds.

Church leaders appear to have called prematurely for reconciliation while the mass slaughter was still continuing. In mid-April the All-Africa Conference of Churches appealed to international agencies "to ask your governments to... restore order and work for lasting peace and reconciliation" (*Church Times*, 22 April). In mid-May the Pope issued a statement: "God awaits from all Rwandans, with the help of the countries that are their friends, a moral awakening – that is, the courage to pardon and of brotherhood" (*The Universe*, 22 May).

A study of the British religious press at the time raises many troubling issues. One is that of nomenclature. Whereas the Catholic press and the evangelical *Church of England Newspaper*, following Oxfam and other aid agencies, identified the killings as "deliberate genocide" around 6 May, the *Church Times* continued to refer to them as "tribal conflict" and acknowledged only on 17 June that they were a "campaign of genocide." The *Baptist Times* led with Rwanda on 14 April ("Baptists urged to pray for Rwanda"), described the killings throughout as "tribal violence," "slaughter" and "civil war," not referring to "acts of genocide" until 21 July. Although following the request of the Evangelical Alliance in Britain, it called on Christians (28 April) to pray for the "genocide taking place in Bosnia," and spoke of genocide in Sudan and "ethnic cleansing" in Bhutan. Only on 21 July, when the massacres were over, did the *Baptist Times* talk of "acts of genocide" in Rwanda and call "for an immediate end to all killings." It did not identify Tutsis as prime victims; its view tended to mirror that of the General Secretary of the Bible Society in Rwanda, who was quoted on 7 July as saying "that all sections of the community, and both ethnic groups, had been hit by the killings." (Ironically, unaware of the role of Churches in the genocide, on 21 July it asked for prayers for, among other things, "the churches of Rwanda as they seek to be agents of the good news of God's healing and reconciling love.")

Another issue is that of balance. While *The Tablet*, the leading left-of-centre Catholic journal, treated the genocide fully and in depth, noting for example the role in the genocide of *Radio Mille Collines*, the education system and drugs (14 May), other Christian papers were more haphazard, particularly in the early period. Reflecting their richer sources of information, the Catholic press had often more accurate details than the Protestant press. (It is worth noting that at any one time there are approximately 800 more foreign press correspondents covering Israel/Palestine than in the whole of sub-Saharan Africa). On 16 April *The Tablet* stated that probably over 20,000 Rwandans had been killed in ethnic violence, mostly Tutsis who had been killed in "an orgy of violence and killing against the Tutsis." Yet the *Church Times* stated on 15 April that 1,000 had died and on 22 April that "thousands of people have been killed." On 6 May *The Universe* counted up to half a million dead, whereas on 20 May the *Catholic Herald* cited "up to 200,000" deaths in the "bitter war," not citing an estimated 500,000 dead until 27 May, and still citing only "the slaughter of an estimated 200,000-500,000 people – most of them Tutsis" on 22 July.

A troubling tendency was to value the lives of individual religious more than those of the mass of laity. This followed a pattern set by the Vatican, which described the deaths of religious as "innocent victims of an absurd hatred" (*The Universe*, 17 April). Typical mid-April headlines were the cover story "19 religious massacred in Rwanda" (*Catholic Herald*, 15 April) and "Many priests killed in tribal revenge" (*The Tablet*, 16 April), doubtless highlighting the shock at clergy being targeted for the first time. Later headlines such as "Lost priest – fear grows" (*Catholic Herald*, 10 June), "Bishops and clergy perish in slaughter" and "The martyrs of Rwanda" (*The Tablet*, 18 June) and "Darlington-born Marist brother lost in Rwanda" (millions of Rwandans were "dying of disease or starvation," *Catholic Herald*, 5 August), all followed a similar pattern. One story, printed in both *The Tablet* and the *Baptist Times* ("A death on the road to Kigali," 2 June), rather shockingly described how escaped French Franciscans had allowed their Tutsi colleague to be killed at a Hutu roadblock.

More disturbing was a widespread pattern of seeking "good news" stories – especially those involving Westerners, which deflected attention from the tragedy. On 17 April the lead story in the mass-publication *The Universe* was "Vatican says 'Yes' to altar girls." Its coverage of Rwanda was under the headline "Hopes grow for Rwanda missionary," Irish-born Thomas O'Donaghue. That same weekend the *Church Times*, under the caption "Tribal divide bridged," had a photograph of an American couple reunited before fleeing Rwanda. On 24 April *The Universe*, while mentioning the deaths of 20,000 Tutsis, highlighted the safety of two Western individuals, de la Salle Brother Thomas O'Donaghue, (headline: "I prayed I would not be hacked to death") forced to leave a school in which 300 orphans had sought shelter (and presumably died), and charity consultant Danny Lillis (headline: "How I escaped murder gang"). This initial press empathy with fleeing European or American missionaries, aid workers or priests (very few Westerners were in fact killed), rather than with murdered and maimed Africans, was common. It was paralleled by a tendency to highlight the fate of individual clergy of the same denomination as the readers. The first long article on the genocide in the *Baptist Times* came only on 19 May, headlined "Rwandan Baptist tells of escape from bloodshed" and highlighting the trek of Rev. Ziharembere, General Secretary of the Rwanda Baptist Union, to safety through his "corpse-strewn" country; his escape was "little short of a miracle." On 10 June the *Catholic Herald* mentioned the slaughter of 20,000 in one convent under the headline: "Lost priest – fear grows." Furthermore, because nearly all aid workers and missionaries were evacuated, including those of Oxfam, Christian Aid and the British-based Anglican missionary society, Mid-Africa Ministry, there were few neutral eyewitnesses left in Rwanda to report on the slaughter of lay Rwandan Christians. Hence, perhaps, the preoccupation with sums raised for aid rather than with accounts of lay Rwandan suffering.

Empathy with Rwandan suffering was deflected, too, by a tendency to focus on international stories which highlighted Church success. Typical were articles in the *Baptist Times*, "Churches help Malawi to be 'truly free and so happy'" (2 June) and the *Church of England Newspaper* on 13 May, whose front page story was "Tears of joy for Mandela," with news of 200,000 murdered Rwandans on page three. Equally typical was the *Church Times* on 22 April; the editorial was on South Africa – "there is much to be thankful for" – matched by the lead story: "Input of prayer in run-up to South Africa elections." News of half a million Rwandans threatened with drought and famine and one and a half million displaced was relegated to the inside cover. Similarly, the editorial in *The Tablet* on 30 April was on South Africa, "High stakes for Africa's big player"; it expressed fears "that South Africa could descend into mass bloodshed and carnage," like Rwanda, "where a terrible example is being given at this moment of what can happen when tribal hatreds break out into warfare. But South Africa is a great country, with huge creative potential... "

The *Church Times*, like much of the religious press, was relatively poor in its early coverage of the genocide. On 29 April it said nothing on Rwanda; on 6 May it had one small article on the "tribal warfare" ("Senior clergy among dead in Rwanda"). On 13 May, when *The Tablet* recognised that half a million were dead and that the slaughter of Tutsis was systematic and supported by radio propaganda and even drugs, the *Church Times* again included nothing on Rwanda, but did carry an article on "Churches held key to peace in South Africa." On 27 May and 3 June the *Church Times* again carried no articles on Rwanda. On 10 June a short article by Rupert Shortt was headed "Rwandan bishops call for talks to end war," yet the same edition carried a long article on Southern Sudan, headlined "Where black people fear extermination," arguing that if no international action was undertaken, "then the blacks of Sudan will be wiped off the face of the earth." (Interestingly, here too the killing is attributed not to the Islamist radicalism of the Sudanese government but to racial factors, the conflict between southern blacks and northern lighter-skinned Arabs). In the *Church of England Newspaper*, however, Dee Sullivan of Christian Aid had already pointed out on 22 April that the Rwandan conflict was not simply tribally motivated, but included ideological, political and regional factors.

Reporting in the religious press could occasionally appear partisan. On 20 May the *Church Times*, in a short article headlined "Rwanda: rain and ruin," included an appeal from the Anglican bishop of Kigali to the Anglican communion to ask the Patriotic Front and the Rwandan government to sit together and stop fighting. But the only killing highlighted was that committed by the Patriotic Front rebels, who were "destroying everything, killing everybody they meet." Sometimes reports on the violence were ambiguous, apparently attributing blame to the wrong parties, perhaps inadvertently. *The Tablet* (23 April), for example, appeared to implicate the Tutsi militia as the main culprits in genocide: "... Hutu attacks on Tutsis were sparked off by the shooting down of... Habyarimana... Forces of the Rwanda Patriotic Front (RPF), made up of Tutsis, have now arrived... in the capital, Kigali, where they too have embarked on an orgy of bloodletting. Scenes of unbridled carnage have been particularly frequent in or outside churches..." "There are massacres all over the place," said one witness. "The army's delight is to murder civilians, while civilians turn on one another in ethnic revenge..." (*The Tablet*, 23 April).

This partisan reporting, whether deliberate or accidental, raises the thorny issue of neutrality of the religious press. It does seem as though the identification of some senior Catholic leaders, the Anglican hierarchy and the Baptist Church in Rwanda with the genocidal Habyarimana government, noted subsequently in the 1999 Human Rights Watch report, did affect the coverage of the genocide in parts of the British Christian press. This may be valid particularly for the *Church Times*, the *Baptist Times* and *The Universe*. In the latter two papers the former domination of Tutsis was stressed: "This has been the cause of conflict going back several decades" (*Baptist Times*, 14 April), and *The Universe* consistently stressed that the RPF were "rebels."

It is interesting to note how the press dealt with accusations of Church complicity by deflection rather than by analysis. In early June *The Observer*, the secular weekly broadsheet newspaper, blamed the Anglican Archbishop of Rwanda and the Bishop of Kigali for failing unequivocally to condemn the assault of Rwandan government militias on members of the Tutsi minority tribe: "Even the most senior members of the Anglican Church were acting as errand boys for political masters who have preached murder and filled the rivers with blood" (cited in *Church of England Newspaper* 10 June). On 10 June the *Church Times* – which in the two previous weeks had no coverage at all of Rwanda – quoted the Rwandan Anglican bishops' statement from Nairobi on 3 June "expressing 'sadness' over the carnage that has gripped their country." The *Church Times* then quoted unnamed "clerical sources in England," where the two accused bishops had been staying, as attributing the bishops' reticence to "a need to foster national unity" and "devotion to the memory of the country's murdered President, Juvenal Habyarimana," who supported inter-tribal ties. "I think they have shown naivete, rather than direct collusion with their government," one senior [English] cleric said. On 17 June the *Church Times*, for the first time, at last carried a long, excellent article on Habyarimana's "campaign of genocide," on the Arusha Accord and the work of relief programmes. Similarly, the World Council of Churches' sharp critique of both Protestant and Catholic Churches during their mid-August visit to Rwanda for being "... tainted... too closely aligned with the Hutu regime," guilty "of passive indifference and active connivance" was followed the next week by articles in *The Tablet* and *Church Times* on the self-sacrifice of Zaire Christians for Rwandans.

As with the secular press, coverage of the Rwandan genocide was extensive in all Christian newspapers only following killings of (mainly Hutu) clergy in mid-June and the exodus of mainly Hutu refugees (including many of those who had perpetrated the genocide) in May and especially in late July, when dramatic photographs from Zaire accompanied equally dramatic eyewitness accounts of cholera and other epidemics in vast refugee camps. The Pope and other Christian leaders described the refugee crisis in late July as "unimaginable," and only when television images emerged from Ngara, Benaco and other camps did empathy really emerge – primarily, of course, with Hutus. The Day of Prayer for Rwandans was not called until 31 July. Even then, when it was already known that only a fraction, probably no more than twenty percent, of Tutsis had survived, some of the Christian press still highlighted Hutu suffering and vulnerability, with the "rebel RPF driving Hutus before them" (*Church of England Newspaper*, 22 July) and "fear of RPF reprisals... still rife" (*Church Times*, 12 August).

While the coverage of the genocide in several of the religious newspapers discussed was patchy at best, and poor at worst, nevertheless certain aspects were excellent. All papers regularly and strongly covered the appeals for money by Christian aid agencies for Rwandan refugees. The *Baptist Times*, uniquely, included maps. Several papers commissioned outstanding background articles by leading aid workers or specialists such as Alex de Waal of Africa Rights (*Church Times*, 5 August – a lengthy and superb analysis), Richard Dowden, *The Independent*'s Africa editor (*The Tablet*, 28 May and 18 June), Dee Sullivan of Christian Aid (*Church of England Newspaper*, 22 April) and Kevin Hartley (*Catholic Herald*, 17 June). Eyewitness accounts from escaped missionaries or aid workers from Trocaire, Oxfam and Christian Aid gave invaluable, though all-too-brief, glimpses of Tutsi suffering. At an early stage the *Catholic Herald* (15 April) already cited the plea of Dr. Ian Linden, director of the Catholic Institute for International Relations, for protected food-aid convoys and for a boost in the UN peacekeeping force, and continued to report the pleas of CAFOD, Trocaire, Pax Christi and other aid agencies for international political intervention. Catholic aid workers were especially outspoken; Eamohn Meehan of Trocaire pleaded that "Catholics throughout the world must raise their voices to stop the genocide taking place in Rwanda. We must... demand that our governments take positive steps to stop the massacres. Not since the killing fields of Cambodia has there been a human rights issue on such a scale" (*Catholic Herald*, 17 June). Indeed, the *Catholic Herald* (26 August) even published an article by Gerard Noel critical of the Pope's donation of £250,000 to Rwanda, arguing that it should have been "something like a hundred times that amount."

Yet the overriding impression is that, with the exception of *The Tablet* and the *Catholic Herald*, the Christian press failed either to convey adequately the scale and horror of the genocide or true moral outrage against it. Coverage of the genocide was often relegated to short articles on inside pages, contrasting with whole page features on Anglican Church cricket or Sligo convents, church fêtes or the Pope's health. Without irony *The Universe* dedicated an entire issue on 8 May to the martyr Father Damien de Veuster, having two weeks before (24 April) led with the story of an escaped British Catholic charity worker who "was saved by the sacrifice of a man he had never met." Danny Lillis watched for half an hour while an "unknown victim" pleaded for his life and then died instead of him. But irony lay in Lillis' own words on arrival in the West. Noting that churches were packed for Mass, Lillis commented: "Perhaps the people believe that only God and the Church can save them." Further irony lay in a brief admission (*The Universe*, 29 May) that over seven percent of the Rwandan population had been murdered, while the main story of the entire issue was devoted to "The Pope's reign of pain," accompanied by huge photographs of the ailing Pope.

Papal pronouncements were generally strong and were covered in full in the Catholic press. Particularly notable was the Pope's statement in mid-May that "one is dealing with a true and proper genocide, for which sadly also Catholics are responsible... Everyone will have to respond for their crimes before history, and above all before God... Stop the bloodshed" (*The Universe*, 22 May). (The guilt of some Anglicans in the camps was acknowledged in the *Church of England Newspaper* on 1 July). Yet Archbishop Paul Tabet, Vatican envoy to UN agencies based in Geneva, was reported in the *Catholic Herald* (3 June) as referring in his speech to the UN Human Rights Commission to Geneva only to "massacres" and to "serious violations of human rights," not to genocide. Moreover, the Pope was not reported as having discussed Rwanda with President Bill Clinton at their meeting in early June, their first since August 1993. The Archbishop of Canterbury, who in April affirmed his "public role"– "Christian leaders must speak out on topical issues, he says" (*Church of England Newspaper*, 29 April) – was "said to be appalled at the continuing loss of life in Rwanda" (*Church of England Newspaper*, 6 May) following the killing of the Anglican bishop of Kigeme. Dr. Carey had already berated poor preaching (*Church of England Newspaper*, 22 April) and in subsequent weeks made statements in favor of such things as daily church services (*Church of England Newspaper*, 3 June), the environment (*Church of England Newspaper*, 10 June) and new music in black-led Anglican churches, but made relatively few public statements on Rwanda, each time in conjunction with Cardinal Basil Hume (*Church of England Newspaper*, 27 May) or other Church leaders. This may to a slight degree account for the relatively poorer coverage of the genocide in the Anglican press. Dr. Carey's strongest statement was issued at the end of July, just prior to the launch of the Primate's Relief Fund and the Day of Prayer for Rwanda on 31 July. Together with the Secretary General of the Anglican Communion, the Archbishop issued an appeal for prayer and for financial donations to help alleviate "an unprecedented human tragedy."

There may have been other factors militating against adequate moral outrage. The Christian press echoed the Pope and other religious leadership in calling for an early date for peace and swift reconciliation, often as though there were an equality of wrongdoing on both sides and as though justice and punishment were irrelevant. Indeed, given the prevalence of terms such as "tribal killings," there may have been a subliminal and racist assumption that collective murder in Africa was somehow normative and less culpable than in Europe. Few newspapers other than *The Tablet* grappled with the fundamental issue of why genocide could occur in one of the most evangelised countries in Africa, over three-quarters Christian and two-thirds Roman Catholic.

One of the greatest ironies during the period of the genocide was that it more or less coincided with the arrival of the Toronto blessing in Britain in early May, and publicity about it in the religious press from mid-June onwards. This phenomenon, which spread through Anglican, non-conformist and some Roman Catholic Churches, was hallmarked by prolonged swooning, shrieking, weeping and, especially, uncontrollable laughter: as the *Church Times* put it in a headline on 12 August, "Lots and lots of laughter." A Baptist minister attacked it as "more like mesmerism and shamanism than Christianity... differing little from pagan cults" (*Church of England Newspaper*, 1 July). On 29 September the *Baptist Times* noted that other characteristics of the Toronto blessing were "lack of Scripture reading" and "abstention from intercessory prayer."

At the time of the genocide I remember being struck by how little intercessory prayer there was and how parochial the local concerns seemed, even in Anglican churches untouched by the Toronto blessing. It seems to me possible that the Toronto blessing simply enhanced an already prevalent characteristic within some Western Churches, that of preoccupation with happiness, with one's own individual feelings and the petty concerns of one's immediate community, rather than an overriding and prayerful awareness of being part of the family of God in all nations and of sharing the pain of all who suffer. Such a preoccupation reflected a natural but problematic trend within Christian and secular international agencies within Rwanda. The

All-Africa Conference of Churches stated in a message to the aid agencies in April: "The international community has displayed little concern other than the evacuation of their nationals" (*Church Times*, 22 April). Dr. Donal Murray, Auxiliary Bishop of Dublin, argued in August that the world's response to the disintegration of Rwanda had been "totally inadequate... a scandal" (*Catholic Herald*, 19 August). Bishop Obiefuna of Nigeria argued during the Rome African Synod that the "blood of family and tribe" was often stronger in Africa than the water of baptism. Perhaps that is often true, too, for Christians in the West and for much of the British religious press in 1994.

Notes

1. Linda Melvern, *A People Betrayed: The Role of the West in Rwanda's Genocide*, (London/New York: Zed Books, 2000), 20.

2. Timothy Longman, "Christian Churches and Genocide in Rwanda," revised paper prepared for the Conference on Genocide, Religion and Modernity, US Holocaust Memorial Museum, May 1998 (http://faculty.vassar.edu/tilongma/ Church&genocide). Samuel Isaac of the World Council of Churches stated in August 1994: "the Church stands tainted, not by passive indifference but by errors of commission as well... Anglican and Presbyterian ministers were also implicated..." (*Church Times*, 19 August 1994)..."[F]rom what we have heard and seen [this claim] was valid for all churches in Rwanda, Protestant and Roman Catholic alike." (*Baptist Times*, 18 August 1994); "If Western governments' approaches to the crisis have been far from blameless then so too has that of the Anglican church in Rwanda," article by Penny Dale in *CEN*, 29 July 1994.

3. For convenience, I will cite references to publications within the text of my essay. References are for the year 1994.

12

CHURCHES AS MEMORIAL SITES

A PHOTO ESSAY

James M. Smith and Carol Rittner

> "Human life is more important than bricks and mortar.
> The lives of those who were hiding in the churches,
> whether they were Christians or not,
> are greater than bricks and mortar."
>
> *Father Pierre, Rwanda, 2003*

During the 1994 genocide in Rwanda, churches, once sanctuaries from violence, became repositories of brutalization and death. The Rwandan Ministry of Local Government in a report issued in 2002[1] states that eleven percent of the victims of genocide were killed in churches. Thousands of Tutsis were shot, burned, blown up, and hacked to death in Catholic and Protestant churches, in church halls and schools, and in convents and clinics. One survivor of the 1994 genocide, Eugénie Musayidire, said that in 1959 when she was seven years old and murderous ethnic violence broke out in Rwanda, she, her mother and other members of her family found refuge in the Catholic church in Nyanza near Butare. Those who made it to the church were not physically harmed, although her father, a doctor, who did not make it to the church, was killed by Hutu extremists. In 1959, people who sought sanctuary in Rwanda's churches survived such outbreaks of violence, but thirty-five years later, the exclusionary Hutu ideology had developed to the point that when ethnic violence erupted on 6 April 1994, no Tutsi was safe, no matter who he/she was or where he/she sought sanctuary. During the 1994 genocide, no Tutsi was intended to survive the slaughter of the *genocidaires*, not even those who fled to "God's house" for safety.

After the genocide, many churches where killings took place were cleaned up, the dried blood, tattered clothing and rotting corpses removed, the buildings re-consecrated by the local bishop and the churches re-established as places of prayer and worship. But this was not without its problems. Some survivors wanted to leave churches as they had been found when the genocide ended, with rotting corpses and desecrated sanctuaries untouched. They were afraid that cleansing the churches and burying the dead would lead to "forgetfulness," even denial that a genocide had occurred. It was better, they argued, to leave the victims' remains exposed where they had been massacred, even if it had been in churches. Others, however, felt that would be disrespectful, even sacrilegious. They wanted to provide a "proper" burial for the victims, although one wonders what could possibly be a "proper" burial for the thousands brutally murdered in churches, indeed, anywhere in Rwanda in 1994. There is little agreement among survivors, much less among Church leaders, about such issues.

At most churches where *genocidaires* did their gruesome work, the victims have been buried, often in mass graves. But there are some churches in Rwanda where people were slaughtered that have been preserved by the government as memorial sites. Sometimes the remains of the victims are deliberately left exposed, as a "memory marker" of what happened there, and throughout Rwanda, during those hundred horrible days in 1994.

In June 1999, an article published in *L'Osservatore Romano*[2] highlighted the controversy surrounding the use of churches as genocide memorial sites. According to the author, turning churches into memorial sites is part of the Rwandan government's project of defamation against the Church:

The obvious intent is to link the church with the genocide in the memory of the Rwandans. The Holy See is opposed to this pretense, pointing out that the churches are places of worship and reconciliation for the whole community (Tutsis and Hutus) and cannot be monopolized as charnel-houses by part of the population. In July 1997 the government nevertheless requisitioned the church in Nyamata with the obligation that every celebration in the shrine be conducted for the dead, and only for dead Tutsis massacred in 1994.

Not everyone agrees with *L'Osservatore Romano* on this matter, however. Father Pierre Habarurema, a priest now living in Brussels, was the pastor of a parish in Cyangugu province (south-west Rwanda) during the genocide. His parents and all his siblings perished in the genocide. On 11 April 1994, 1,500 parishioners who had gathered outside his church in Cyangugu were murdered. While the politics and controversies over remembrance of the victims and justice for the perpetrators were raging in the world press between 1994 and 2000, he served a parish in Kigali. During those six years, he spent most weekends traveling backwards and forwards across Rwanda to the sites of genocide, celebrating Mass and helping to bury the dead.

"Nobody helped us," he said. "In all that time all these NGOs and foreign governments were doing many things in Rwanda, but nobody considered it was their obligation to help." He continued, "My thoughts are that this is too big to explain. I'm tired now. I can only say that when I think of those sites and the people, it is all too much to comprehend. All I can do sometimes is sit down and cry." But Father Pierre is adamant about one thing: churches should be kept as memorial sites because so many people were murdered in them. It would communicate an important message, he believes: "Human life is more important than bricks and mortar. The lives of those who were hiding in the churches, whether they were Christians or not, are greater than bricks and mortar."[3]

Perhaps keeping churches as memorial sites of the 1994 genocide could help "the Church" – bishops, priests, nuns and laity alike – to confront some of the difficult and sensitive questions about the role of the Church in Rwandan society, before, during, and after the genocide. Was the Church's emphasis in Rwanda on quantity (number of people baptized) rather than on quality (people evangelized)? Was the Catholic Church racist in its teachings and its practices? Did the Church "help" to prepare the seed ground for genocide? Were members of the hierarchy so intertwined in partisan politics that even when confronted with grievous human rights violations, they were unable to "speak truth to power"? Did a patriarchal Church help to reinforce a patriarchal society, and vice versa? As a result, were women devalued in Church and society? Has the Catholic Church tried to protect bishops, priests and nuns accused of genocide? Why has the Church in Rwanda failed to live out Jesus' Great Commandment, "You shall love your neighbor as yourself" (Mark 12:31)?

Kibuye
This church at Kibuye, Diocese of Nyundo, was built in 1963 with stone quarried from the hill on which it stands. On the left side, off the balcony walkway, are the doors to the bedrooms of the priests who work in the parish. On 17 April 1994, several thousand Tutsis, including two priests from the parish, were massacred in and around the church. Their bodies were left unattended for a week. Prisoners were forced to remove the bodies from the church. A bulldozer pushed the bodies into a mass common grave behind the church. In 2001, a memorial, seen in front of the church, was built to commemorate the victims of the 1994 genocide killed in and around the church. *Photo © James Smith*

This is the front entrance of the church in Kibuye, as seen from the main road. After the genocide, the political authorities wanted to keep the church as a memorial to the victims, but after much negotiation and appeals from the local bishop and the people of Kibuye, the authorities permitted the resumption of religious services in the church on the condition that "another" memorial be built. The people of the parish, including the religious working there, helped to build the memorial. The words written on the wall of the memorial are taken from a song composed for the synod of the Nyundo diocese. *Photo © James Smith.*

On each side of the center aisle of the memorial are two large burial vaults containing the remains of 4,000 victims, exhumed by forensic experts seeking evidential proof of the 1994 genocide for the International Criminal Tribunal for Rwanda in Arusha, Tanzania. For some time, the skeletons remained unburied, wrapped in plastic and stored in the dining room of the former rectory behind the church. Almost all the remains were re-buried in the large vaults in the memorial, although as can be seen in the window under the cross, some remains were left exposed as part of the memorial.

The text of the words on the wall is: (Left) "Let us remember that this horror of killing trampled humanity underfoot"; (Center) "We lacked brotherhood"; (Right) "Let us ask for mercy so that this horror does not happen again." *Photo © James Smith*

The skulls and bones behind the window are those of victims murdered in and around the church in Kibuye. The figure of Jesus crucified, carved by a child from the center for Kigali's street children, run by the Salesian brothers, does not close His eyes, but seems to be crying out His suffering to God, His Father ("My God, my God, why have you forsaken me?" Mark 15:34). After the Nyundo Diocesan Synod of 2000, prisoners awaiting trial for genocide and crimes against humanity, in the spirit of reconciliation encouraged by the diocese, offered to do manual work on the memorial building. *Photo © James Smith*

Ntarama
During the 1994 genocide, thousands took shelter in this little church in Ntarama and in its surrounding outbuildings in rural Kigali province, central Rwanda. No one was removed from the church. Instead, the militia smashed holes through the walls so they could throw grenades into the body of the church, killing the people inside. Even in 2004, human remains are still scattered all over the floor of the church. The church continues to deteriorate as the rain drips through the bullet-ridden tin roof and holes in the walls. *Photo © Glen Powell*

This is the interior of the church in Ntarama. Between the benches where people sat during the celebration of Mass and other worship services are the scattered remains of the victims. In the center is the altar, behind which the priest stood when celebrating Mass. To the right of the altar, against the back wall, stands the tabernacle, where the Blessed Sacrament was reserved; to the left of the altar is the Ambo (lectern) where the priest, deacon or lay reader proclaimed the Holy Scriptures during Mass. On the back wall can be seen pictures depicting biblical scenes. *Photo © Glen Powell*

This is a close-up of the altar in the church in Ntarama. Propped up by a brick on the altar is the skull of one of the victims of the 1994 genocide, a silent witness to what human beings are capable of doing to each other, even within a house of worship. On the wall are pictures of biblical scenes, including the Baptism of Jesus by John the Baptist (Mark 1:9) and the Visit of the Magi at the time of Jesus' birth (Mathew 2:9-12). *Photo © Glen Powell*

These are remains of victims massacred by Hutu extremists inside the church in Ntarama. Fragments of clothing are mixed in with the piles of bones. Flowers often are left by relatives and friends of the victims. On top of both the altar and the tabernacle are single skulls. Today the church is more or less cleaned up, but remains of the victims have been left in the body of the church. *Photo © James Smith*

Nyamata

This is the church in Nyamata in the Diocese of (rural) Kigali. In 1997, church authorities handed the church over to the Rwandan government for use as a memorial to the 20,000 people killed in and around Nyamata, thousands of them inside the church itself. The outside memorial, seen in this photograph, is built on the tomb of the victims. On the memorial wall are the names of some of the victims who could be identified. At the end of the list, on the right, is written, "... and all the others whose names we do not know... " *Photo © James Smith*

The altar in this photograph is in the sanctuary in the church at Nyamata. Carved into the front of the altar, which is covered with a blood-stained altar cloth, is a representation of Jesus with his disciples at the Last Supper. Behind the altar is the partially opened tabernacle, its right front door desecrated and broken. Its stand is pock-marked with bullet holes, as is the damaged and disfigured baptismal font on the right of the photo. *Photo © James Smith*

Behind the altar, draped with a blood-stained altar cloth, is the statue of Our Lady of Banneux, also known as Our Lady of the Poor. Nyamata was known for its beautiful and pious women, many of whom could often be found in church. After the genocide ended, the body of a woman with a spear brutally thrust through her vagina, piercing up to her chest, was found inside this church – a powerful reminder of the brutal and degrading acts of rape inflicted by male *genocidaires* on women all over Rwanda during the genocide. *Photo © Glen Powell*

These shelves, located outside the church at Nyamata, are part of the memorial honoring the victims of the genocide. On the first shelf are two coffins containing the remains of victims; on the second shelf are the skulls of some of the victims killed in the church; and on the third shelf are bones – arms, legs, hands, feet, etc. The remains of more than 10,000 victims of the genocide are buried in two large crypts behind the church. *Photo © James Smith*

Nyange
The church at Nyange in the Diocese of Nyundo, Kibuye Province, is on the road between Kibuye and Gitarama. The priest, Father Athanase Seromba, allegedly encouraged Tutsis to seek refuge in the church. Once they were inside, he allegedly worked with the army and militia, who threw grenades through the church's windows, maiming and killing hundreds of people. When an attempt to burn down the church failed, some refugees climbed up into the church tower to escape the smoke and flames. Father Seromba allegedly ordered the killers to "clean up the rubbish," with the result that bulldozers were brought in and used by the Hutu militants to reduce the church to rubble, crushing thousands of victims. *Photo © James Smith*

What is left of a church window is buried in the remains of the church at Nyange. The massiveness of the original church structure is evident from the very large piece of rubble on the left side of the photograph. A community of Assumption Sisters worked in the parish at Nyange, but at the time of the genocide in 1994, the Sisters fled to Kibuye, from where they were evacuated to Goma by the French. As of 2004, the Assumption Sisters have not returned to the parish. *Photo © James Smith*

Amidst the pile of bricks and rubble can be seen the remains of two pillars from the original church at Nyange. The crosses adorn two of the burial vaults holding the remains of thousands of victims of the genocide killed in and around the church. *Photo © James Smith*

Today the church ruins remain on the side of the main Kibuye road, surrounded by a fence. The three crosses in the photograph sit on top of the burial vaults dug after the 1994 genocide. One survivor objected to the crosses, saying that they were erected without a context. "The impression is that they were martyrs," he told James Smith. "The people died despite their faith, not because of it. We must tell the story of what happened here." Flowers planted in the rubble commemorate the victims. *Photo © James Smith*

Nyarubuye

The church at Nyarubuye is in the Diocese of Kibungo, south-east Rwanda. It is a massive structure. On a spring afternoon in April 1994, the killers came to this church. Thousands of Tutsis were killed here. For several weeks the dead and rotting bodies, terribly twisted, lay where they fell, their skulls smashed, their arms and legs severed, their faces frozen in the last terrible expression of violent death. The church at Nyarubuye was one of the first genocide sites discovered by foreign journalists. *Photo © James Smith*

The parish at Nyarubuye was a large complex. It was made up of a number of buildings, including the Convent of the Benebikira Sisters, a diocesan religious congregation founded in 1919 by the White Sisters of Africa (Sisters of Our Lady of Africa) who are the largest order of nuns in Rwanda. Nineteen Benebikira Sisters were killed during the 1994 genocide. Sisters were working in this parish in 1994, but they did not return after the genocide. The convent, now a genocide memorial, holds the remains of many of the victims. *Photo © James Smith*

Skulls and skeletal remains of victims of the genocide are arranged on slatted tables, lined against the wall in this room in the former convent of the Benebikira Sisters. On the bottom of some of the tables are encased objects and clothing of the victims. On the right are two piles of clothing, shoes, and other possessions of the victims killed in and around the convent area. *Photo © James Smith*

These are the shoes, 'flip-flops,' and sneakers of victims massacred in April 1994 at the church complex of Nyarubuye. They are waiting for Nyarubuye to be turned into a permanent memorial exhibition. *Photo © James Smith*

The conflict between Church authorities, survivors, and the government of Rwanda about the existence of churches as memorial sites seems to be lessening with the passage of time. "It is not the blood of my murdered family that has profaned the church," said one young woman whose aunt lies on the floor of the church in Ntarama. "It is the acts that led to their murder that are the profanity. The hatred and evil acts should be cleaned away, not the remains of my family."[4]

Survivors want their dignity as human beings restored. They want those who were involved, particularly perpetrators and bystanders, to sincerely reckon with the past, to acknowledge the horror that was perpetrated, to make amends, and to change their attitudes and behaviors so that such things do not happen again. Memorialization has an impact on the collective memory of a people and on the next generation.

There is no general agreement about the right way forward. Some survivors want the remains of their loved ones exposed, so these remains can "speak" and bear witness to the failure of the global community to respond to the anguished cries for help of so many people during the months of genocide, not to mention the failure of so many Christians "to love your neighbor as yourself."

Ten years after the genocide, there is still no story told inside the church at Nyamata, other than what the building and the bones tell for themselves. There is no text, no photographs, and no description of what happened, or to whom – only a deteriorating building to provide evidence of a tragic past. And this is true for other churches throughout Rwanda as well. François Ngarambe, head of *Ibuka*, the survivors' association, thinks displaying bones is a "banality of genocide memory."[5] But other survivors think the only way to prove that genocide occurred in 1994 is to preserve the evidence, including the human remains found during and after the genocide in churches where people sought sanctuary from the killers. The churches and convent shown in this photo essay, with their bullet-scarred, bloodied walls and desecrated sanctuaries, their piles of rotting clothing, neatly exposed arm and leg bones, and their carefully displayed human skulls, are part of that evidence.

Notes

1. *The Counting Of The Genocide Victims*, Final Report, Rwanda, Kigali, November 2002. See Republic Of Rwanda, Ministry For Local Government, Department for Information and Social Affairs, B.P. 3445 Kigali, http://www.bsos.umd.edu/gvpt/davenport/genodynamics/minaloc_report.doc

2. Unsigned editorial, *L'Osservatore Romano*, weekly edition in English, 2 June 1999, 8; also at http:/www.ewtn.com/library/ISSUES/RWANDA.HTM

3. Private conversation between James Smith and Father Pierre Habarurema, formerly of Muyenge Parish, Cyangugu, Rwanda, now based in Brussels, January 2004.

4. Personal conversation with James Smith, July 2003.

5. François Ngarambe, President of *Ibuka*, the survivors' association in Rwanda, in conversation with James Smith, April 2003.

THE
CHURCH
AND
COMPLICITY?

"The Church . . . cannot be held responsible for the guilt of its members that have acted against the evangelic law; they will be called to render account of their own actions. All Church members that have sinned during the genocide must have the courage to assume the consequences of their deeds they have done against God and [their] fellow men."

Pope John Paul II, Rome, May 1996

Nothing Guaranteed

John K. Roth

The reverberations of genocide continue long after mass murder stops. Few episodes in the aftermath of the Rwandan genocide better illustrate that judgment than a trial that took place in Belgium from 17 April to 20 June 2001. During those proceedings, two Rwandan nuns from the Benedictine Monastery of Sovu were convicted of genocide. Sister Gertrude (Consolata Mukangango) and Sister Kizito (Julienne Mukabutera) were sentenced to prison terms of fifteen and thirteen years, respectively. It does not follow that justice was done, at least not completely, for in addition to the protest that the Vatican filed on behalf of the two nuns, there is Martin (François) Neyt's essay, "Two Convicted Rwandan Nuns," a contribution to Part IV that reminds us of the complexity involved when the question is about the complicity of the Churches in the Rwandan genocide.

Complicity is not a welcome word. It neither inspires confidence nor produces joy. No person or institution wants to be complicit because *complicity* refers to partnership in wrongdoing. Hence, allegations of complicity are usually controversial and contested, and not without reason, because saying that someone is complicit in wrongdoing typically raises as many questions as it answers. To be complicit is to be an accomplice. An accomplice, however, is not the instigator, mastermind, or main perpetrator of a crime. Typically, an accomplice plays a subordinate or tangential but nonetheless significant role, one that aids and abets crime and usually in ways that are necessary if the criminal action is to have much chance of success.

No individual or small group can commit genocide. It takes many people and institutions to commit a crime so far-reaching and vast. In addition, since genocide does not erupt from context-free spontaneity, complicity in it can include conditions – social and political, economic and religious – that have long been in the making. Those conditions, moreover, do not exist abstractly. They are created – sometimes well in advance of the act of genocide itself – by persons and their intentions, by institutions and their policies. The resulting actions have consequences that may not be the acts of genocide itself but still are genocidal because they tend in that direction. Thus, the question of complicity, like the reality of genocide, reaches far and wide.

Differences of opinion remain about the two nuns convicted of genocide. The same is true about the complicity of the Church – its history, extent, degree, and scope – in the Rwandan genocide. Where complicity is concerned, it is important at every turn to pose questions thoughtfully, to consider responsibility carefully, to assess evidence critically, and to draw conclusions judiciously. As Part IV takes up explicitly the topic of "The Church and Complicity," the authors work in that spirit. One of their most sober and somber – in David Gushee's words, broken-hearted – findings is that the existence of Churches and Christians guarantees nothing.

It would be comforting to think that Churches and Christians guarantee that the world will be more secure, peaceful, just, and loving than it would be if they did not exist. That challenge, of course, is not exclusive to Christianity. Versions of it face all religions, every nation, and each economy as well. Nevertheless, the Rwandan genocide puts the challenge before Christians in direct and explicit ways. So much depends on what Churches actually teach and on what Christians really do. As Gushee's eloquent and pointed chapter underscores, "The spiritual journey is never over, and the Christian is never free from the possibility of careening over the cliff into moral disaster, until he breathes his last breath."

Nothing is guaranteed. If it is arguable that the two Rwandan nuns were unjustly found guilty of genocide, nothing guarantees that Christians will be innocent, let alone resistant, when that crime is planned and committed. Instead, taking all of the reasonable differences of opinion into account, the evidence of Christian complicity in the Rwandan genocide remains more than sufficient to make everyone broken-hearted, whether they are Christian or not. But again nothing is guaranteed. The Rwandan genocide may not break our hearts, or not do so enough. Complicity may be denied. Memory of the genocide may dwindle. Life will go on. There is nothing guaranteed.

210

13

FROM KIBEHO TO MEDJUGORJE

THE CATHOLIC CHURCH AND ETHNO-NATIONALIST MOVEMENTS AND REGIMES

Léon D. Saur

Kibeho, Rwanda and Medjugorje, Yugoslavia – two places where the Blessed Virgin Mary reportedly appeared in 1981. The purpose of this essay is not to address the question of the authenticity or inauthenticity of Marian apparitions at either site, but to address the appropriation of these apparitions by conservative, Catholic, authoritarian, ethno-nationalist movements and regimes. Apparitions such as those at Kibeho and Medjugorje illustrate how Marian devotion, promoted in certain places and aided by movements connected with the so-called "new evangelization" favored by Pope John Paul II, can be misappropriated by such movements and regimes, particularly when countries experience terrible civil conflicts, as did both Rwanda and (former) Yugoslavia in the 1990s.

Kibeho

The College of Kibeho, a Catholic school located in the prefecture of Gikongoro, is dedicated to "Mary, Mother of God." It is situated in the parish of Kibeho, in the Roman Catholic diocese of Butare. The school, directed by the *Congrégation des Filles de la Vierge* (Congregation of the Daughters of the Virgin), trained girls to become secretaries or primary school teachers and was financially dependent on the Rwandan Ministry for National Education in Kigali. School facilities were minimal. It had neither a chapel nor running water. Every day, pupils had to fetch water from a well, two kilometers away from the college. Many of the teachers, both men and women, were lay people. Devotion to Mary, the Mother of Jesus, was at the heart of the school's teaching, even though some of the teachers were Protestant and several were Moslems. The parish of Kibeho had produced many religious vocations for the Catholic Church, and organizations such as Catholic Action, the Catholic Scouts, the Legion of Mary[1] and the Charismatic Renewal[2] were all active in the parish and in the college.

Saturday, 28 November 1981. Midday. Students of the College of Kibeho were having lunch in the refectory, when suddenly one of the girls, sixteen-year old Alphonsine Mumureke, rose from her chair, walked to the middle of the room and knelt down. With arms outstretched, she gazed fixedly at a point in space while the other girls looked on flabbergasted. They saw nothing but a young girl on her knees, speaking into the void. Alphonsine later explained that she had a feeling of being somewhere else, in a well-lit place. She saw, she said, a white cloud and a beautiful, unknown woman dressed all in white. The woman wore a veil of the same color which covered her hair, but not her face. She approached Alphonsine, who said the woman seemed to glide along the ground.

When Alphonsine asked, "Who are you?" the woman in white answered, "I am the Mother of the Word." At that moment, the girl recognized the apparition as the Blessed Virgin Mary, the Mother of Jesus. Alphonsine and the woman conversed. Then Alphonsine said three *Ave Marias* and the *Veni, Creator Spiritus*. When she "came to," Alphonsine was subjected to a torrent of questions by her friends and by Sister Blandine, the principal of the College of Kibeho, who had partially witnessed the scene.

The following day at about twelve noon, Alphonsine saw another apparition, this time in the dormitory of the College of Kibeho. Sister Blandine and Marie-Claire Mukangango, another pupil, were present. Over the following days, all conversations at the College focused on the apparitions. What accounted for them? Illness, hysteria, hallucination, mythomania, mental deficiency, simulation, trickery or black magic were some opinions expressed to explain Alphonsine's visions. In the first weeks, *suspicion* was the general sentiment expressed about the apparitions, according to Abbé Augustin Misago, author of the most important and best documented book on the Marian apparitions at Kibeho.[3]

According to Alphonsine, at the Virgin's request, she joined the Legion of Mary in February 1982. Two other students, Anathalie Mukamazimpaka and Marie-Claire Mukangango, also had visions of Mary in February and in March 1982. Thereafter, the number of visionaries multiplied outside the College, at the nearby primary school, and even in the hills. Seventeen-year-old Valentine Nyriamukiza said she also saw the Virgin, from 15 May 1982 on. The first time she saw her was in the parish. Later, fourteen-year-old

Stéphanie Mukamurenzi said she also conversed with the Mother of God, again in the parish.

On 31 May 1982, the first important popular gathering of pilgrims took place in Kibeho. At that time, five visionaries were known: three from the College (Alphonsine, Anathalie and Marie-Claire) and two from the parish (Valentine and Stéphanie). Others also made themselves known: Vestine Salima (twenty-two years old) and Segatashya, later baptized Emmanuel (fifteen years old). Pilgrims arrived from all over Rwanda. The phenomenon of the apparitions was publicized by the regime in power. Christophe Mfizi, director of ORINFOR,[4] the government information service, had the location wired for sound so the crowd could follow the conversations between the visionaries and the Virgin Mary.[5] From April 1982 on, *Imvaho*, the government-controlled daily newspaper, published articles about the apparitions at Kibeho, while the national radio also covered at length the apparitions. In July, the bishop had a platform built in the college courtyard so the public could see the visionaries in ecstasy during the apparitions. Foreign observers who were present noted that ORINFOR "went beyond simple information and launched a quasi-official Marian cult in the country."[6]

President Grégoire Kayibanda and Major General Juvénal Habyarimana, encouraged by the Church's support and proclaiming their Catholicism loudly, imposed an authoritarian and conservative regime on Rwanda. Philosophically, their regime was strongly Catholic and anti-liberal, evocative of Salazar's Portugal, Franco's Spain, and Vichy France during World War II.[7] For the Rwandan government, closely involved with a Church which was always ready to promote devotion to the Mother of God, one of the best means of reinforcing its own legitimacy was to ensure that the apparitions had a strong impact. Because Marian devotion can be used as a tool of Church propaganda,[8] when that happens, the Church can be said to lend a regime an ideological alibi and a moral legitimacy.[9] Therefore, it was not surprising that in the Rwanda controlled by Juvénal Habyarimana's regime,[10] national radio and governmental press promoted the Marian apparitions at Kibeho. Members of the presidential family went so often to Kibeho that caustic tongues spoke of "Our Lady of the Second Republic."[11] Later, during the 1994 genocide, the Mother of the Word, to some extent, literally became "Our Lady of the Hutus."

The Charismatic Renewal movement contributed to the international fame of Kibeho.[12] Father Daniel Ange, a French national who has lived in Rwanda for a long time, is one of the great figures of the movement in the

French-speaking world. At the invitation of Monsignor Jean-Baptiste Gahamanyi, Bishop of Butare, Father Ange visited Kibeho, then wrote a short, edifying work on the apparitions of Mary, published in France in 1985 by one of the Charismatic Renewal communities[13] which also later published a videocassette on the same subject.[14]

On 15 August 1982, 20,000 people were present at Kibeho to witness the Marian apparitions, previously announced to Alphonsine on 28 June. By August, seven visionaries were listed by the Church. Five were on the platform: Anathalie, Alphonsine, Marie-Claire, Valentine and Stéphanie. The Marian apparitions lasted from 4:00 p.m. to 11.30 p.m. It was an ordeal for the young women, as Mary appeared separately to each one. Mary, they said, seemed sad, displeased, even angry. Alphonsine added that several times Mary cried. The visionaries were deeply upset and frightened. In the apparitions, they saw crowds of people thrown headlong into pits, rivers of blood, thorny bushes, the flames of hell, people killing each other, decapitated bodies, and threatening monsters, among other terrors.

According to the visionaries, Mary went into greater depth concerning the messages she had spoken to them since May: "The world is going badly. It is running towards its destruction because of sins committed there. The world needs love and peace; men must repent and convert; they must pray and obey the divine will." According to the visionaries, the Virgin Mary had become more and more insistent with each appearance. On 15 August 1982, she invited the five visionaries to mortify themselves so as to expiate for the sins of the world.

Marian visionaries proliferated. By the end of 1982, religious authorities counted fourteen. By the end of December 1983, there were thirty-three. In total, about fifty visionaries were identified. However, Marian apparitions began to occur less frequently or to stop altogether for almost all the first visionaries: Alphonsine's became rare; Anathalie's ceased on 15 October 1982, Marie-Claire's on 15 September 1983, Vestine's on 24 December 1983 and Emmanuel's on 1 August 1983. Only Valentine continued to see apparitions. In 1994 she was apparently still active and even talked about during the genocide.

According to canon law, it was the Bishop of Butare's responsibility, Monsignor Jean-Baptiste Gahamanyi, to manage the dossier and to study the question of possible recognition by the Catholic Church of the authenticity of the Marian apparitions at Kibeho because the parish was within his diocese. On 30 July 1983 and 30 July 1986, he published two pastoral letters on the subject.[15] On 15 August 1988, he authorized a public service. When the parish of Kibeho was incorporated into the new diocese of Gikongoro in 1992, responsibility passed to Monsignor Augustin Misago, the diocese's first ordinary. On 29 June 2001, Monsignor Misago published a *Déclaration portant jugement définitif sur les apparitions de Kibeho*. According to Monsignor Misago, "in the case of these three visionaries (Alphonsine Mumureke, Anathalie Mukamazimpaka and Marie-Claire Mukangango), who were finally the source of Kibeho's renown, there was nothing said or done by them during the apparitions which was against Christian faith or morality. Their message coincides satisfactorily with the Holy Scriptures and the living Tradition of the Church...."[16]

Genocide in Rwanda

On 6 April 1994, an unidentified person, or persons, shot down the plane transporting President Habyarimana. The genocide started: some killers wore Marian medallions; others wore rosaries around their necks or tied rosaries on their weapons. When a nun asked a soldier how he could kill with a rosary around his neck, he replied that the Virgin was helping him to discover his enemies.[17] Many *interahamwe* militia struck their victims carrying a crucifix in one hand and a machete in the other. Murderers and victims prayed to the same God. Killers attended mass between massacres.

The sadly famous *Radio Télévision des Mille Collines* (RTLM), the Hutu Power radio station, broadcast announcements that God and his Mother were fighting on the side of the Hutus. The RPF (Rwandan Patriotic Front) and the Tutsis were demonized as instruments of Satan and the incarnation of the Antichrist. Extremist newspapers wrote the same. Although Monsignor Misago had emphasized as early as 1991 that the Kibeho visionary Valentine was a "contradictory sign,"[18] in the midst of the genocide, Hutu Power media reported that Valentine affirmed that the Blessed Virgin Mary had told her to fight on the front line with the Hutus and prophesied their victory. From the Hutu extremists' point of view, the civil war was the final combat between good and evil, between God and Satan. To convince their followers of the justness of the Hutu fight, all means were legitimate, including using the words of a "contradictory sign" to support their cause.

Medjugorje

Medjugorje is a small village in the Herzogovinian part of Bosnia, one of the five republics of former Yugoslavia. On 24 June 1981, six children of Medjugorje, four girls and two boys (aged between ten and seventeen), said they had seen a young woman at the place called "Podbrdo," on a stony hillside near the village. She had introduced herself to them as "Our Lady," in Serbo-Croatian, "*Gospa*." The following day, two of the children saw the Lady again. Two days later, they all saw her again. On 29 June, 1981, 15,000 people gathered on the hill where the apparitions had taken place.

For more than twenty years, *Gospa* has appeared in Medjugorje and wherever the visionaries are in the world. Three of them continue to see her daily; the three others still have an apparition once a year. Every 25th of the month since June 1981, *Gospa* sends a message to the world, which is passed on piously to the four corners of the universe through electronic bulletins and websites.

Medjugorje is part of the diocese of Mostar-Duvno. When the Marian apparitions began, Monsignor Pavao Zanic was the ordinary. When he referred to Medjugorje, he spoke of "supposed apparitions" and "possible hallucinations." He also spoke of "manipulations orchestrated by a small group of Franciscans" and said that he had uncovered a "series of lies and contradictions"; he confirmed that he had "reached moral certainty of the falseness of the apparitions." He viewed Father Tomislav Vlasic, the replacement for Father Jovo Zovko, the parish priest at the time of the first apparitions in Medjugorje, as a "mystifier and a charismatic magician" who had been given the mission at a May 1981 meeting of charismatic leaders in Rome of making the Virgin appear in Yugoslavia.[19] Fathers René Laurentin and Ljudevit Rupcic confirmed the substance of the Rome meeting to which Monsignor Zanic referred.[20]

In 1986, after an investigation into the matter, Monsignor Zanic gave a negative decision on the apparitions of Medjugorje and transmitted his report to the Vatican. Cardinal Joseph Ratzinger, Permanent Prefect of the Congregation for the Faith, sent the file to the Yugoslav bishops' conference.[21] In June 1993, Monsignor Ratko Peric succeeded Monsignor Zanic. He also declared that there had not been any supernatural phenomenon at Medjugorje. In October 1997, Monsignor Peric sent a letter to the French magazine *Famille chrétienne*: "My conviction and my position are not only *Non constat de supernaturalitate*, but indeed *Constat de non supernaturalitate* concerning the apparitions or revelations of Medjugorje."[22]

Ethno-nationalist appropriation of the message of Mary of Medjugorje

If one wants to understand what happened in Kibeho, it is necessary to make a detour via Medjugorje. *Gospa*'s messages are presented by their partisans as an infinite variation on prayer, fasting and penitence, renunciation and faith, conversion and peace. These themes are in accord with the ecclesial magisterium; they have as a common objective to bring each person to a life of holiness. "I love you," assures the Virgin, "That is why I want you to be holy. I do not want Satan to block your path."

The French sociologist Gérard Getrey in *Kibeho ou la face cachée de la tragédie rwandaise* provides invaluable evidence of the deterioration of the situation: "During my first stay [in Medjugorje] in June 1985, you had the impression of being in a corner of paradise which had fallen to earth. It was really a haven of peace. It has subsequently deteriorated considerably: many have turned towards materialism, extracting dollars or *deutsche-marks* from the purses of defenseless pilgrims: 'business' everywhere, a formidable passion for everything American or German... But above all, what was increasing was Croat nationalism. Virulent nationalism, fanned by certain old people in the village... "[23]

During the Bosnian war, men in military uniform were to be seen in Medjugorje. With rosaries on their rifles or around their necks, they paraded in the uniform of the HOS extremist militia (the armed branch of the Croatian right-wing party, heir of the *Ustacha*, supported by the traditionalist disciples of the late Monsignor Marcel Lefebvre, and the Catholic wing of Jean-Marie Le Pen's National Front),[24] sporting badges and stickers celebrating Our Lady of Peace. These nationalists proclaimed that Croatia was their native land. "Under *Gospa*'s high patronage," they were fighting for the addition of Herzegovina to Croatia and practiced ethnic cleansing to purify the country of Moslems. In so doing, they were scarcely different from the *interahamwe*, who claimed that Rwanda was the land of the Hutus alone, and prayed to the Mother of the Word to help them find the Tutsis so they could kill them.

Some reasons why Medjugorje and Kibeho can be compared

Some people may be astonished that one can compare a place of Marian devotion located in the western Balkans with another in the heart of Africa, but even more stunning is seeing how the apparitions were appropriated by extremist groups in both countries:

1. Leaders of the charismatic movement, as well as Fathers René Laurentin and Daniel Ange, followers of *Theotokos*, are all aficionados of Kibeho and Medjugorje.[25] Father Laurentin, in an essay he wrote, highlighted the doctrinal and theological links between the two sites, as well as those between the sites and the Charismatic Renewal.[26]

2. Gérard Getrey emphasized the common message between *Gospa* and the Mother of the Word.[27]

3. At the beginning of the 1980s, Rwanda and Yugoslavia were countries which experienced an economic upturn, but then, when world markets changed, were plunged into a profound political, economic and moral crisis.[28] In Rwanda, political scandals and the increasing corruption of a regime which till then had been relatively honest, combined with the fall of the price of raw materials on the world market, a mounting public debt, the forced liberalization of the economy, and the inhumanity of the structural adjustment programs (imposed by the international financial institutions) made the situation worse. The war of October 1990 did the rest.[29]

In Yugoslavia, the death of Marshal Tito in May 1980 left an economy riddled with public debt and ethno-nationalist movements which had never really been extinguished.[30] Yugoslavia was organized, at that time, as a federal system of six republics and two autonomous provinces that brought together a mosaic of nationalities. It was directed by collegial federal authorities with a revolving presidency, in which each republic and autonomous province had one representative. In short, just as Rwanda practiced the system of "ethnic quotas," Yugoslavia was built on an "ethnic key." Once the iron hand of Tito released its grasp, it was not long before ethno-nationalism exerted its strength.

Thus, the Marian apparitions of Medjugorje and Kibeho occurred in societies which were ethnically divided and in political, economic and social crisis. According to Getrey, the apparitions of Kibeho and Medjugorje revealed "the sociological, psychological and polemological state of their societies,"[31] and the apparitions of Mary "should in consequence be taken seriously or at least into consideration on that level."[32]

4. The supporters of the supernatural nature of the Medjugorje and Kibeho apparitions have drawn attention to the massive and spontaneous character of religious conversions which they caused.

A parish priest in Rwanda, Gabriel Maindron, wrote, "Mary is known more than ever, loved, sung about, prayed to, although before they had wanted her to be forgotten." He also wrote, the "sensational conversions which are reported here and there, this wave of prayer, this deepening of faith which are appearing in Rwanda and beyond its borders around the apparitions, are they not Kibeho's greatest miracle?"[33]

5. In both Rwanda and Yugoslavia, the Church reaffirmed its presence and power. The Yugoslav regime was Marxist, atheist and anticlerical. It had long had a relationship of conflict with the Church and continued to be wary of it.[34] In Rwanda, at the beginning of the 1980s, the institutional Church was struggling to adapt to rapid changes of sentiment about its place

in society.[35] While it continued to train young people in its colleges, seminaries and movements, it no longer seemed able to control them longer term, nor did it have the same attraction for the Westernized elites.

The apparitions of Mary at Medjugorje and Kibeho happened at a time which allowed the institutional Church to reposition itself within countries which were in serious crisis and in societies uncertain of their future. Moreover, the apparitions fell within the so-called "new evangelization" that Pope John Paul II wanted and tradition-oriented organizations and movements like *Opus Dei*, the Charismatic Renewal, and *Focolari* helped to promote. Devotion to the Blessed Virgin Mary played (and still plays) a central role in the strategy for the reconquest of hearts and minds, which the "new evangelization" represents. Devotion to Mary often is a first step on a return to the Church, an expression of tradition against reason and modernity. It is the principal weapon of the devout against the intellectuals within the Church.[36] Carl Bernstein and Marco Politi stress that the traditions linked to Marian devotion were permanent sources of pride and inspiration for Pope John Paul II. In his eyes, they were tangible proof of the privileged bonds that the Virgin weaves with the humblest and weakest.[37]

Marian apparitions "are not situated on the margins of the Church or in a reactionary or retrograde perspective, but in the avant-garde. They lead and carry out true evangelization, something which does not always succeed in the institutional Church, and they contribute at its very heart to peaceful, discrete but effective renewal." In Gérard Getrey's view, John Paul II perfectly understands what is at stake in Marian apparitions.[38] We should also add that the cult of Mary represents an opportunity for the Polish pope to promote the traditional and patriarchal Church concept of woman: the Virgin Mary as a paradigm of the "true nature" of woman and her "specific vocation" as wife and mother[39] – according to some, the very incarnation of the obedient and submissive woman![40]

The appropriation of Marian apparitions by conservative and extreme-right movements

In both her Rwandan and Yugoslav apparitions, Mary exhorted people to prayer, repentance, conversion and obedience to the will of God. She never preached protest or revolt. Instead, she taught pacifism and non-violence. Despite this, however, devotion to Mary was appropriated both by Hutu and by Croat nationalists, extreme-right, conservative and ethno-nationalist parties and movements. Her words of peace and reconciliation in Medjugorje fell on deaf ears: "In this milieu of mounting hatred, *Gospa's* message... to reconcile oneself with the Serbs, the Moslems, the atheist Communists was unacceptable for many Croats. [Their] reconstruction of the message and significance of the apparitions... [confirmed by] certain preachers [was that] if the Virgin appeared in Medjugorje, in a Croatian village, it meant that she had appeared for them, and specially for them, to liberate them from Communism, the Serbs, [and] the Gypsies who poisoned their lives."[41]

In Rwanda, political powers and Church leaders were closely associated. Their proximity helped to give legitimacy to the regime's ethno-racist ideology which made Rwanda the land of the Hutus. From the start of the 1990s, the press mobilized religion in the service of the Hutu cause.[42] During the genocide, the presenters on RTLM and national radio repeatedly explained why it was obvious that the Virgin had appeared in Rwanda for the benefit of the Hutus. In Rwanda, a society still traditional and strongly hierarchical, people were accustomed to obeying orders.[43] It was easy to transmit this message.

Other Catholic national regimes have appropriated Marian worship, e.g., Our Lady of Fatima, in Salazar's Portugal. In 1943, an Argentinean junta promoted the Virgin to the rank of army general.[44] In 1982, the Argentinean generals gave the name Operation *"Azul"* to the reconquest of the Falklands, the word describing the color of the Mother of God's blue robe. In 1941, it was the *"Azul"* division which Franco sent to fight beside the *Wehrmacht* against the Soviet Union. The US section of the Blue Army aims to fight the moral decline of the United States and to bring people back to respect for the divine plan.[45] In December 2000, the Blue Army offered a national novena for the election of George W. Bush, the "pro-life candidate."[46]

Conclusion

In principle, there is no common ground between the Church and the ethno-nationalist or any other extreme right wing.[47] However, in Catholic milieus favorable to it, the cult of Mary is seen as an effective weapon against the tireless activity of Satan and, consequently, as an effective instrument for what Pope John Paul II calls a "new evangelization." Thus, it is somewhat easier to understand the close ideological links between the "new evangelization" and Marian devotion as promoted in places like Medjugorje and Kibeho.

For the Catholic right, the Mother of God "will crush the head of the snake" and vanquish "the forces of evil." Only divine intercession and prayer can act effectively in the apocalyptic combat between good and satanic forces.[48] In spite of its evolution, the post-conciliar Vatican II Church and its head, Pope John Paul II have remained imprisoned by a traditional,[49] hierarchical vision of the world, inherited from the *Ancien Régime*. This anti-modern vision is founded on a medieval concept of society. Political power is ceded to Caesar while the Church provides the religious and moral framework within a biological order, presented as immutable, in which the female obviously cannot be the equal of the male. The persistent anti-modernism which the Roman Catholic Church shares with the political right makes it easier to understand the relative ease with which ethno-nationalist movements, as vehicles of conservative, traditional and hierarchical values, can divert the apparitions of Mary from their initial goals and use them for their own ends. The Church – eager to combat, in this instance, Communism in Yugoslavia and the Patriotic Front in Rwanda, and happy to have allies with whom it believes it has common values – is more or less consciously complicit.[50]

Translated by Wendy Whitworth

Notes

1. The Legion of Mary was created in 1921 by Frank Duff, an Irishman. This movement of popular piety intended for laymen spread in the Third World, especially in Rwanda, where it was launched in May 1950. Jean-Pierre Chrétien, in "Hutu and Tutsi in Rwanda and Burundi," in Jean-Loup Amselle and Elikia M'Bokolo eds., *Au Coeur de l'ethnie. Ethnie, tribalisme et Etat en Afrique* (Paris: Ed. La Découverte, 1985; 2nd ed. La Découverte Poche, 1999), 154, recalls that this "apparently anodyne network spread its net over the country" from the 1950s onwards and emphazises that it was involved in the structuring of the Hutu contra-elite which fomented the 1959 revolution. Grégoire Kayibanda was president of the Legion of Mary. He took advantage of it to criss-cross the country under this cover and propagate everywhere the good news of the Hutus' political awareness, see Ian Linden, *Christianisme et pouvoirs au Rwanda (1900-1990)*, translated and revised by Paulette Gérard, (Paris: Ed Karthala, 1999), 337 and 350; 1st ed.: *Church and Revolution in Rwanda*, (Manchester: Manchester University Press and Africana Publishing Company, 1977).

2. The Charismatic Renewal had its origins in the Protestant world and is of recent formation among Catholics. In 1906, the American Baptist Pastor Charles Parnham and some friends wanted to break with the theological and religious practices of the Protestant Churches and to get back in touch with the fundamental truths of the Scriptures. They thus reinvented the baptism of the Spirit as Christ had done it. The Pentecostal movement was born. It is composed of independent local churches, the Assemblies of God. In 1967, the Spirit descended on a group of Catholic students from the faculty of theology at

Duquesne University, Pittsburgh, Pennsylvania. They were gathered together for a weekend of prayers. Grace overcame them, transforming them in their deepest beings. They spoke of a "baptism in the Holy Spirit." There was talk of Catholic Pentecostalism. The Charismatic Renewal had been born. It reached Europe at the start of the 1970s and Rwanda in 1974. Attracting believers in need of spirituality, the movement was initially looked upon with mistrust by the Holy See. Soon, however, the Holy See understood the advantage to be gained from it and tried to use this new form of spirituality to its own benefit. The movement is subdivided into several communities, of which Emmanuel is the most important in Belgium and France. It depends on its members who are often well established professionally and willing activists in parish life. Each year, it brings together several thousands of pilgrims at Paray-le-Monial, a small Burgundian locality in Sâone-et-Loire. Globally, Emmanuel presents "an image of a community which is both very modern in its organizational method and very traditional in its concept of the Church and Catholicism" (Christine Pina, *Voyage au pays des charismatiques*, (Paris: Editions de l'atelier/Editions ouvrières, 2001), 53).

3. Abbé Augustin Misago, *Les Apparitions de Kibeho au Rwanda*, (Kinshasa: Facultés catholiques de Kinshasa, 1991).

4. ORINFOR: *Office rwandais d'information* (Rwandan office of information).

5. To avoid any misunderstanding, it should be clarified that the spectators could only see the visionaries and only heard the questions and replies formulated by them. The Virgin was only seen and heard by the visionaries. They then reported what the Virgin said.

6. François Imbs, François Bart et Annie Bart, "Le Rwanda: les données socio-géographiques," in *Hérodote*, LXXII-LXXIII, 1994, 262.

7. Several authors referred to Salazar's Portugal and Vichy to describe the Rwandan republics which resulted from the All Saints' Day Revolution of 1959: Kayibanda, Salazar and Vichy: Gérard Prunier, *Rwanda 1959-1996: Histoire d'un génocide* (Paris: Ed. Dagorno, 1997), 78 (1st ed.: *The Rwanda Crisis, History of a Genocide*, (London: C Hurst and Co, 1995); Habyarimana and Salazar: Jean-Pierre Chrétien, *L'Afrique des Grands Lacs: Deux mille ans d'histoire*, (Paris: Ed. Aubier, 2000), 269-271. Without necessarily establishing an explicit link with Franco's Spain or Salazar's Portugal, several authors who knew the country well from having lived there highlighted the oppressive weight of the Church on Rwandan society, which evoked some reminders of the Church's weight in Iberian and Lusitanian society. This applied to both Kayibanda's regime (G. Prunier, *Rwanda 1959-1996: Histoire d'un génocide*, 77-79; Claudine Vidal, "Situations ethniques au Rwanda" in J. L. Amselle and E. M'bokolo, *Au coeur de l'ethnie*, 17) and to that of Habyarimana (G. Prunier, *Rwanda 1959-1996: Histoire d'un génocide*, 104-105; Pierre Erny, *Rwanda 1994. Clés pour comprendre le calvaire d'un peuple* (Paris: Ed. L'Harmattan, 1994), 79-80 and 120-130).

8. See below.

9. See especially G. Prunier, *Rwanda 1959-1996: Histoire d'un génocide*, 103-107.

10. With Rwanda, "you have to forget all the current clichés about the joyful shambles of tropical countries [...] administrative control was probably the strictest in the world for a non-Communist country. "(G. Prunier, *Rwanda 1959-1996: Histoire d'un génocide*, 99).

11. I. Linden, *Christianisme et pouvoirs au Rwanda*, 396-397.

12. Gérard Getrey in *Kibeho ou la face cachée de la tragédie rwandaise* (Paris: Ed. François-Xavier de Guibert, 1998), 44 and note 14, stresses that the Charismatic Renewal and the Legion of Mary contributed towards giving an international, and even global impact, to the apparitions of Mary and Christ at Kibeho.

13. Père Daniel Ange, *Kibeho, le ciel à fleur de terre!: Des apparitions de Marie au cœur de l'Afrique?* (Nouan-le-Fuzelier: Ed. Lion de Juda), 1985. The Lion of Juda is the former name of the present-day Community of the Beatitudes.

14. Videocassette: *Kibeho. Marie au cœur de l'Afrique* (Nouan-le-Fuzelier: Lion de Juda Productions, 1985).

15. Published in *Dialogue*, N°101, November-December 1983, 31-41, et N°120, January-February 1987, 60-68.

16. On the procedure for recognition of apparitions and the criteria which diocesan theological commissions must take into account to assess the divine origins of apparitions, see Père René Laurentin, *Multiplication des apparitions de la vierge aujourd'hui. Est-ce elle? Que veut-elle dire?* (Paris: Ed. Fayard, 1988), 18-48.

17. See "Le Récit effaré du père Maindron," in *La Croix*, Paris, 5 juillet 1994; Nicolas Poincaré, *Gabriel Maindron, un prêtre dans la tragédie* (Paris: Les Editions de l'Atelier, 1995) et André Sibomana, *Gardons espoir pour le Rwanda* (Paris: Desclée de Brouwer Ed., 1997), 113 et 147. See also *Rwanda: Not So Innocent. When Women Become Killers* (London: Ed. African Rights, 1995); G. Prunier, *Rwanda 1959-1996: Histoire d'un génocide*, 175-177 and notes, as well as J. P. Chrétien, *L'Afrique des Grands Lacs*, 291.

18. Misago, *Les Apparitions de Kibeho au Rwanda*, 487.

19. "Interview of Monsignor Zanic," in *La Libre Belgique*, Bruxelles, 11 April 1985.

20. René Laurentin and Ljudevit Rupcic, *La Vierge apparaît-elle à Medjugorje? Un message urgent donné au monde dans un pays marxiste* (Paris: Ed. ŒIL, December 1984), 26: these authors reported that on that occasion, Sister Briege McKenna prophetically saw Father Vlasic seated in the midst of a crowd, with rivers of water flowing from his seat; God whispered a prophecy to Father Tardif: "Do not be afraid, I will send you my Mother." In fact, the translation of a book written in Serbo-Croat by Ljudevit Rupcic, (*Gospina Ukazanja u Medjugorju* (The Apparitions of Our Lady in Medjugorje), Samobor: Imprimerie A.G. Matos, 1983) served as matrix to the original edition of R. Laurentin and L. Rupcic, *La Vierge apparaît-elle à Medjugorje?*, as the authors themselves indicate, pp. 21-27, 190.

21. This initiative provoked a dispute of interpretation which is still ongoing between the partisans and opponents of the authenticity of the Medjugorje apparitions. According to R. Laurentin (*La Vierge apparaît-elle à Medjugorje?*, 2002, 290), this referral was an important first, which reveals papal interest in Medjugorje. Joachim Bouflet on the other hand in *Faussaires de Dieu. Enquête* (Paris: Ed. Presses de la Renaissance, 2000) 86-89, and especially 92-95, considers that Ratzinger simply restricted himself to applying a new canonic arrangement in the procedure for recognition of Marian apparitions which was in force since 1978.

22. Letter dated 2 October 1997 of Monsignor Ratko Peric, bishop of Mostar, to *Famille chrétienne*. It is published in "Miracles. Apparitions. Que croire? Qui croire?" in *Les Cahiers d'Edifa*, Paris (hors série de *Famille chrétienne*), I, novembre

1997, 92 and in René Laurentin, *Dernières nouvelles de Medjugorje*, XVII bis, *Medjugorje. L'hostilité abonde, la grâce surabonde, plus que trois voyants* (Paris: Ed. François-Xavier de Guibert, 2nd revised edition, November 1998), 150-152.

23. G. Getrey, *Kibeho ou la face cachée de la tragédie rwandaise*, 240-242.

24. See René Monzat, *Enquêtes sur la droite extrême* (Paris: Le Monde-Editions, 1992), 30-32 et Jean-Yves Camus, *Le Front national. Histoire et analyses* (Paris: Ed. Olivier Laurens, 1996), 248-250.

25. It is not our intention here to determine if and to what extent the visions of the world circulated by Fathers Laurentin and Daniel Ange promoted (as we think) or not, *volens nolens*, the depoliticisation of the faithful and the emergence of strong regimes. For the moment, it is sufficient to state that both stressed the existence of links between Kibeho and Medjugorje.

26. See René Laurentin, "Préface" in Gabriel Maindron, *Des Apparitions à Kibeho. Annonce de Marie au cœur de l'Afrique* (Paris: Ed. O.E.I.L., 1984), 9-17. Laurentin does not hide the fact that the evidence of Father Maindron "was, with that of Daniel Ange (whose mission in Rwanda was long, and he speaks the language) illuminating," for the reflections he made. "Kibeho, like Medjugorje, is not a particularist African message, in spite of its African form. It seems to me to have a global dimension, in spite of the isolation of a small people with no border on the sea. All universal human and Christian messages are rooted in the particular." On the evidence of Daniel Ange, see above.

27. G. Getrey, *Kibeho ou la face cachée de la tragédie rwandaise*, 184.

28. On this and the following comments, see especially Peter Uvin, *L'aide complice? Coopération internationale et violence au Rwanda* (Paris: Ed. L'Harmattan, 1999; 1st ed.: *Aiding Violence. The Development Enterprise in Rwanda*, New York, 1998); Léon Saur, *Influences parallèles. L'Internationale démocrate-chrétienne au Rwanda* (Bruxelles: Ed. Luc Pire, 1998), 38-42; and F. Imbs, F. Bart et A. Bart, "Le Rwanda: les données socio-géographiques," 262-269; Stefaan Marysse, Tom de Herdt et Elie Ndayambaje, *Rwanda. Appauvrissement et ajustement structurel* (Bruxelles: *Cahiers africains*; formerly *Cahiers du CEDAF*), XII, 1994.

29. On the ephemeral and superficial nature of Rwandan prosperity in the 1970s and 80s, as well as the ethnic, vote-seeking system of ethnic quotas in force in Rwanda, see Human Rights Watch and Fédération Internationale des Ligues des Droits de l'Homme, ed. Alison Des Forges, *Aucun témoin ne doit survivre. Le génocide au Rwanda* (Paris: Ed. Karthala, 1999), 59-61; 1st ed.: *Leave None to Tell the Story* (New York: Human Rights Watch, 1999).

30. On the following, see Vidosav Stevanovic, "Les Métamorphoses de Slobodan Milosevic," in Predrag Matvejevitch, ed., *Ex-Yougoslavie: Les seigneurs de la guerre. Milosevic, Tudjman, Karadjic, Mladic, Seselj, Arkan, Susak et les autres...*, (Paris: translated from Serbo-Croat by Mauricette Begic, Nicole Dizdarevic et Sasa Sirovec, Ed. L'Esprit des péninsules, 1999), 19-69; Joseph Krulic, *Histoire de la Yougoslavie. De 1945 à nos jours* (Bruxelles: Ed. Complexe, 1993), 127-151.

31. G. Getrey, *Kibeho ou la face cachée de la tragédie rwandaise*, 244.

32. G. Getrey, *Kibeho ou la face cachée de la tragédie rwandaise*, 92.

33. On the following, see G. Maindron, *Des Apparitions à Kibeho*, 1984, 34 and 79. See also "Discours de Monsieur Christophe Mfizi, directeur de l'Office rwandais d'information," in *Discours prononcés à l'occasion de la visite du pape Jean-Paul II*

au Rwanda. 7-9 septembre 1990 (Kigali: Ed. Présidence de la République rwandaise. Service de l'information et des Archives nationales avec la collaboration du Comité pour la visite du pape de l'Eglise catholique au Rwanda, septembre 1990), 40-44, as well as the postscript given by Christophe Mfizi to Maindron's *Des Apparitions à Kibeho*, 1984, 239-242; et E. de Viron (père), "Le Rwanda, Bretagne de l'Afrique," in *Vivante Afrique*, n° 270, Nov-Dec 1970, 44-46. See also P. Erny, *Rwanda 1994*, 120-130, et Gabriel Maindron (père), *Des Apparitions à Kibeho. Annonce de Marie au cœur de l'Afrique. L'avertissement donné au Rwanda dès 1982* (Paris: Ed. François Xavier de Guibert, 3rd ed., 1994), 82-83.

34. On the tempestuous relations between the Holy See and the Tito regime, especially concerning Cardinal Stepinac, see (among many others) Jean-François Furnemont, *Le Vatican et l'ex-Yougoslavie* (Paris: Ed. L'Harmattan, 1996), 22-28 and 134-140, as well as J. Krulic, *Histoire de la Yougoslavie de 1945 à nos jours*, 78-83.

35. Father Maindron leaves no remaining doubt on the decrease in Church congregation at the time of the first apparitions in Kibeho: "The intellectual elite and the newly rich are deserting our churches," he lamented. And he specified, "I thought then with sadness of our Sunday gatherings in which the young, the intellectuals, civil servants and tradesmen were now poorly represented." At the time of Pope John-Paul II's visit to Rwanda in September 1990, Christophe Mfizi witnessed with apparent sincerity: "The churches were gradually emptying, especially of intellectuals; we only went there now for weddings, funerals, first communions and the confirmation of children; it had all become a social ritual. Until Kibeho came to astonish us and tear us from our indifference." ("Discours de Monsieur Christophe Mfizi," 40-44). See also the references cited in note 33 and I. Linden, *Christianisme et pouvoirs au Rwanda*, 396.

36. See especially Sylvie Barnay, *La Vierge, Femme au visage divin* (Paris: Ed. Gallimard, 2000). See also Sylvie Barnay, *Marie* (Paris: Ed. La Table Ronde, 2001, coll. *Les petits livres de la sagesse*); Sylvie Barnay, *Le Ciel sur la Terre. Les apparitions de la Vierge au Moyen Age* (Paris: Ed. du Cerf, 1999) and Sylvie Barnay, *Les Apparitions de la Vierge* (Paris, Ed. du Cerf, 1992, coll. Bref); René Laurentin, *Multiplication des apparitions de la Vierge aujourd'hui. Est-ce elle? Que veut-elle dire?* (Paris: Ed. Fayard, 1988).

37. Carl Bernstein et Marco Politi, *Sa Sainteté Jean-Paul II et l'histoire cachée de notre époque* (Paris: transl from American by Frank Straschitz, Ania Ciechanowska, Fabienne Vimeren and Martine Leroy-Battistelli, Ed. Plon, 1996), 339-341; 1st ed.: *His Holiness and the Hidden History of our Time* (New York: Doubleday, 1996).

38. G. Getrey, *Kibeho ou la face cachée de la tragédie rwandaise*, 213-215, 243-244, 249, 251-252.

39. On the vocations of woman according to John Paul II, see *La Femme: Textes choisis par les moines de l'Abbaye de Solesmes* (Paris: Ed. Le Sarment, 2001, coll. Ce que dit le pape).

40. It is necessary at this point to discuss Our Lady of Guadalupe. From what we know of her remarks, she no more preached revolt than her counterparts of the ancient world: she restricted herself to demanding that a sanctuary be built to her and to promising her compassion and help to the inhabitants of the country and to those who would love her, call upon her and have confidence in her. According to American theologian Megan McKenna (*Mary: Shadow of Grace* (New York: Orbis Books, 1995), 10-11), she is nevertheless a unique case, because

she seems to aim to "to throw the powerful down from their thrones and raise the poor in their place." In McKenna's view, the Virgin of Guadalupe is "a strong Marian apparition, which transforms the structures of power and resists evil." We must then specify that it would be a mistake to think that *Nuestra Senora* might essentially escape from a right-wing, conservative reading. Pro-life associations, which continue to praise the "eternal female" and the "true nature" of woman as wife and mother, see in her the protector of unborn children and pray to her for the victims of abortion. Thus, the French association *S.O.S Tout-Petits* (well received in the Vatican and close to the French extreme right-wing) placed its electronic website in the protection of Our Lady of Guadalupe, because she is "one of the rare representations of the pregnant Mother of God" (see: http://www.sos-tout-petits.org/sommaire.html – August 2003). In December 2001, the very conservative *Blue Army of Our Lady of Fatima* (USA) committed the final election of George W. Bush (the "pro-life" candidate for the presidency of the United States) to the auspices of Our Lady of Guadalupe (http://www. bluearmy.com/right_to_life_march.htm – August 2003). The approach adopted in reading thus appears to be a determining element in the interpretation of *Nuestra Senora*'s ultimate message. Just as a right-wing reading appears likely to overturn the emancipatory perception of Our Lady of Guadalupe, in the same way it would be useful for the conservative image of the Virgin traditionally circulated in the old world to be reinterpreted in a radically different perspective by the liberation theologians, including Megan McKenna. She has become the *bête noire* of conservative Catholics in the USA, whom she shocked by her strong comments on the more traditional theologies (she does not hesitate to castigate Mother Teresa for her total disinterest in the structural causes of social injustice). Moreover, in December 2002, she co-signed a letter addressed to George W. Bush, along with 16 US congressmen and more than 200 personalities. The letter supports the Venezuelan president Hugo Chavez and invites the White House not to recognize any government in Caracas which has not been democratically elected. "Miracles are not well thought of by our theologians," notes Father François Brune in *La Vierge du Mexique ou le miracle le plus spectaculaire de Marie*, (Paris: Ed. Le Jardin des Livres, 2002), 14. And they are right, I would tend to add! Yet the fact remains that given the proven potential of the attractiveness of the cult of Mary for a people in search of direction, the "leftist" theologians would be well advised in their turn to take an interest in the apparitions of Mary, in order to propose a reading of them which is no longer the "conversion-withdrawal-resignation" pattern, but one of "awareness-emancipation-participation." In that, it is possible to join the fight of feminist theologians who – like Elizabeth A. Johnson CSJ, in *Truly Our Sister: A Theology of Mary in the Communion of Saints* (London and New York: Continuum International Publishing Group, 2003) – dispute the Church's traditional teaching. They see Mary as a source of liberation for women and consequently work to "liberate" the Mother of God from the image of submission and obedience in which the patriarchal theology of the institutional Church has confined her for centuries.

41. G. Getrey, *Kibeho ou la face cachée de la tragédie rwandaise*, 242. See also Joachim Bouflet, *Medjugorje ou la fabrication du surnaturel* (Paris: Ed. Salvator, 1999), 189-191.

42. On this and the following comments, see Jean-Pierre Chrétien et al, *Rwanda. Les médias du génocide* (Paris: Ed. Karthala, 1995; rev. ed., 2002), 324-330, 324-330 and 372-373.

43. A. Sibomana, *Gardons espoir pour le Rwanda*, 59.

44. This phenomenon of Marian appropriation for partisan ends is not new. François-Michel Van der Mersch in *La Révolution Belgique. Chronique d'une famille entre France et Flandres* (Bruxelles: Ed. Racine, 2000), 176-179, reports that in October 1790, the sovereign congress of clerical theocracy which tried to take advantage of the so-called Brabançon revolution to impose itself in the short-lived United States of Belgium, named the Virgin Mary the *"généralissime de l'armée patriote"* (generalissimo of the patriotic army), charged with confronting the offensive return of the Habsburgs of Vienna. One can easily imagine the consequences. On 2 December of the same year, Austrian troops entered Brussels. On relations between the Church and the armed forces in Argentina, see Emilio F. Mignone, "Le 'national-catholicisme' argentin. Actualité de Charles Maurras," translated from Spanish by Daniel Gilbert, in Ignace Berten et René Luneau, eds., *Les Rendez-vous de Saint-Domingue. Les enjeux d'un anniversaire (1492-1992)* (Paris: Ed. du Centurion, 1991), 227-240, et Emilio F. Mignone, *Les "Disparus" d'Argentine. Responsabilité d'une Eglise. Martyre d'un peuple*, translated from Spanish by Daniel Gilbert (Paris: Ed. du Cerf, 1990).

45. See website: http://www.bluearmy.com/ – August 2003.

46. See website: http://www.bluearmy.com/right_to_life_march.htm – August 2003.

47. On this point, see especially Xavier Ternisien, *L'Extrême droite et l'Eglise* (Paris: Ed. Brepols, 1997).

48. Claudie Lesselier, "De la Vierge Marie à Jeanne d'Arc. L'extrême droite frontiste et catholique et les femmes (1984-1990)," in Claudie Lesselier et Fiammetta Venner, eds., *L'Extrême droite et les femmes. Enjeux et actualité* (Bruxelles/Villeurbanne: Ed. Golias, 1997), 64. On the tangible reality of the combat between the Virgin and Satan in the world concept of John Paul II, for whom it was the Virgin's hand which deflected the bullet fired by Ali Agça, himself an instrument of Satan, see C. Bernstein et M. Politi, *Sa Sainteté Jean-Paul II*, 252 and 339-341, as well as André Frossard, *"N'ayez pas peur!" Dialogue avec Jean-Paul II* (Paris: Ed. Robert Laffont, 1982), 327-374, especially 373.

49. John Paul II is an ageing Pope, "whose ideas are those of Poland of the 19th century." This comment – strong precisely because it is not devoid of meaning – is by Mark Eyskens, Belgian minister of State and Flemish Social-Christian Deputy, in an interview given to the newspaper *Het Laatste nieuws* during Holy Week in 2001.

50. For this, the history of relations between Catholicism and the thought of Charles Maurras remains a significant lesson.

14

THE CHURCH'S BLIND EYE TO GENOCIDE IN RWANDA

Tom Ndahiro

"Will all these evil doers never learn,
they who eat up my people just as they eat bread?"
(Psalm 14)

All over Rwandan hills, valleys and mountains, thousands of crosses mark the mass graves of victims of the 1994 genocide. During the genocide, many Tutsis were massacred in or around places of worship, including Catholic churches – paradoxically, in a country which was the most Christianised in Africa, with Christians constituting more than eighty percent of the population. Catholic bishops in Rwanda have sometimes claimed that all Rwandans believe in God.[1] There are hundreds of churches and chapels everywhere and almost every day the faithful repeatedly recite the prayer, "Our Father who art in heaven," pleading with God, the Father to deliver them from evil (Matthew 6:13). From where, then, did the malevolence at the root of the genocide come? How and by whom could it have been overcome? Part of the answer to these questions lies with the Church and its members.

In the book of the prophet Isaiah, we read, "... reject evil and do what is good" (Isaiah 7:15), an admonition that can bring authentic deliverance. It is an unfortunate fact that most of those involved in organising the whole process leading to the genocide were people who were baptised Christians. Some were in the Church hierarchy, particularly in the Roman Catholic Church, which is the focus of this paper. By omission and/or commission, some members of the Catholic Church's leadership were involved in the 1994 genocide against Tutsis. Considering what genocide is – by definition, or as a crime[2] – the involvement of an institution like the Catholic Church demands painstaking analysis.

The role of the Church in the creation of exterminationist ideology

According to Jean-Pierre Karegeye, a Jesuit priest, genocide is morally hideous, an evil expressed by forgetting God, and hence a new form of atheism. Karegeye asks several pertinent questions which merit consideration: "Christians killing other Christians? How could Rwandan Christians who manifested commitment to their faith have acted with such intense cruelty? How did ordinary people come to commit extraordinary evil...? Does the sin of genocide disturb the relationship between God and the perpetrators in official Catholic Church discourse? How can we explain the strange situation of priests involved in the crimes of genocide who are still running parishes in Western countries? Why are they protected by the Vatican against any legal proceedings?" He concludes: "The Church's attitude towards genocide seems to suggest that the hierarchy of religious values is not usually in proportion to the hierarchy of moral standards."[3]

Generally, in Rwanda, the leadership of the Christian Churches, especially that of the Catholic Church, played a central role in the creation and furtherance of racist ideology. They fostered a system which Europeans introduced and they encouraged.[4] The building blocks of this ideology were numerous, but one can mention a few – first, the racist vision of Rwandan society that the missionaries and colonialists imposed by developing the thesis about which groups came first and last to populate the country (these are the Hamitic and Bantu myths); second, by rigidly controlling historical and anthropological research; third, by reconfiguring Rwandan society through the manipulation of ethnic identities (from their vague socio-political nature in the pre-colonial period, these identities gradually became racial). From the late 1950s, some concepts became distorted; thus, democracy became numerical or demographic democracy. The philosophy of *rubanda nyamwinshi*, a Kinyarwanda expression which politically came to mean "the Hutu majority," prevailed after the so-called social revolution of 1959 and ignored the basic tenets of democracy. In my view, recurrent genocides in Rwanda since 1959 were meant to maintain the "majority" by killing "the other." Distributive justice became equivalent to regional and ethnic quotas, and revolution came to mean the legitimised genocide of the Tutsis.

Church authorities contributed to the spread of racist theories mainly through the schools and seminaries over which they exercised control. The elite who ruled the country after independence from Belgium in 1962 trained in these schools. According to Church historian Paul Rutayisire, Church authorities maintained a tight network of communication with many ramifications. Church teachings culminated in massive conversions (*irivuze umwami*) and in the establishment of Catholicism as a state religion, especially from 1946 with King Mutara III Rudahigwa's consecration of Rwanda to Christ the King.[5]

King Rudahigwa, a replacement for his exiled father, was baptised in 1943, and a wave of conversions (including those of chiefs) followed his baptism. But these conversions were not the result of profound faith; the missionaries were only interested in baptising as many people as possible.[6] As a result, there was an increase in the number of geographical centers to disseminate Christianity, as well as an increase in Church personnel. In these circumstances, the evangelisation could not reach the hearts of the people; it was superficial. This quantitative rather than qualitative growth of the Catholic Church became a source of future disaster.[7]

It is unfortunate, says Rutayisire, that these bearers of "good news" promoted and legitimized political regimes which supported the racist ideology: first, the colonial regime, based on racial discrimination between the coloniser and colonised, and on the division of Rwandans into "races" or "castes"; then the First and Second Republics which prided themselves on being "Hutu" regimes.[8]

In colonial times (1930s), missionaries used their influence and power to help secure the banishment of the King of Rwanda, Yuhi Musinga, for the simple reason that he refused to be converted to Christianity. The King was exiled by the colonisers following the advice of Bishop Léon Classe, advisor of the colonial administration.[9] The King later died in Belgian Congo, thousands of kilometers from his country of birth.

Triumph of evil

Stereotypes used by the Hutu-dominated Rwandan government to dehumanise Tutsis were also spread by some influential clergymen, bishops and priests, before and after the genocide.[10] The Catholic Church and colonial powers worked together in organizing racist political groups like the Party for the Emancipation of the Hutu (Parmehutu).[11] When the first acts of genocide were carried out in Rwanda, at the beginning of 1959 and in the early 1960s, there were some brave Church voices against them, most notably that of Bishop Aloys Bigirumwami who wrote several pastoral letters condemning the events.

In his pastoral letter of 15 November 1959, Bishop Bigirumwami expressed his exasperation with those who were to blame for the atrocities in the country. He also warned about the dangers of racism. *"The greatest culprits are those* (my emphasis) who incited others to kill, to burn houses. Those who allowed themselves to be tempted to take part in the attacks, massacres and arson, bear great guilt; they are the enemies of Rwanda, they have sinned against God and against their neighbour... Those who brought the country to fire and blood will perhaps face no consequences here on earth, but if they do not commend themselves to God's mercy, and even man's mercy, they will not escape on the day of judgment of the truth... Reasonable people, especially Christians, should not bear a grudge against others for their birth and origin..."[12] Again on 25 January 1960, Bishop Bigirumwami wrote another letter, this time referring to the guilt of Christians and tackling the issue of racist-related crimes and attitudes.

Christians, understand clearly that it is not the misfortunes that have befallen Rwanda that are the worst of disasters. The worst disaster was rather to persevere in the evil and to brag about it wickedly. The worst disaster for Rwanda was that the proponents of the acts of stupidity of which I spoke, were not pagans, nor notorious apostates who have abandoned Christianity, but rather Christians who were known as good elements among others. These Christians who incite others to evil, who preach hatred in Rwanda, they never miss mass on Sundays, and moreover, they are not afraid to take communion often. This is the worst disaster in our country and in our church. These Christians discredit us among pagans and members of other religions.[13]

The Bishop's appeal at the time also went beyond pastoral letters. In his *Memorandum* of 15 March 1960 to the United Nations Mission to Rwanda, he said that Rwanda was under a "road roller." Yet again, racism and hate propaganda was the crux of the matter. "One thinks that internal violence and subversive propaganda are all out to spark off hatred, divisions between Hutu, Tutsi and Twa – real racism, whatever one may say – and yet these three social groups have always lived together in symbiosis and should pursue and complete it."[14]

As things turned from bad to worse, and the involvement of priests and nuns in the cataclysm became more discernible, the Bishop wrote another letter on 10 June 1960, this time focused on religious: "Fellow Rwandans, priests and the religious... and you the missionaries..." He pleaded with those who gave in during the "recent events" to examine their consciences, to open their eyes and ears, free themselves from temptations, renounce the temptation to sow discord in families by claiming that this was the best way to save Rwanda and its inhabitants. In strong terms, he demanded:

Let us fight wickedness and hatred because they will sink Rwanda and weaken the Church. Evil and hatred continue to increase; it is said that a Muhutu cannot live with a Mututsi, that he must no longer be the teacher of his child at school, that they can no longer meet, share, trade, buy from each other, be in solidarity. This disaster that has befallen us, ward it off through the God of Rwanda, conquer it through the Gospel of love, truth and justice... Let us stop being divided into parties, which disseminate the Hutu-Tutsi ethnicity because this would mean us sinking in the worst filth. Things have gone wrong and we keep quiet, we remain bystanders, we laugh it off, how will this end? People are tracked in every corner, refugees of all sorts flock in such numbers that we do not know where to put them and we tell them to move on, while they do not know where to go. How is this going to end? This happened first in Rwanda and now it is also happening in Congo. Rwanda has known no peace since November. What will be the consequences of these elections? If we have praised Rwandans who chased away other Rwandans, are we going to frown on those who will chase non-Rwandans? With what is happening in Rwanda, and if this continues, do you think that people are going to be able to live together? Let us start by saving what was lost; let us stand up and look for friendliness of Rwandans among themselves; let us look ahead, the sky is getting dark, the storm is brewing, let us put under shelter what is not covered... Let us strengthen the links of unity... if we do not succeed at home, we will have nothing else to do but sink into the sea with the millstone round our necks...[15]

The Bishop wrote this letter at the time when the referendum to bring the monarchy to an end was drawing close. Many Rwandans (including myself) were either already refugees or would soon be. Bishop Bigirumwami's supplications vanished into the wilderness. Why? His colleague, Bishop André Perraudin,[16] had a more influential voice, one that was more listened to even than Bishop Bigirumwami's. Bishop Perraudin, it should be noted, was a mentor of PARMEHUTU (*Parti du Mouvement et de l'Emancipation Hutu*, formerly MDR/PARMEHUTU), formed on 16 November 1959.[17]

It is significant that Bishop Perraudin's language echoes that of the sponsors and perpetrators of genocide. Talking about genocide in his book *Mgr. André Perraudin – Un Evêque au Rwanda*, and referring to the attack by the Rwandan Patriotic Front (RPF) in October 1990, Perraudin states,

Tutsi leaders have never abandoned this project [the idea of returning to power]. It became manifest on 1 October 1990 with the whole army organised in Uganda... This unshakable will of returning to power is the key to all the events that plunged Rwanda into a bloodbath, including the genocide of Tutsi which began on the very evening of 6 April 1994 when President Habyarimana was killed... The argument often put forward and exploited, that is the protection of the Tutsi inside Rwanda, was only a pretext. The true motive of the attackers was to retake power. It cannot be overemphasised enough; it is the explanation of everything that happened. Without any doubt, it must be stated that the first and main cause of the genocide of Tutsi in April 1994 was the attack on the country by the Tutsi themselves. Without 1 October 1990 and all that followed, especially the killing of President Habyarimana, neither the genocide of the Tutsi, nor that of the Hutu, would have happened ...[18]

It is disquieting to note that a Church leader of that caliber, instead of conveying a message of consolation to the victims of the 1994 genocide, implies that the Tutsis were the cause of their own extermination.

Archbishop Perraudin remained influential in all regimes. On 20 June 1976 he was replaced in the archdiocese of Kigali, by Archbishop Vincent Nsengiyumva,[19] a staunch member of the ruling MRND's (*Mouvement Révolutionnaire National pour le Développement*) Central Committee in General Habyarimana's regime.[20] Bishop Perraudin retired in 1989, and was replaced in his diocese of Kabgayi by Bishop Thaddée Nsengiyumva on 7 October 1989. MRND was the party which in the mid-1970s had introduced and institutionalized policies of racial discrimination which they termed "*équilibre éthnique et régional*" (ethnic and regional equilibrium, a quota system). It was a system advocated by Catholic priests in April 1972, including by Monsignor André Havugimana, the current vicar-general of the Catholic Archdiocese of Kigali.[21]

The Church supported the quota system, as expressed in the Bishops' letter of 28 February 1990: "One hears, at times, people complaining that due to their ethnic origin, employment, or admission to school has been refused them. They have been deprived of an advantage, or justice has not been impartial towards them...You do not ignore the fact that the policy of ethnic balance in places of employment and schools is aiming to correct this inequality that might favor one to the detriment of the other. It is evident that such a policy cannot please everybody, nor produce immediately all the results they were hoping to gain."[22]

On 30 April 1990, five Catholic priests from Nyundo diocese broke the silence. In a letter to the Church's bishops in Rwanda, they called the quota system "racist" and argued that it was high time "the Church of Jesus Christ established in Rwanda proclaimed aloud and tirelessly" to denounce it, since it constituted "an aberration" within their Church. They further said that the only sure justice in schools and employment was the one which only took account of individual capacities, regardless of people's origins, and that it was on this condition that the country could have citizens capable of leading it with competence and equity. In conclusion, they said, "The Church should not be the vassal of the secular powers, but it should be free to speak with sincerity and courage when it proves necessary."[23] The authors of this letter were Father Augustin Ntagara, Father Callixte Kalisa, Father Aloys Nzaramba, Father Jean Baptiste Hategeka, and Father Fabien Rwakareke. The first three were killed during the genocide; the last two survived.

Within the Catholic Church, this discriminatory policy had long been in the seminaries. According to Father Jean Ndolimana, enrollment of Tutsis in the Nyundo diocese was limited to four percent. On the school card, every seminarian had to indicate his father's ethnic group.[24]

Racial discrimination is something that has to be condemned because, as it has been stressed: "...any doctrine of superiority based on racial differentiation is scientifically false, morally condemnable, socially unjust, and dangerous and there is no justification, in theory or in practice, anywhere... [it] is an obstacle to friendly and peaceful relations among nations and is capable of disturbing peace and security among peoples and the harmony of persons living side by side, even within one and the same state. Its existence is repugnant to the ideals of any human society ..."[25] The Church should have been aware of this. Instead of condemning those who were against the racist system, instead of playing an important role in institutionalizing injustice by convincing their congregants to accept a morally reprehensible racist policy, Church leaders should have spoken out against racist discrimination. Regrettably, the Church took the side of the political regimes, and thus was unable to exercise its prophetic role. It did not denounce political and social injustices, nor did it condemn the first mass killings, nor those which followed.

After 1 October 1990, the Government's ideologues launched a hate campaign intended to polarize Rwandan society as preparation of the genocide was underway. The trigger was the publication of the so-called "Hutu Ten Commandments" in the magazine *Kangura*,[26] whose Chief Editor, Hassan Ngeze, was a Moslem.

The last three "commandments" are significant. The eighth commandment said that "The Bahutu should stop having mercy on the Batutsi," while the ninth read: "The Bahutu, wherever they are, must have unity, solidarity and be preoccupied by the fate of their Hutu brothers; the Bahutu, both inside and outside Rwanda, must constantly look for friends and allies for the Hutu cause, starting with our Bantu brothers; they must constantly counteract the Tutsi propaganda. The Bahutu must be firm and vigilant against their common enemy who are Batutsi."

The tenth commandment went back to the roots. "The 1959 social revolution, the 1961 referendum and the Hutu ideology must be taught to every Muhutu and at all levels. Every Muhutu must spread widely this ideology. We shall consider a traitor any Muhutu who will persecute his Muhutu brothers for having read, spread and taught this ideology."

President Habyarimana's speech to the MRND Congress of 28 April 1991 alluded to Hutu unity, saying: "It is imperative that the majority forge unity, so that they are able to ward off any attempt to return them into slavery."[27] The issue of Hutu Unity was key. The front cover of *Kangura* of May 1991 (Issue No. 16) reads, "Hutus' unity is their only hope" (*Ubumwe bw'abahutu niyo mizero yabo*). Referring to the party line that the Tutsis premeditated the extermination of the Hutus, the front cover of *Kangura* (Issue No. 17) bore the message "If it was not for the God of Rwanda who is always on the alert, the Hutus would be in great danger." Again, on the front cover of Issue No. 25, there was a portrait of President Habyarimana wearing a Bishop's chasuble and miter with the word "*Ubumwe*" (Unity). He said that his "Christian faith" had made many Rwandans consider him a "Catholic priest" and added, "The ungrateful should know that the Hutus would take action if he (President Habyarimana) removed his priestly clothes."[28]

Hutu extremists, who perhaps wanted the extermination of the Tutsis earlier than April 1994, portrayed President Habyarimana as soft, with sympathy for the Tutsis, although this was not the case. At the peak of the genocide, in a long exhortation, the RTLM (*Radio Télévision Libre des Mille Collines*) announcer Valerie Bemeriki described what was going on as "holy." She claimed that before the beginning of the war many Hutus believed that the Tutsis were "disturbing" them because of the support they had from President Habyarimana. And she added: "And yet they killed the father for no good reason, for the Blessed Virgin Mary said recently that he was in fact a father, that he was our father, that she had received him... I will repeat the words of the Holy Mother, such as she said them..."[29]

In January 1992, *Kangura's* front cover featured a conversation between Jesus Christ, the Virgin Mary and her husband St. Joseph about how Hutu unity could be achieved.[30] Not a single protest came from either the Catholic or Protestant Churches. In 1991, priests from the diocese of Kabgayi had initiated a Pastoral Letter, which audaciously condemned the evil practices in the country, but they did not get sufficient support from their superiors.[31]

In the same year, a Catholic journal, *Kinyamateka*, published an article that challenged the Church to act or be declared "asleep" or "dead beat."[32] Church leadership remained silent. By then, genocidal killings in Bugesera, Kibuye and Gisenyi were occurring with impunity. In the same month, on 22 November 1992, Dr. Léon Mugesera, a vice-president of the ruling party MRND in Gisenyi prefecture, overtly called for the extermination of Tutsis, for them to be sent to Ethiopia (their alleged country of origin) via the Nyabarongo River.[33]

It is difficult to describe the position taken by the institutional Church just before and during the genocide. It is appropriate to take note of a declaration made by some "Christians" who met in London in 1996: "The church is sick. The historical roots of this sickness lie in part with the 'mother churches.' She is facing the most serious crisis in her history. The church has failed in her mission, and lost her credibility, particularly since the genocide. She needs to repent before God and Rwandan society, and seek healing from God."[34]

This diagnosis offers a good summary of the situation. The Church lacks a sense of remorse and therefore cannot repent; hence, its active involvement, in my view, is the last stage of genocide – denial. At the time when the Church's voice was needed most, its authorities abided by the Commandment to maintain Hutu "unity" in order to fight the common "enemy." Since October 1990, the Church had employed the official language of hate propagated by the government. The minor difference was in the medium of communication. While the government used national radio and other print media, the Catholic Church made use of Pastoral Letters.

The writings of the Catholic bishops just after 1 October 1990 read like an official text from the state publishing house. After the attack by the RPF, President Habyarimana continually referred to them as "aggressors" or "assailants." The official media followed suit. The French fortnightly *La Relève* commented, "During the morning of October 1st, 1990, Rwanda was attacked by assailants including Rwandan refugees, members of the Ugandan army who rallied with Ugandan elements, members of this army."[35]

In the Catholic bishops' letter of 7 November 1990 entitled "Happy are the artisans of peace, for they will be called Sons of God,"[36] the same words were used, with some emphasis to confirm that the President had spoken nothing but the truth in his speech on 5 October 1990. But that was not the only similarity. The President had also said: "Aggression against our country is not only of military nature. It also rests on international media manipulation and disinformation... we were surprised by the violent manipulations, being prepared a long time ago, as we now know, by certain media from the West and not of the least minimal. Our country is still being subjected to attacks and calumnies, to systematic lies, that we can only qualify as diabolic in nature."[37] And in their letter, the bishops said: "In these difficult times, it is our duty to remain in solidarity in the defense of the truth... False information and rumors, libel and lies have been spread in Rwanda ... We strongly deplore disinformation, cleverly and maliciously organized by those who have attacked Rwanda, about certain facts and events which some of the media have transmitted."[38]

Remaining in solidarity with the government that planned genocide was not limited to speeches in the name of defending "the truth." The "comité de contacts," bringing Catholics and Protestants together, was created as a messenger of the government. This ecumenical movement is hailed in several documents as proof that "the Church did something" during the genocide. Father Joseph Ngomanzungu recently dedicated almost a whole book to this committee.[39] His publication exhibits the failures and complicity of an institution he is trying to defend.

On 2 March 1993, a delegation of the "comité de contacts" met the RPF at the Papal envoy's residence in Bujumbura, Burundi. The aim was for the representative Church leaders to discuss with the RPF ways and means of bringing the collapsed peace process back on track. Deliberations centered on the circumstances that had led the RPF to attack the government forces on 8 February that year, and what could be done to reverse the trend. This twelve-hour meeting followed another that had brought together the RPF and the four opposition parties. In the latter, it had been agreed that: "Despite the content of the cease-fire accord concluded between the Rwandese Government and RPF on 12 July 1992, the blood of innocent persons continues to be shed in all regions of Bugesera, Ruhengeri, Gisenyi and Kibuye. This organised terrorism, which has totally paralysed the government, has been transformed into a real genocide which has shocked and revolted the universal consciousness and which constitutes a serious violation of the cease-fire accord."[40]

Despite explanations and requests to the bishops at least to condemn what was happening,[41] there was no positive response. With the exception of Bishop Alexis Birindabagabo of the Anglican Church, who proposed that there had to be a statement to condemn the killings that were by then common knowledge, others remained indifferent. It is disquieting to read that in that meeting, Bishop Augustin Misago of the Diocese of Gikongoro said that the death of Tutsis was not enough reason to justify the usurpation of power.[42] Misago's comments in fact give the impression of a racist without scruple, who attached no value to the life of Tutsis. He remained committed to the Hutus rather than to God's commandment. During the genocide, he refused to hide any Tutsis, for "lack of space" in his bishop's residence.[43] Except for Bishop Birindabagabo, this *comité de contacts*," whose president was Bishop Thaddée Nsengiyumva of Kabgayi, remained loyal to the regime that committed genocide. Their statements, available today in the publications of Father Joseph Ngomanzungu, are a testament to the team's sympathy with the perpetrators of genocide – before, during and after the genocide.

Like Archbishop Perraudin, Bishop Focas Nikwigize of Ruhengeri was unequivocal in supporting the ideology of genocide. While in exile in Goma, Zaire, he told a Belgian newspaper,

The Batutsi would like to restore their power and to reduce the Bahutu to slaves! Their objective was to take Kigali by force, whatever the cost; not to share power, but to govern. In order to fulfil this objective they used two sorts of weapons: their guns, which came from Europe, and their women. They gave their women to Europeans and so remained in a strong alliance with them. That is how bad they are! A Muhutu is simple and right but a Mututsi is cunning and hypocritical. They seem fine, polite and charming, but when the time comes, they force themselves on you. A Mututsi is deeply bad, not because of her education, but because of her nature.[44]

The above statement bears witness to the racist views of this priest. Considering a people as naturally bad is similar to the explanation used by the Nazis to justify the extermination of Jews in order to maintain the purity of the Aryan race. Bishop Nikwigize continues: "What happened in 1994 was something very human. When someone attacks you, you have to defend yourself. In such a situation, you forget that you are a Christian; you are first a human being."[45]

There has been no condemnation of Bishop Nikwigize's denial and endorsement of the genocide from the Church hierarchy as a whole, nor has there been an admonition from any individual bishop. Since "silence implies consent," one might rightly say that the Church leaders who have said nothing have espoused Nikwigize's ideas. It was all the more disquieting that the justification of the genocide came from a senior Church leader whose influence was great among refugees.

Besides the writings of Father Ngomanzungu, there is a letter written by an interdenominational group called "Representatives of the Church of Christ" in Katale Camp, in former Zaire. Written on 10 November 1995, the letter was full of praise of the Church and condemnation of the RPF, which was accused of all the crimes committed in 1994. The letter says that during the "war" and "tragedy," the Church did not cease to appeal to "the people to live in love, harmony, and mutual respect, despite menaces from the RPF and its supporters who aimed at taking power by force to the point when they started eliminating politicians who did not share their opinion." The word genocide does not appear in the letter.[46]

The letter's signatories are Rev. Archdeacon Canon Charles Samson Muzungu and Rev. Archdeacon Alphonse Barasebwa of the Episcopal Church of Rwanda, Father Jean Baptiste Rwamayanja of the Roman Catholic Church, Rev. Paulin Nkezabera and Rev. Simon Pierre Bimenyimana of the Baptist Churches Association in Rwanda, Pastor Jonas Barame of the Seventh Day Adventist Church, Rev. Innocent Mukumira of the *Communauté des Eglises de Dieu en Afrique Centrale au Rwanda*, Rev. Joël Nkeramihigo of the *Eglise biblique de la vie profonde au Rwanda*, Rev. Joseph Habineza of the Pentecostal Churches Association in Rwanda, Rev. Uziel Nkenyereye of the Evangelical Churches Community in Rwanda and Daniel Mugema, an evangelist in the Free Methodist Church in Rwanda.

On the role of the Church in Rwandan society, the letter's authors say that the missionaries' presence was considerably felt in "the educational and socio-cultural sectors" without discrimination. Here, they add, the Church accomplished its mission in the light of the gospel, appealing to the people to live in brotherhood, love and trust. On the Church and politics, they claim that the Church never failed in its mission of love and truth at the "political level" until the "murderous and devastating invasion of the RPF in 1990." It is true that the Church had built more schools than any other institution, including the government. But it was in these very schools that the hate ideology was taught.

Father Rwamayanja, one of the letter's signatories, was also among the twenty-nine Rwandan Catholic priests who, from Goma, Zaire, wrote a letter to the Pope in August 1994, demanding that the Rwandan government should allow all refugees home and then hold a referendum to determine the country's political future.[47] The authors of this letter had no good program for the country. All they wanted was to hold in contempt the Pope's acknowledgment of the genocide. As early as 15 May 1994, the Pope had declared that the massacres in Rwanda were indeed genocide.[48]

The priests wrote to the Pope: "Everybody knows, except those who do not wish to know or understand it, that the massacres which took place in Rwanda are the result of the provocation of the Rwandese people by the RPF." These priests, contaminated by the genocidal ideology, placed His Holiness the Pope in the category of "those who did not wish to know," to cover up their own shortcomings, and those of the government they served.

Among the signatories of that letter, there was also a vicar general from the diocese of Ruhengeri, Monsignor Simon Habyarimana, who was clear-cut in denying the genocide. In early 1995, from his residence, room 119, in the Major seminary of Buhimba, a few kilometers from Goma, he was asked what he thought about the genocide. For him, it was simply RPF propaganda to mould international opinion, and the Tutsis had perished because of *"la colère populaire"* – meaning "popular anger" following the death of President Habyarimana. This is a view shared by many genocide deniers. As if giving the position of the Church, Monsignor Habyarimana said: "There may be talk of a genocide of Tutsis. It was not so, it wasn't deliberate... what you had was a hidden genocide of Hutus."[49] While in Rome, he keeps on reinforcing a hate discourse to justify his stay in exile. "The plan of the present government of Rwanda is to destroy the Hutu intelligentsia, to get rid of people who are educated. Clearly, they want to eliminate us."[50] When he says the "present government," he refers to the government they identify with Tutsis.

Almost seven years later, Dr. Pascal Ndengejeho and Father Serge Desouter replicated the words of the so-called "Church of Christ" when they appeared as witnesses before the International Criminal Tribunal for Rwanda (ICTR). Dr. Ndengejeho was a Minister of Information in the early 1990s and a member of MDR (*Mouvement Démocratique Républicain*[51]) Power, a faction that was a partner in the genocide. By the time he went to testify before the ICTR, he was, and still is, the director of communications in the Episcopal Conference of Namibia. Father Desouter, an influential White Father and a known genocide denier,[52] had gone to Arusha, Tanzania, to testify for Pastor Elizaphan Ntakirutimana of the Seventh Day Adventist

Church, and his son Gerard Ntakirutimana. The two suspects were found guilty and convicted by the tribunal for genocide and related crimes.

Desouter told the ICTR that the "real" problem in Rwanda had nothing to do with ethnic hatred. "The invasion of 1990 [by the RPF] was a catastrophe for two reasons. The ethnic aspect was introduced into the politics of Rwanda and weapons were also introduced... the fight for power by extremists on both sides is what destroyed Rwanda." He also commented that after the death of Burundi's President Melchior Ndadaye, you could not trust Tutsis.[53]

Father Desouter, who was at one time accused of being a racist and a revisionist by a Catholic journal,[54] publicly states his dislike for the idea of making Rwanda for Rwandans, rather than for Hutus, Tutsis and Twa. In a paper entitled "The usurpation of the term genocide," published in March 2002, Desouter says, "Denial of ethnic character often serves to establish a sordid agenda... Replacing a majority regime with a minority regime that is even more intolerant and cruel resolves nothing."[55] He insists that his congregation is more knowledgeable, that others who have analysed and tried to be part of solutions to Rwandan problems are simplistic, and base their judgment on conventional wisdom. In his view, it is the missionaries "who have a better understanding of the reality of the situation, of the culture and the local language."[56] In 1996, Father Desouter, then president of the Committee of Belgian Missionary Institutions, claimed, like Monsignor Habyarimana, that he did not know if the genocide of the Tutsis was planned. And commenting on the estimated death toll, he said: "[T]hey talk about a million dead Tutsis... There have never been that many Tutsis in Rwanda."[57] This is the language often used by many *genocidaires* and apologists, who play about with victim numbers to blur the criminal act.

Accepting failure is a virtue. Even so, it is difficult for institutions like the Catholic Church that are known to command respect worldwide – above all when such institutions have been party to policies of racial discrimination and genocide. The Church decided to adopt silence and slander as defense mechanisms. The question is why the Vatican has accepted or tolerated such tendencies.

The call for remorse and repentance still seems unnecessary and problematical for the Catholic Church. In March 1996, Pope John Paul II told the Rwandan people, "The Church... cannot be held responsible for the guilt of its members that have acted against the evangelic law; they will be called to render account of their own actions. All Church members that have sinned during the genocide must have the courage to assume the consequences of the deeds they have done against God and fellow men."[58]

Had this been accepted and done, it would have helped to end a culture of impunity that has characterised Rwanda for more than thirty-five years. This could have been an established warning to anyone who harbored the archaic racist ideology. It could have acted as a deterrent to foreign mentors, warning that continuation of such politics contravenes the principle of natural justice and is liable to be punished by law. Thirdly, it offers the only premises on which durable reconciliation, rehabilitation and reconstruction could take place or be cemented.

In April 2001, a magazine called *Fête & Saison* published by *Aide à l'Eglise en Détresse (AED)*, a powerful Catholic organization[59] specified the countries in the world where the Church was persecuted. On a world map, a number of countries were marked in red, including Rwanda, Afghanistan, Sudan, Saudi Arabia, etc... implying that somehow the government in Kigali was no different from that of the Talibans! In that fund-raising advert, AED called for a minute's silence on 10 April, in memory of martyrs and Christians under persecution. Incidentally, this is also the time when Rwandan genocide survivors mourn their murdered relatives and remember the darkest days of their lives.

The hostile propaganda against the government of Rwanda started immediately after the genocide. Papal envoys in Kigali, the lobby group of White Fathers, and other Church organisations, like the MISNA News Agency and *Fides*, went so far as to accuse the government of Rwanda of persecuting the Church.[60] They were well aware that the Church was not persecuted, but they were trying to avoid the repugnant facts about the failures of their institution. Far from being persecuted, the Church was being challenged over its responsibility.

In 1999, Bishop Augustin Misago was arrested and subsequently tried for the crime of genocide. After some months, a court in Kigali acquitted him – for lack of evidence, not as the Papal Nuncio, Archbishop Salvatore Penacchio, claims, because he was innocent.[61] On several occasions Misago told the press that through him the government was targeting the Church.[62] Cardinal Josef Tomko, one of the Pope's close "lieutenants," also said that the Church was "targeted" in the trial, but the Church was not afraid – "welcoming even the destiny of martyrdom."[63] Both concocted such distortions that were disseminated with impunity by the Vatican's propaganda machine.

The protection of Bishop Misago was not the Church's only move to shield it from the arm of the law. The most common move was to facilitate the departure of the accused to foreign countries. These included Father

Wenceslas Munyeshyaka, who is in one of the parishes in France,[64] Monsignor Simon Habyarimana, living in Rome, and many others who are fugitives around the world. On many occasions, whenever a member of the clergy was arrested and imprisoned, the Church alleged that they were innocent without any credible proof.[65] In *Obstruction of Justice: The Nuns of Sovu in Belgium*,[66] clergymen are among those accused of trying to cover up crimes committed by the two nuns, Sister Julienne Kizito and Sister Gertrude Mukangango, who were found guilty of genocide and related crimes, and convicted by a Belgian tribunal.

Given their moral authority and role as educators of society's sense of right and wrong, Church leaders could act in such a way as to commit Christians to a genuine path of repentance, if they themselves recognised the role played by the Church in contributing to divisions and conflicts in Rwandan society. After repentance, the Church could then preach reconciliation.

On 20 June 1994, a Rwandan radio announcer, Kantano Habimana of *Radio Télévision Libre des Milles Collines*, called upon his listeners to join him in singing a song praising genocide. "Friends, let us rejoice... All *Inkotanyi* have perished... Friends, let us rejoice. God is fair." On 2 July, the same announcer was not only praising genocide, but also using God's name to justify it. "Let us rejoice: the '*Inkotanyi*' have been exterminated! Oh dear friends, let us rejoice, God is equitable... The Good Lord is really equitable. These evildoers, these terrorists, these people with suicidal tendencies will end up being exterminated... In any case, let us stand firm and exterminate them, so that our children and grandchildren do not hear the word '*Inkotanyi*' ever again."[67]

Soon after the genocide, some non-Catholic Churches recognized and confessed their collusion with the powers that carried out the genocide, their silence and the involvement of their members in the massacres. The Catholic Church did not do this immediately, even though some of its leaders spoke out as individuals. It was only at Christmas 1995 that the Rwandan Episcopal Conference, officially but vaguely, acknowledged that there had been genocide – more than a year after the Pope and international community had acknowledged it. In February 2001, a confession of collective accountability was formulated in nebulous language. Since then, as Rutayisire says, investigations conducted in Catholic communities have never ceased to show the existence of revisionist tendencies among them.[68]

Conclusion

I chose to write about the Catholic Church and the genocide in Rwanda because I would argue that it was the only institution involved in all the stages of genocide. As a layperson, it is astounding to hear about the "love, truth and trust" that the Church has achieved[69] in a country where genocide took more than 800,000 lives in just a hundred days, and to see the institutional Church protecting, instead of punishing or at least denouncing, those among its leadership or in its membership who are accused of genocide.

There is no doubt that throughout the history of Rwanda, Church leaders have had ties with the political powers in Rwanda. The Church was also involved in the policy of ethnic division which degenerated into ethnic hatred. In order to succeed in its mission of uniting people, the Church in Rwanda and elsewhere must examine its attitudes, practices, and policies that have too often encouraged ethnic division. If all Christians belong to the same family of God whose head is Jesus Christ, the message that must prevail in the Church, to paraphrase the Apostle Paul, is that there is no Hutu, Twa, and Tutsi – but simply Rwandans. The Church should embody and emulate what St. Paul says: "There is neither Jew nor Greek, there is neither slave nor free, there is neither male nor female; for all you are one in Christ" (Galatians 3: 28).

When the sexual abuse scandal about pedophilia involving Roman Catholic priests hit media headlines in 2002, Pope John Paul II issued a very strong statement: "As priests, we are personally and profoundly afflicted by the sins of our brothers who have betrayed the grace of ordination in succumbing even to the most grievous forms of evil at work in the world..."[70] It was effective. Bernard Cardinal Law of Boston (USA) was forced to resign because of how he mishandled the cases of priests in his diocese who had been accused of pedophilia.[71]

And that is not the only time recently that Church leaders have taken strong positions. In April 2002, Bishop Olivier de Berranger of France spoke out against racism, xenophobia, and other prejudices and accused Jean-Marie Le Pen of being "the heir to a totalitarian and anti-Christian" tradition.[72] And when Archbishop Emmanuel Milingo of Zambia flaunted the Church's rule of celibacy for priests by marrying a woman in a public ceremony, he was, in accord with Church discipline, threatened with excommunication for his misbehavior. Paradoxically, Rwandan priests accused of genocide and related crimes against humanity still publicly celebrate Holy Mass in Rome and in countries like France, where other priests are infuriated by Le Pen's racist rhetoric.

Church leadership should both be on the side of *and be perceived* to be on the side of justice and the victims of injustice rather than on the side of genocide perpetrators and deniers. The Church must remember what Dietrich Bonhoeffer said in his April 1933 essay, "The Church and the Jewish Question." As he wrote, one way in which Churches can fight political injustices is to question state injustices and to call the state to responsibility. Another is to help the victims of injustice, whether they are members of the Church or not. To bring an end to the machinery of injustice, he said, the Church is obliged not only to help the victims who had fallen under the wheel, but also to fall into the spokes of the wheel itself.[73]

Since justice is an integral element in the process of reconciliation, the Church should be among those asking that the perpetrators of genocide be brought to justice. If the Church contributes to the process of justice, unity can be re-established among Rwandans in general, and among Christians in particular. It is the only way that the Church can restore its credibility, and thus be what it is called to be: a witness to faith, hope and love, to truth and justice. Only in this way will the Catholic Church in Rwanda be able to help save the people of Rwanda – *all the people* – from future suffering and bloodshed.

Notes

1. See further, *Kinyamateka* (a journal owned by the Rwandan Episcopal Conference of the Catholic Church), No. 1614, January 2003, 6.

2. See further, *Convention on the Prevention and Punishment of the Crime of Genocide,* www.unhchr.ch/html/menu3b/p_genoci.htm

3. This priest gave me this answer in January 2003 in response to a question I had asked. On the issue of priests accused of genocide, who are currently living in Europe and elsewhere, see *Les Dossiers de Golias – Rwanda: L'honneur perdu de l'Église* (Édition Golias-France, April 1999).

4. See further, André Sibomana, *Hope for Rwanda: Conversations with Laure Guilbert and Hervé Deguine* (London: Pluto Press, 1999), 78-85.

5. Paul Rutayisire, *La Christianisation du Rwanda* (1900-1945) (Editions Universitaires Fribourg, 1987), 321-346.

6. Ibid., 328-333.

7. Ibid., 333-336.

8. Paul Rutayisire, "Silence et compromissions de la hiérarchie de l'Eglise Catholique du Rwanda," *Au Coeur de l'Afrique*, (No 2-3, 1995), 427.

9. Paul. Rutayisire, *La Christianisation du Rwanda*, 167-190.

10. See further, Sibomana, *Hope for Rwanda*, 77-98.

11. Rutayisire, "Silence et compromissions," 428.

12. Venuste Linguyeneza, *Lettres Pastorales et autres Declarations des Eveques Catholiques du Rwanda 1956-1962* (Waterloo, February 2001), 159-162.

13. Linguyeneza, *Lettres Pastorales et autres Declarations*, 190-191.

14. Monseigneur Aloys Bigirumwami, *Memorandum Remis à la Mission de Visite de l'ONU Concernant la Tragique Situation Actuelle du Rwanda*, Nyundo, 15 March 1960.

15. Linguyeneza, *Lettres Pastorales et autres Declarations*, 236-241.

16. Perraudin became Archbishop of Kabgayi on 1 May 1960.

17. Along with Father Ernotte, Bishop Perraudin was also behind the creation of the *Mouvement Social Muhutu* (Hutu Social Movement) on 1 May 1957. Its chairman was Grégoire Kayibanda who was also head of the Legion of Mary. The same clique drafted the *Manifeste de Bahutu* (Hutu Manifesto) in the same year.

18. (Saint-Maurice: Edition Saint Augustin), February 2003, 277.

19. Vincent Nsengiyumva was ordained as a priest on 18 June 1966, consecrated as Bishop of Nyundo diocese on 3 May 1976 and became the Archbishop of metropolitan Kigali on 20 June of the same year. See *Jubilé de 100 Ans d'evangelisation au Rwanda 1900-2000: 83 Ans de Sacerdoce au Rwanda 1917-2000* (Palloti Presse, 2000), 64.

20. MRND was Juvénal Habyarimana's single party, later revamped by the addition of a second D, to signify "democratic." Many of its leaders were among the main organizers of the genocide.

21. Havugimana's letter, the source of this statement, remains unpublished, but see "Shameful Silence of the Rwandan church," *The Guardian*, 28 August 1999.

22. *Le Christ, Notre Unité, Recueil de Lettres et Message de la Conférence des Evêques Catholiques du Rwanda publiés pendant la période de guerre* (1990-1994), edited by the Secrétariat Général de la Conférence des Eveques Catholiques du Rwanda, 1995, 11-12.

23. Father Jean Ndolimana, *Rwanda 1994: Idéologie, Méthodes et négationnisme du génocide des Tutsi* (Edition Vivere, February 2003). The letter is published in full, pp. 220-224.

24. Ndolimana, *Rwanda 1994*, 216.

25. "Preamble of the International Convention on the Elimination of All Forms of Racial Discrimination" of 21 December 1965. This is a human rights instrument which the Rwandan government ratified in March 1975.

26. *Kangura* (No 6, December 1990).

27. See the weekly newspaper *Imvaho*, No 893, 6-12 May 1991.

28. Reading through all the Pastoral letters and declarations written or made between 1990-1994, nowhere can one find a reproach to the hate media or condemnation of genocide.

29. Valerie Bemeriki of RTLM, 20 May 1994. See Prosecutor's Closing Brief in Case No. ICTR-99-52-T, 83.

30. *Kangura*, International Version, No 3.

31. The diocese of Kabgayi published it on 1 December 1991 under the Title *Twivugurure Tubane Mu Mahoro*.

32. *"Kiliziya Gatolika niba idasinziriye iraboshye,"* *Kinyamateka*, (No. 1381, November 1992).

33. International Commission of Inquiry into Human Rights Violations in Rwanda since October 1, 1990, *Report* (March 1993), 9-10.

34. Conference declaration: "The Church's Role in the Reconstruction of Rwanda." Conference organized by the Newick Park Initiative, Ashburnham, UK, June 1996.

35. *La Relève*, No. 143-144, 1990, 2.

36. *Recueil de Lettres*, 1995, 119-133.

37. *La Relève*, no. 143-144, 1990, 7.

38. *Recueil de Lettres*, 1995, 123-124.

39. Joseph Ngomanzungu, *Effort de Médiation Oecuménique des Eglises dans la Crise Rwandaise: Le Comité de Contacts* (1991-1994) (Palloti Presse, February 2003).

40. Final communiqué published at the end of the Bujumbura meeting held from 25 February - 2 March 1993 between the political parties MDR, PSD, PDC, PL, and the RPF.

41. See Joseph Ngomanzungu, *Effort De Médiation Oecuménique.*

42. I was present at that meeting. For the list of participants see Ngomanzungu, *Effort De Médiation Oecuménique*, 45.

43. *Rwanda: The Betrayal*, a documentary film produced by Lindsey Hilsum for Channel 4 Television UK, 1995.

44. Interview with Els De Temmermen, *De Volkskrant*, 26 June 1995.

45. Ibid.

46. The author obtained an original copy of this letter in 1996 from Mugunga Camp, Goma, Zaire. This is the first time that details of this letter have been published.

47. The text of this letter, with signatures of the authors, was published by Father Jean Ndolimana in *Rwanda, L'Eglise Catholique dans le Malaise: Symptômes et Témoignages* (Edizioni Vivere, July 2001), 170-175.

48. *L'Osservatore Romano*, N° 20 (2315), 17 May 1994.

49. Unpublished document.

50. http://ilrestodelcarlino.quotidiano.net/chan/cronaca_nazionale:347596.3:/1999/11/24.

51. *Mouvement Démocratique Républicain* – MDR – was the main opposition party, later to become the main coalition partner in the July 1994 government.

52. See Jean Damascene Bizimana, *L'Eglise et le Génocide au Rwanda: Les Pères Blancs et le Négationnisme* (L'Harmattan: Paris-Montreal, 2001).

53. *Internews*, 11 February 2002.

54. *Kinyamateka*, No. 1583, September 2001.

55. http://www2.minorisa.es/inshuti/desoutera.htm.

56. Ibid.

57. *Le Vif L'Express*, 7 October 1994, 61.

58. Letter of 14 March 1996 to Monsignor Thaddée Ntihinyurwa, Bishop of Cyangugu and President of the Rwandan Episcopal Conference. It was this letter that caused some Rwandans, myself included, to write "A Memorandum to His

Holiness Pope John Paul II: Concerns about the attitude of the Catholic Church with regard to the social and political development of the country after the genocide," Kigali, 23 March 1996. See also African Rights: "An Open Letter to His Holiness, Pope John Paul II," 13 May 1998. The latter is available on http://www.africanrights.unimondo.org/html/pope_en.html

59. See Issue No. 554.

60. "A Memorandum to His Holiness." An unpublished source.

61. http://www.catholic.net/rcc/Periodicals/Igpress/2000-08/wrwanda.html

62. One example is where he is quoted as saying, "I'm innocent. But through me, the Rwandan government is targeting the Catholic church." See http://www. cathtelecom.com/news/909/47.html The same statement is repeated in a revisionist feature with the title "Decapitating the Church" by Michael S. Rose. See http://www.catholic.net/rcc/Periodicals/Igpress/2000-07/rwanda2.html.

63. See *Catholic World Report*, August/September 2000: http://www.catholic.net/rcc/Periodicals/Igpress/2000-08/wrwanda.html.

64. See African Rights, *Father Wenceslas Munyeshyaka: In the eyes of the Survivors of Sainte Famille. (Witness N° 9 , 1999)*. In this report, Father Celestin Hakizimana describes Father Munyeshyaka as someone who "didn't behave like a priest during the genocide," describing how he insulted Tutsi refugees as '*Inyenzi*' (literally meaning cockroaches). Munyeshyaka also told this priest (who is among the few courageous Hutu clergymen) that he, (the latter) supported the *interahamwe*; see page 95.

65. See the example of Father Anasthase Seromba, now in the detention facility of the International Criminal Court for Rwanda, Arusha, Tanzania. For years he was protected by the church hierarchy in Italy. See *Father Anasthase Seromba, A priest in Florence, Italy* (African Rights, Charge Sheet N° 2, November 1999) and *The Guardian*, 16 July 2001. See also http://www.cathtelecom.com/news/ 107/61.php where Mr Ricardo Bigi, the spokesperson for the Archdiocese of Florence, defends Seromba, claiming, "It's highly improbable that the accusations against him are true."

66. African Rights, February 2000.

67. Translation from RTLM transcripts.

68. Interviewed in Kigali, January 2003.

69. Letter from the camp in Zaire.

70. See abcNEWS.com, 21 March 2002.

71. "Resignation of Cardinal tipped to become Pope fuels sense of betrayal among American churchgoers," *Guardian Newspapers*, 13 December 2002, on http://www. buzzle.com/editorials/text12-13-2002-32156.asp and further information on "Pope accepts Law's resignation. 'I both apologize and ... beg forgiveness,'" 13 December 2002 on http://www.cnn.com/2002/US/12/13/law.resigns/.

72. *The Observer*, 5 May 2002.

73. http://www.ushmm.org/bonhoeffer/b3.htm.

15
TWO CONVICTED RWANDAN NUNS

Martin (François) Neyt

The passing of time makes it easier to situate the tragic events which took place during the Rwandan genocide at the Benedictine monastery of Sovu in Rwanda. It leads us to consider the sentences for genocide received by the Prioress and one of her Sisters.

Everyone is profoundly wounded by what happened in Rwanda. Much suffering, trauma and grief were caused by that tragedy. We must preserve the memory of the victims, of the people who gave their lives to save their neighbors, of those who survived with the memory of so many loved ones assassinated. We must ask how we can prevent the repetition of such tragedies on earth?[1] What can the religions do? The Rwandan genocide of 1994 raises a fundamental question for the Catholic and Anglican Churches. It reveals an ignorance of the human creature and the mechanisms which prompt human behavior. Our objective must be to consider the moral duty of the Churches and to embark upon a dynamic "of healing and repair."[2]

As André Malraux wrote concerning art, "Just as sharks are preceded by their pilot fish, our own view is preceded by a pilot-view, which suggests a meaning for what we see ... We believe quite wrongly that we are free to break away from this view..." Ludwig Wittgenstein commented on the reading of signs and meaning, and developed the idea that the same signs can be read in different ways. This brief essay seeks to recall the facts regarding the events at the monastery of Sovu, to ask questions about the community's earlier history and to clarify certain elements which carried a great deal of weight in the legal verdicts. The judgement given in 2001 related to four Rwandans: two men and the two Sisters of Sovu, Sister Gertrude (Consolata Mukangango) and Sister Kizito (Julienne Mukabutera). Sister Gertrude was sentenced to fifteen years in prison and Sister Kizito to thirteen years. They were immediately arrested and imprisoned on 8 June 2001.

Many questions spring to mind. Who are these Benedictine Sisters? What happened at the monastery of Sovu? How did the legal proceedings begin? What was the context of this trial? Why did it take place in Belgium? What legal and human support did the Sisters receive? What was the position of the Benedictine order? Why were the judgements of these two men and the two Benedictine Sisters linked together?

The observations that follow are based on some knowledge of Africa, where I was born and grew up until I was seventeen years old. I later returned as a monk, teaching both in a college and at the university of Zaire, where I gave courses on the arts and cultures of Africa. An art historian by training, I also maintain good contacts with the School of Oriental and African Studies in London. When I was the Superior of our monastery in Belgium, a new monastic community was founded in Kinshasa, Democratic Republic of Congo. It now comprises twenty monks, eighteen of whom are African. I teach at the Catholic University of Louvain, am a member of the *Académie Royale des Sciences d'Outremer* in Belgium and have published several works on Central Africa and Nigeria.

I. The accusation and beginning of the lawsuit

Sister Gertrude, prioress of the Sisters of Sovu, did not apply for the post. She was persuaded to accept it by part of the community and by some European Sisters who returned to Europe before the events of the genocide. Another part of the community was represented by a separate group of Sisters, and it was one of this group who made the main accusation of genocide against the prioress. This Sister had an influential member of her family in state security, close to President Kagame. This information, however, was not highlighted by the Benedictines of the Congregation to which Sovu is attached.

Does one bring family disagreements into the public arena? One could also ask questions about the entry requirements to the community, the training the Sisters received, and, more broadly still, about the place of women in Rwandan society. The young prioress was thirty-five years old and had everything to learn, both on a personal level and about the art of managing a community, with the multiple situations which can develop there.

In August 1994, the Sisters of Sovu (nine of whom were massacred on the journey) arrived in Belgium at the abbey of Maredret after spending a few weeks at the abbey of Jouarre in France. That was when many in the Benedictine community learned in more detail about the dramatic events which had taken place at the monastery of Sovu in April/May 1994 and the great number of victims of the genocide killed near the monastery.

In December 1994, two Sisters returned to Rwanda without the permission of the Superior or the community, which had chosen to remain in Belgium. These two Sisters had accused their prioress of responsibility for the deaths of some victims, amongst whom were members of their own families. One of these Sisters was the unsuccessful candidate for election as prioress. In 1995, a journalist published an article declaring, "The abbey of Maredret is hiding Sisters guilty of genocide." In February of that same year, Sister Gertrude, who had resigned as prioress, lodged a complaint for slander on the advice of a lawyer. This act further attracted the attention of the Belgian judge charged with the Rwanda file. A legal investigation on Sister Gertrude was begun.[3] From the month of August 1995, the mass media began to exaggerate the accusations against the Sisters and a press campaign developed, whilst the Benedictines remained silent and allowed no contact with the Sisters. The press also expressed strong opposition to the Church and the Benedictines.

I accompanied Sister Gertrude on two occasions when she described to the legal authorities what she had lived through: first to the police to obtain a visa and refugee status, and then to the judge in charge of the investigation, D. Vander Meersch. I waited in the corridor until the cross-examination was finished in order to take Sister Gertrude back to Ermeuton. When she came out of the interrogation, I spoke to the judge to ask him what the situation was. My intention was simply to envisage the future of this Sister, who at any rate could not return to her country. The reply I received was indicative of his state of mind: "Are you trying to influence the course of justice?" I kept quiet and realised how difficult it was for a Benedictine to say anything about this affair, without being accused of protecting people suspected of genocide. It was one of the main reasons why there was no Benedictine representative during the trial.

II. The Belgian context

For forty years, Belgium had a government in which the Social Christian parties were in power. A law referred to as the law of "universal competence" was initiated in 1990 and finalized in 1993, at a time when the Social Christians were still in power, to provide the legal basis for the trials which were to take place.

By 1999, the Socialists and Liberals found themselves in power without the Social Christians. In Rwanda at the same time, a new government had taken power after the death of the president and the subsequent genocide. It had its roots partly in Uganda where many Rwandans had been in exile. New links were created between the Belgian and Rwandan governments. The first use of the law of universal competence occurred in the trial – the only one, to date – which has become an example for Belgium and the whole world. It focused on the two Rwandan Benedictine Sisters, a university professor and an industrialist. One can already question the reason for bringing this group of people together in a single lawsuit, since the offences occurred in quite different places. For the Benedictines, it was a linkage which generated confusion and an obvious shift in direction towards what was to happen later.

This law of universal competence was severely contested. It provoked the anger of Ariel Sharon, Yasser Arafat, Colin Powell and President Bush to the point where today it is almost repealed. In the words of Professor Pierre d'Argent, professor of international law at the Catholic University of Louvain, "since no legal reason justifies such a broad law, there has to be a political motive which justifies this choice." In Arusha, Tanzania, a Belgian judge who was also due to try a case involving massacres of women and children by the new Rwandan army in the Democratic Republic of Congo, was dismissed. As for Carla del Ponte, she was removed from her post as prosecutor at the Criminal Tribunal for Rwanda (ICTR).[4] Political pressures are brought to bear everywhere, even in the heart of Africa and in a UN court.

The competence of Belgian juries could also be discussed. How can Belgians consider such complex situations, in which the facts are mingled with history and with so many painful socio-political realities?

III. Mass media

From the outset, this lawsuit started with significant media coverage. The world was shaken by what had happened in Rwanda and the presence in this first trial of two Benedictine nuns evoked the Churches' responsibility in the genocide. In Sovu, where more than 3,000 people had been killed by the militia, there was great trauma. Belgian television interviewed the widows of Sovu, and the two Sisters were presented as to some extent responsible for a place where people had come to seek refuge and were massacred. Belgium brought these widows to testify at the trial. The evening before they gave evidence, after the 8 p.m. television news, interviews with the widows were broadcast. Did the press fail in its duty of neutrality by presenting the Sisters as "monsters, possessed by the devil"?

The Benedictines and those in charge of our Congregation were denounced in the press as "complicit in lodging and hiding these genocidal Sisters." These statements, before the end of the trial, had a great impact in Belgium and abroad. Personally, knowing that the Benedictine Sisters of Sovu had come to testify in Belgium for or against their colleagues, I consulted a high-ranking Belgian magistrate to ask whether I could visit them in the Military School where they were housed. The wise advice was: "Wait until they have testified so you are not accused of wishing to influence their evidence." The Sisters left Belgium without having seen a Benedictine and the new prioress reproached me later for leaving them all alone in Brussels.

IV. The Congregation of the Annunciation

The Benedictine order is part of a Confederation of monasteries grouped in twenty-one Congregations. Its organisation is therefore decentralised, as are the convents of nuns. A few convents, like Maredret and Sovu, depend on a male Congregation, in this case, the Congregation of the Annunciation. In these international Congregations, it is the founding or nearby monasteries that know the situation best, that follow events and make crucial decisions. Each Congregation elects a President who creates a council to deal with the life of the communities.

In the Council of which I am a member, we deliberated many times about the tragic events of Sovu, not really knowing what to think of the prioress's decisions, but remaining convinced that she had never touched a weapon and had no authority over the groups who were circulating around the monastery. What could we suggest? Since the White Father P. André Comblain had lived for several decades in the country, the president of our congregation, Father Abbot Nicolas Dayez, OSB, and the new prioress of Sovu, Sister Anastasie, asked him to meet the Sisters to alleviate internal dissension and rebuild the community's unity. It was an error on our part and showed a deep lack of understanding of what was happening in Rwanda. Even Father Comblain did not understand. He went there, but his intervention was interpreted by some as a desire to conceal the genocide. Father Comblain was arrested by Security. His visa was not renewed and he was expelled.

The situation worsened. In March 2001, Father Abbot of Maredsous envisaged returning to Rwanda. He abandoned the idea at the request of the prioress of Sovu, for fear that it might be interpreted as pressure on the legal proceedings.

Gradually, the Benedictines shut themselves off. Maredret closed its doors to journalists, but also to other well-intentioned people. Although we did not realise it (on the contrary, we thought that justice would prevail), this policy of silence led to the condemnation of the Sisters. This ignorance of the link between the inter-community tensions of Sovu and the impact of the genocide made the two Sisters the scapegoats for all that happened. Under the new law of universal competence, the Sisters were associated with two other people who were condemned alongside them. They were judged less for what they were unable to do to help the victims, than for being representatives of the genocide who could finally be tried in Belgium. In addition, they were members of the Church.

V. The isolation of the accused Sisters

From the very outset of the accusations, whether they were true or false, neither the abbey of Maredret, nor the Congregation of the Annunciation made any public statement, except in the following circumstances.

In August 1995, Father Célestine Cullen, OSB, president of the Congregation, published a short press release. The Prioress of the monastery of Ermeuton (near Maredret, where Sister Gertrude took refuge for a while) and I were interviewed by Catholic TV. We defended Sister Gertrude and at the time, almost all the Sisters of Sovu who were still in Europe said nothing to the contrary.

Father André Comblain, who had lived many years in Rwanda and knew the community of Sovu well, stated that Sister Gertrude was not guilty.

But the general climate, described above, required silence and waiting for justice to do its work. The result, alas, was that throughout the trial which took place from 17 April to 20 June 2001, no Benedictine was present. Because of this, the Sisters were really abandoned. They lived in a Carmelite order near the law courts. I went to visit them in secret for fear of the press and frenzied journalists. Could we have made ourselves heard in the context of the time?

VI. What really happened and what are the main accusations?

For three months, the monastery was encircled by armed groups, likely to kill at any moment, day or night. The Sisters saw death before them and knew their last hour could occur at any moment.

Sister Gertrude saved all her community, despite what was happening all around. Her own father was killed, as well as other members of her family. Events were described on many occasions by those who were there.

In the beginning, all the Sisters believed they would die. They put on their prayer habits and spent the night in the chapel. They were not killed, but there was a massacre in the health center at the monastery entrance.

The community shut itself away in the monastery. All negotiations were led by the Prioress and a novice who helped her, Sister Kizito. They gave everything that was demanded: food, money, fuel. Sister Gertrude was even authorised to leave on one occasion on an errand.

Among the armed groups, there was a temporarily professed Benedictine[5] who gave Sister Gertrude advice as best he could to save her community. Following this advice, she never allowed the nuns' families to enter the monastery. The signs of a general massacre were all too predictable. She kept in touch with the mayor of Butare whom she thought would be able to help the monastery.

In the extreme tension which led to the massacre of 3,000 people, this ex-novice wrote a letter asking the mayor to intervene to allow those who had sought refuge to leave the monastery. In despair, Sister Gertrude signed it. The letter only asked that people should be able to leave the monastery compound. "In any case," Sister Gertrude told me, "we could do nothing and our opinion carried no weight."

The Belgian judge found this letter and considered it decisive proof of collaboration with the mayor and the armed groups. As Father Comblain explains, "She wanted to inform the mayor, thinking that he had the authority to protect the refugees."

Conclusions

This essay raises a certain number of questions which throw a different light on these events. Not to have foreseen the genocide and to have been incapable of stopping it was an immense failure on the part of the Churches. It is terribly painful to see that the people who hoped to find refuge in the monastery of Sovu – and also in other churches – were massacred. Let us keep the memory of those victims and be vigilant to prevent such a genocide happening again.

What about the community of Sovu today? They have to find a way of living which both comes to terms with the past and turns towards the future. The solidarity of Benedictine nuns is there to help and support them.

The Congregation of the Annunciation did not want to bring the internal disagreements of a community into the public arena. These became public during the trial, in which the Sisters of Sovu testified, some in favor of their former prioress, others against her. This community continues its work but remains silent about the past. Should the Benedictines have brought everything into the open before the legal proceedings? Would the outcome have been different?

Sister Gertrude would have liked to have an African lawyer. Two Belgian lawyers were chosen for each of the Sisters, one of them a former pupil of Maredsous. The trial thus took place in a Belgian atmosphere.

Sister Gertrude is in prison in Namur, Sister Kizito in Bruges. Both repeat that they are innocent, that the Benedictine Congregation defended them badly and that they are victims both of their community and the judicial proceeding. The government has let them know that they will be expelled from Belgium once they have completed their sentences. Where might they be made welcome?

On the legal front, the Court of Appeal rejected their appeal and so the matter is closed in Belgium. Another appeal was taken to the Court of Human Rights in July 2002. This was accepted, which is a first step. The following stages will take two to three years, but this European Court examines only whether human rights have been respected. It will not interfere at all in the sentence delivered in Belgium. This decision could possibly have an influence on whether parole is granted to the Sisters, which could occur as soon as half the sentence is complete.

Translated by Wendy Whitworth

Notes

1. Carol Rittner, John K. Roth, James M. Smith, *Will Genocide Ever End?* (St Paul, Minnesota: Paragon House and Aegis, 2002).
2. "To engage in healing and reparation" (*Tikkun olam*, in Hebrew).
3. Sister Kizito was charged later by the King's Prosecutor.
4. See the newspaper *La Libre Belgique*, 31 July 2003.
5. He was a monk for nine years before leaving the community.

16
WHY THE CHURCHES WERE COMPLICIT

CONFESSIONS OF A BROKEN-HEARTED CHRISTIAN

David P. Gushee

To ask why the Churches were complicit with the Rwandan genocide that annihilated 850,000 people in three months is to reveal the assumption that the Churches could have been expected to do better. Indeed, the question is usually asked from the stance of an outraged conscience.

To question Christian complicity is peculiarly appropriate in this case. Rwanda was the most heavily Christianized country in Africa. Some ninety percent of the people were self-identified Christians. The Roman Catholic Church (home to sixty-five percent of the population, by one estimate) played a huge role in Rwandan society, while various Protestant Churches also attracted large numbers. Missionaries were immensely influential in Rwandan society from their arrival in the late 19th century, and a large missionary presence has been found in Rwanda throughout its modern history. Christian churches, seminaries, schools, and other institutions were sprinkled throughout the land. And yet all of this Christianity did not prevent the most rapid and in some ways most horrific genocide of the 20th century, a genocide which leading Church officials did little to resist, in which a large number of Christians participated, and in which more people "died in churches and parishes than anywhere else."[1]

So the churches were everywhere in Rwanda, as were the Christians who claimed allegiance to them. Whence then came genocide? The question reveals a logic that goes something like this: Churches are ____(fill in the blank), which means that by their very nature they should be opposed to genocide. Churches believe____(fill in the blank), which means that their doctrines teach against genocide. If Churches are____ and believe ____, how could they be complicit with genocide?

259

DAVID P. GUSHEE

Long may the question be posed. Long may onlookers, both Christian and non-Christian, have high enough hopes for the faith to expect that the character and doctrine of Christianity should produce justice and love, or at least *not produce genocide*. I personally will continue to teach such justice and love to students and parishioners at my college and church. I personally will continue to exhort students and parishioners to reject any other understanding of Christianity with all their hearts – and with their *lives*.

But long study of the Holocaust, and now fresh study of the Rwandan genocide, has led me to the heartbroken realization that the presence of Churches in a country guarantees exactly *nothing*. The self-identification of people with the Christian faith guarantees exactly nothing. All of the clerical garb and regalia, all of the structures of religious accountability, all of the Christian vocabulary and books, all of the schools and seminaries and parish houses and Bible studies, all of the religious titles and educational degrees, they all guarantee exactly *nothing*. The desecrated churches and parish houses and seminaries and church schools and prayer books and Bibles of Rwanda will survive (unlike the murdered people who once used them) as the enduring memorial to this fact.

A deeply committed Christian never begins here. I certainly did not begin here. I had great confidence in the moral productivity of the Christian faith. But the conclusion has become inevitable, after a long journey to places like Auschwitz and Treblinka and Majdanek, and now Kigali and Kabgayi and Kibuye.

As a Christian, one normally starts with the assumption that the teachings of the Christian faith demanding love of neighbor and respect for life – as embedded in the Scriptures and Church tradition – are actually taught with accuracy and fidelity everywhere the Churches gather. Then one assumes that the people gathered together to hear these teachings are serious about listening to them and putting them into practice. Then – and this is a belief certainly aided by a reading of the Bible itself – one assumes that the Holy Spirit, the third Person of the Trinity, is at work in the hearts of God's people to work divine truth into their hearts and souls.

But then comes Auschwitz and Kigali. Careful examination of the role of the Churches both in Nazi Germany and Rwanda (to name but two places) reveals that none of the above can be assumed.

First, it cannot be assumed that the Christian faith is taught in such a way as to emphasize love of neighbor (*all* neighbors) and respect for human life. No agency on earth has ever been able to control what is actually taught in a local church on a given Sunday morning. It is by now more than obvious that a variety of bastardized versions of the Christian message, including hateful ones, have been and continue to be communicated in congregations all over the world. This is true both in Churches where authoritative (and sometimes authoritarian) Church hierarchies supposedly have great power to control what happens in the local church, and in decentralized communions in which the local minister has the final say. Either way, the teaching of the Christian Churches lands all over the map, from richly faithful to blandly mediocre to dreadfully immoral.

Second, it cannot be assumed that the people gathered to hear the Word proclaimed and to participate in the sacraments are serious about the Christian faith. People come to church for a wide variety of reasons. They bring widely varying levels of receptivity to the truth that leaders do communicate from the pulpit and the altar. They bring widely varying moral and spiritual capacities. Jesus himself said that the seed of the Gospel is scattered on all different kinds of ground; only one of the four kinds of soil that he mentions has the quality needed for fruitfulness (cf. Mk. 4:14-20). In light of Auschwitz and Rwanda, that sounds about right. Narrow is the road that leads to salvation; few there are who enter it.

Third, it cannot be assumed that all of the self-identified Christian people (baptized, born-again, converted, members, whatever criteria or name you want to use) gathered in these churches are subject to the influence of the Holy Spirit. I am committed to the authority of the Bible, so I cannot believe that what it says about the work of the Spirit of God is erroneous. But what must be admitted is that there is quite a gap between the list of "Christians" on church rolls or in church pews and the much smaller list of Christians in whom the Spirit of God is working. This is not a novel idea. The concept of the true church within the visible church is an ancient one, and in the shadow of Rwanda's killing fields and the crematories of Belzec, seems irrefutable.

Fourth, it cannot be assumed that Christian faith is the only or even the primary factor affecting the attitudes and behavior of those who claim Christian identity. In fact, Christians, like everyone else, are subject to being blown about by ferocious ideological, economic, social, and political crosswinds. In that light, the teachings of the Christian faith are often more like a candle flickering in a tornado than the sure anchor of the soul – the dominating factor in a Christian's thinking and behavior – that we often assume them to be. Or, to switch images, Christian teaching provides one set of inputs into human consciousness, but other inputs are always cycling through that consciousness as well. Christians often speak of the terrific struggle of the soul *before* a profession of initial faith in Christ; but now we see that this terrific struggle of the soul for faith (and especially faithfulness) continues long after faith commences. The spiritual journey is never over, and the Christian is never free from the possibility of careening over the cliff into moral disaster, until he breathes his last breath.

We must move beyond the general to the particular. Certainly there were specific historical factors in Rwanda that contributed to the disastrous involvement and complicity of the Churches in the 1994 genocide. The most significant appear to be the following four problems:

- *The historic participation of the Churches, especially the Roman Catholic Church, in reinforcing ethnocentric thought and behavior, both in public life and in the Church itself.* This weakened the Church's ability to resist the quasi-fascist genocidal racism that emerged in a sector of Hutu society in the late 1980s and early 1990s.[2]

- *The cozy relationship enjoyed by the leaders of the Rwandan Catholic Church and of several Protestant denominations with the Hutu government.*[3] This led Church leaders to identify their interests with the interests of the then-current government and its leaders. In the end, the outcome was a hesitation on the part of Church leaders to stand up for innocent Tutsis (and moderate Hutus) and say a clear no to genocide.

- *The traditional teaching of the Churches that the Bible mandates unquestioning submission to both churchly and government authority.* This left grassroots Christians very poorly prepared to resist the genocidal commands of local and national leaders.[4]

- *The historic social power of the missionaries and Churches in Rwanda apparently attracted the nearly universal "conversion" of Rwandans to Christianity.* This nearly universal assent to Christianity, we can now see, was clearly more of a "veneer" than a "living reality in people's hearts,"[5] as observers of Rwanda have noted.

As a student of the Holocaust, it is striking that each of these problems was also apparent in the German Churches (and throughout Europe) during the Hitler years:

- German Christianity did not *produce* racist, pseudoscientific Nazi antisemitism any more than Rwandan Christianity produced racist, pseudoscientific Hutu anti-Tutsism. But a misunderstanding of Christianity in Germany (and throughout Europe) that tied it to ethnic identity through historic antisemitism weakened the resistance of Christians to the allure of a much more vicious and hateful genocidal mentality when it emerged.

- The cozy marriage of Church and State that had existed throughout much of Europe was a prize that both Catholic and Protestant Church leaders were loath to give up in a modernizing Europe. In Germany, this left them susceptible to the false promises of a Hitler who at first promised a return to "positive Christianity" in Germany. Here was a conservative leader who would restore traditional German Christian values! It also left them indisposed to resist the unjust decrees and behaviors of the Nazi regime, for fear of weakening their already uncertain influence with the government, as well as their institutional independence and social power.

- The authoritarian understanding of power and the requirement to submit unquestioningly to it in all of its forms was, if anything, worse in Germany than in Rwanda. It certainly inhibited resistance to Nazism and to the Holocaust. Indeed, the same misunderstanding of Scripture as mandating total and unquestioning obedience to government (based on a misreading of Romans 13:1-7) contributed to submission to Nazi mandates among Christians in occupied Europe as well.[6]

- The Europe of the 1930s still bore the marks of the culture of Christendom that had dominated for over 1,500 years. Well over ninety percent of Europeans who lived through World War II self-identified as Christians. When just about everyone is a "Christian" and all agree that they are living in a "Christian" culture, what is the meaning of Christianity? The observation concerning Rwanda, that "the pervasive Catholic institutional and cultural presence... proved little impediment to such mind-numbing savagery" applies equally well to Germany and German Christianity, both Protestant and Catholic.[7]

The fact of the matter is now clear; plenty of evidence is in. When a ruling elite decides to destroy a group of people in a society, most of the people who are not targeted will not resist, whatever their religious affiliation. To put it bluntly: politics usually matters more than religion does; or, politics co-opts religion and thus neutralizes it. To put it even more bluntly: people are sheep. Most will go along with what their elites tell them to think and do. Few have the intellectual, spiritual, or moral capacity to resist either the genocidal thinking of elites or genocide itself once it begins.

But still we must affirm the mission and vocation of the Churches. We must say that the Christian Churches are required to be agents of resistance to genocide or any other kind of social evil. They must do so as a basic expression of faithfulness to their own God, their own sacred scriptures, and their own social responsibility. *We* must do so.

But we cannot start preparing people for resistance only at the point when evil takes the stage. Training in resistance to evil must be a part of the daily teaching and preaching and training that occurs in every Christian congregation. If the lessons of both Rwanda and the Holocaust are taken seriously, the implications are clear. We return to our four problem areas:

- The Churches must do everything they can to destroy racism, root and branch, where they find it in their congregations. Even "mild," subtle, unarticulated racist attitudes are poison. They are poison because they violate biblical norms. They are poison because they weaken or neutralize resistance to more virulent forms of political racism when these emerge.

- The Churches must give up, once and for all, any hope of great social and political power, including a comfortable embrace by government leaders. The dream of Christian political dominance is an alluring one, but now must be recognized as a demonic snare. And a cozy relationship with government almost always comes at far too high a price, either for Christian integrity or for the victims of government injustice, whom we do nothing to protect because we are too busy protecting our privileged position.

- The Churches must teach that government powers, and all other structures of authority, are mandated by God *to serve the well-being of people and communities*. The mandate of government does not require Christians to offer unquestioning obedience. Government leaders and laws are to be respected, yes, but they are only to be obeyed insofar as they advance the common good and act in accordance with the dictates of justice. Otherwise, they are to be cheerfully disobeyed, in the tradition of civil disobedience or even, in extreme cases, justified revolution.

- The Churches must reconsider what exactly we mean when we invite someone to "Christianity" or call someone among us a "Christian." In both Germany and Rwanda, we now see, Christianity was broad and wide, but not deep, like the seed sown on rocky ground that has no root and so endures only for a while, till "trouble" comes (Mk. 4:17). How can we read about this veneer-like faith and not shudder as we compare it to the broad, wide, and often equally shallow "thing" that passes for Christianity in so much of our culture, and in so many of our churches? What if we understood Christians to be only those who "hear the word, accept it, and produce a crop" (Mk. 4:20)? What if we conclude that when Jesus said, "Not everyone who says to me 'Lord, Lord,' will enter the kingdom of heaven, but only he who does the will of the Father in heaven," (Mt. 7:21), he knew exactly what he was talking about?

The Churches must teach their members to stop their ears to the siren song of any ideology, such as racism or tribalism or xenophobia, that subverts the dignity and equality of all people as made in the image of God and therefore sacred in God's sight. We must be the social institution in any society most sensitive to the rise or spread of ideologies that promote hatred, torture, or genocide. We must be the most fiercely independent and unselfish social institution in society, far more committed to truth-speaking and defending the innocent than to personal self-interest or ecclesial power. We must be the social institution that offers the most careful scrutiny of government and its leaders, and articulates both praise and criticism when they are due. We must be the social institution whose identity and mission are the most closely guarded – not "just" because eternal destinies are at stake (which they are), but also because the earthly well-being of many millions of people depends on our faithfulness to our calling, and our Lord.

DAVID P. GUSHEE

Notes

1. Timothy Longman, "Church Politics and the Genocide in Rwanda," *Journal of Religion in Africa*, XXXI, 2, 163, quoting the authoritative 1995 report on the genocide by African Rights.

2. Longman, 168-170; cf. Michael Chege, "Africa's Murderous Professors," *The National Interest* (Winter 1996/97), 32-36.

3. Longman, 166; John A. Berry and Carol Pott Berry, *Genocide in Rwanda* (Washington: Howard University Press, 1999), ch. 2.

4. Longman, 166 ff.

5. Rwandan faith as a "veneer" – William Knipe, Maryknoll priest, quoted in "Pope Calls for End to Killings in Rwanda," *The New York Times*, 20 September 1995, A 11; "living reality," "Religion and Genocide," *Commonweal* (July 13, 2001), 6.

6. David P. Gushee, *Righteous Gentiles of the Holocaust*, 2nd ed. (St. Paul: Paragon House, 2003), 161-162.

7. "Religion and Genocide," 6.

EPILOGUE

EPILOGUE
WHAT SHOULD BE REMEMBERED?

John K. Roth

As one finishes reading a book, it can be a good to ask, "What should I remember?" No two readers will answer that question identically, but a recapitulation of that kind may provide a helpful summing up, particularly if it points to the future and to ways in which some mending of the world might take place after the carnage of the Rwandan genocide. The authors of this book's sixteen chapters each have important insights to share along those lines, and it will be fitting to allow their words to speak for themselves once more before these pages end. To preface those parting thoughts, the following points seem worthy of recollection, too.

This book has raised questions about the complicity of the Churches in the Rwandan genocide, but it is dedicated to "all Christians in Rwanda, known and unknown, who before, during, and after the 1994 genocide in Rwanda, defended humanity, stood firm against a tide of unprecedented atrocities, and who did not leave God without witnesses." There were many who fitted that description – just not enough of them. There might have been more – and perhaps enough – if Christians, governments, and others outside of Rwanda had recognized that genocide was coming, intervened before it got under way, or at least stopped it before the worst happened. No one who considers the historical evidence carefully is likely to deny that this genocide could have been prevented. Rwandans themselves bear responsibility that it was not, but that responsibility is much more than theirs alone. Dealing with the threats and realities of genocide is a human responsibility, and that responsibility does not start or stop at national borders or with ethnic and religious differences.

Next, as readers turn its last pages, it is important to note that this book had a birth more difficult than might meet the eye at first glance. No one enjoys writing about genocide, even though the responsibility to do so may be strongly felt by those who have witnessed or studied such catastrophes. Assembling the authors for discussion and then producing the manuscript that resulted also had the special difficulties that attend a project involving people from different countries and continents and whose scholarly fields, religious traditions, and languages are diverse. At this juncture, however, the key point lies elsewhere. What needs to be noted is the absence of some voices who at first agreed but then decided not to have their contributions published here.

Genocide is divisive in more ways than one, particularly when issues arise about how responsibility for it and remembrance of it should be handled. As it turned out, this book's focus on the complicity of the Churches in the Rwandan genocide became a topic too "hot" religiously and politically for some to handle. Even as the book was in the final stages of production, pressures were brought to bear to derail it. Some authors withdrew their contributions, including four Rwandan priests. The reasons why are best known to them, but in at least some cases it is clear that the withdrawals were influenced by the conviction that this book comes down too hard on Christianity and the Churches. As a Christian, I do not take that position. On the contrary, my role as one of the book's editors leaves me convinced that this book offers perspectives and insights that are important not only for Christians and Churches but for a world that exists in an age of genocide. Standing in solidarity with the authors of this book's sixteen chapters, I have selected their own words to summarize perspectives and insights that deserve remembering.

1. *Hubert G. Locke:* "If there is a lesson to be derived from the Rwandan experience, it is that religion, in the final analysis, may not be a sufficiently strong inducement to engage in ethically responsible behavior – strong enough at least to outweigh the influence of social class or ethnic and cultural tradition."

2. *Roger W. Bowen:* "Sadly, within the Church itself the mutual fears between Hutus and Tutsis were not faced up to and dealt with... By and large,... the Church had allowed these ethnic tensions to continue unresolved, often below the surface, until conditions occurred where the issue exploded beyond their control in horrific violence."

3. *Octave Ugirashebuja:* "The role of the Church of Jesus Christ... is to reconcile all God's children... Yet, the decisions made – first to ignore the Tutsis and turn toward the Hutus, then to overvalue the Tutsis at the expense of the Hutus, and finally to totally exclude the Tutsis from Rwandan society – were deliberate."

4. *Jerry Fowler:* "As a general matter, the Church hierarchy in Rwanda was closely aligned with the government in the years before the genocide... In addition to the leadership's close identification with the regime, Rwanda's ethnic divisions were reproduced inside the Church. Far from being a force for social unity and respect for human dignity, the Rwandan Church in fact was at least as divided as the society itself."

5. *Charles Petrie:* "In a number of cases the representatives of the Church themselves had led the killers to their prey, some even participating in the murders. A number of these individuals continue to celebrate the sacraments in parishes around the world, protected by the very institutions whose teaching should promote universal peace and forgiveness. Why is this so? And is the Church alone to bear the responsibility for not having lived up to its mission, then and after?"

6. *Marie Julianne Farrington:* "The Gospel itself and the true nature of the Church demand that the memory of genocide be kept alive and that the question be endlessly and objectively pursued."

7. *Philippe Gaillard:* "Memory is the most invisible and resistant material you can find on earth. You cannot cut it like a diamond, you cannot shoot at it because you cannot see it; nevertheless, it is everywhere, all around you, in the silence, unspoken suffering, whispers, and absent looks. Sometimes you can smell it and then the memory clearly speaks like the whisper of silence. Sometimes the smell is still unbearable, even when things have been forgotten for decades."

8. *Marie Césarie Mukarwego:* "What one must understand is that the Church is made up of human beings and thus is not shielded from the fragility and weaknesses of our humanity. Those who massacred others during the 1994 genocide were for the most part Christians killing other Christians. The killers had heard the Gospel, many times, in fact. They were quite conscious of it. Some even spoke about it. Nevertheless, they chose to put the Gospel aside. They allowed themselves to be manipulated by those whose devilish project was the extermination of others."

9. *Tom O'Hara* in his interview with Carol Rittner: "It's not enough to issue pastoral statements, even if the words are so-called 'prophetic.' What's needed is to turn prophetic words into prophetic actions. The reality is that you can promulgate all you want, but it's actions that are going to make the impact on people's lives and in society... Evil was perpetrated; evil occurred. The hierarchy of the Church in Rwanda is not without blame, and neither is the American government and the larger international community. There are no saviors in the sad history of Rwanda."

10. *Matthias Bjørnlund, Eric Markusen, Peter Steenberg, and Rafiki Ubaldo:* "... It seems possible to conclude that the Catholic Church was instrumental in the creation of important preconditions for a genocidal mentality. Also, the Church had... the opportunity to speak against widespread racism, systematic oppression, and frequent massacres. The Church generally failed to do so, perhaps partly out of opportunism. But no matter what the reason(s) were, they were thereby legitimating these crimes, abandoning the victims, and even acting as an accomplice in genocide."

11. *Margaret Brearley:* "Since the national Churches in Rwanda were both complicit and silent, the response of the international Church was likely to be ambiguous at best, and so it proved."

12. *James M. Smith and Carol Rittner:* "During the 1994 genocide in Rwanda, churches, once sanctuaries from violence, became repositories of brutalization and death... Perhaps keeping churches as memorial sites of the 1994 genocide could help 'the Church' – bishops, priests, nuns and laity alike – to confront some of the difficult and sensitive questions about the role of the Church in Rwandan society, before, during, and after the genocide."

13. *Léon D. Saur:* "On 6 April 1994, an unidentified person, or persons, shot down the plane transporting President Habyarimana. The genocide started: some killers wore Marian medallions; others wore rosaries around their necks or tied rosaries on their weapons. When a nun asked a soldier how he could kill with a rosary around his neck, he replied that the Virgin was helping him to discover his enemies. Many *interahamwe* militia struck their victims carrying a crucifix in one hand and a machete in the other. Murderers and victims prayed to the same God. Killers attended mass between massacres."

14. *Tom Ndahiro:* "Since justice is an integral element in the process of reconciliation, the Church should be among those asking that the perpetrators of genocide be brought to justice. If the Church contributes to the process of justice, unity can be re-established among Rwandans in general, and among Christians in particular. It is the only way that the Church can restore its credibility, and thus be what it is called to be: a witness to faith, hope and love, to truth and justice. Only in this way will the Catholic Church in Rwanda be able to help save the people of Rwanda – *all the people* – from future suffering and bloodshed."

15. *Martin (François) Neyt:* "Everyone is profoundly wounded by what happened in Rwanda. Much suffering, trauma and grief were caused by that tragedy. We must preserve the memory of the victims, of the people who gave their lives to save their neighbors, of those who survived with the memory of so many loved ones assassinated. We must ask how we can prevent the

repetition of such tragedies on earth?... Our objective must be to consider the moral duty of the Churches and to embark upon a dynamic 'of healing and repair.'"

16. *David P. Gushee:* "The Churches must teach their members to stop their ears to the siren song of any ideology, such as racism or tribalism or xenophobia, that subverts the dignity and equality of all people as made in the image of God and therefore sacred in God's sight."

★   ★   ★   ★   ★   ★

As the Rwandan genocide makes clear, words may do more to incite genocide than to prevent or stop it. Nevertheless, if genocide is to be prevented and stopped, and if there is to be healing after genocide has happened, words are still important because they can lead to actions that mend the world. Time and human responsibility will tell the tale, but it is the hope of all those who have contributed to this book that their words will encourage steps in those directions.

"The Rwandan people will never be reconciled with each other unless each party accepts to kneel down before the suffering of the other party, to confess their own offenses and to humbly ask forgiveness of their victims. Therefore,

"We, Hutu Christians, present at Detmold [Germany], recognize that our group has oppressed the Tutsi in various ways since 1959. We confess the massacres committed by the Hutu against the Tutsi group at different periods of Rwandan history, culminating in the genocide of 1994. We are ashamed of the horrors and atrocities committed by the Hutu towards the Tutsi: torturing, raping, slitting pregnant women open, hacking humans to pieces, burying people alive, hunting people with dogs as if they were animals, killing in churches and temples (previously recognized as places of refuge), massacring old people, children and the sick in hospital, forcing people to kill their own relatives, burning people alive, denying burial and thousands of other ways of cynically degrading and mockingly putting to death.

"We carry the terrible weight of this unspeakable crime and we accept to bear the consequences without resentment. We implore our Hutu brothers and sisters not to forget this terrible past when they judge the present reality in Rwanda. We humbly request forgiveness of God and our Tutsi brothers and sisters for all the evil we have inflicted upon them. We commit ourselves to do whatever we can to restore their honor and their dignity and to regain our lost humanity in their eyes.

"We, Tutsi Christians, present at Detmold, are happy and feel comforted by the request for forgiveness made by our Hutu brothers and sisters. We likewise request God and the Hutu to forgive the repression and blind vengeance which members of our group have taken, surpassing all claims to legitimate self-defense.

"... We also request of God and of our Hutu brothers and sisters forgiveness for certain arrogant and contemptuous attitudes shown to them throughout our history in the name of a ridiculous complex of ethnic superiority.

"We, western Christians present at Detmold... confess that since the arrival of the first Europeans in Rwanda, we have seriously contributed to the increase of divisions in the Rwandan people. We regret that feeling too sure of our superiority we discriminated between people by generalizing and judging some as good and others as bad. We regret that our countries have conduced violence by delivering arms to all parties. We regret our silence and our neglect of the refugees of the years of the Independence. We also regret our silence and our abandonment of the Rwandan people during the genocide and massacres in 1994. We regret our silence and neglect when it was a question of finding a viable solution to the return of the refugees after the genocide. We regret our failure to listen and to share in the suffering experienced by our Rwandan friends.

"For all this harm, we request God and our Rwandan brothers and sisters to forgive us for not respecting them as they are and we want to commit ourselves with Jesus to a path of listening, respect and solidarity...."

From The Confession of Detmold, Germany, 12 December 1996

APPENDICES

CONVENTION ON THE PREVENTION AND PUNISHMENT OF THE CRIME OF GENOCIDE

Approved and proposed for signature and ratification or accession by General Assembly Resolution 260 A (III) of 9 December 1948 Entry into Force 12 January 1951, in Accordance with Article XII

The Contracting Parties,

Having considered the declaration made by the General Assembly of the United Nations in its resolution 96 (I) dated 11 December 1946 that genocide is a crime under international law, contrary to the spirit and aims of the United Nations and condemned by the civilized world,

Recognizing that at all periods of history genocide has inflicted great losses on humanity, and

Being convinced that, in order to liberate mankind from such an odious scourge, international co-operation is required,

Hereby agree as hereinafter provided:

Article I

The Contracting Parties confirm that genocide, whether committed in time of peace or in time of war, is a crime under international law which they undertake to prevent and to punish.

Article II

In the present Convention, genocide means any of the following acts committed with intent to destroy, in whole or in part, a national, ethnical, racial or religious group, as such:

(a) Killing members of the group;
(b) Causing serious bodily or mental harm to members of the group;
(c) Deliberately inflicting on the group conditions of life calculated to bring about its physical destruction in whole or in part;
(d) Imposing measures intended to prevent births within the group;
(e) Forcibly transferring children of the group to another group.

Article III

The following acts shall be punishable:

(a) Genocide;
(b) Conspiracy to commit genocide;

(c) Direct and public incitement to commit genocide;
(d) Attempt to commit genocide;
(e) Complicity in genocide.

Article IV
Persons committing genocide or any of the other acts enumerated in article III shall be punished, whether they are constitutionally responsible rulers, public officials or private individuals.

Article V
The Contracting Parties undertake to enact, in accordance with their respective Constitutions, the necessary legislation to give effect to the provisions of the present Convention, and, in particular, to provide effective penalties for persons guilty of genocide or any of the other acts enumerated in article III.

Article VI
Persons charged with genocide or any of the other acts enumerated in article III shall be tried by a competent tribunal of the State in the territory of which the act was committed, or by such international penal tribunal as may have jurisdiction with respect to those Contracting Parties which shall have accepted its jurisdiction.

Article VII
Genocide and the other acts enumerated in article III shall not be considered as political crimes for the purpose of extradition.
The Contracting Parties pledge themselves in such cases to grant extradition in accordance with their laws and treaties in force.

Article VIII
Any Contracting Party may call upon the competent organs of the United Nations to take such action under the Charter of the United Nations as they consider appropriate for the prevention and suppression of acts of genocide or any of the other acts enumerated in article III.

Article IX
Disputes between the Contracting Parties relating to the interpretation, application or fulfillment of the present Convention, including those relating to the responsibility of a State for genocide or for any of the other acts enumerated in article III, shall be submitted to the International Court of Justice at the request of any of the parties to the dispute.

STATUTE OF THE INTERNATIONAL TRIBUNAL FOR RWANDA

Established by Security Council Resolution 955
Acting under Chapter VII of the UN Charter
8 November 1994

Article 1: Competence of the International Tribunal for Rwanda

The International Tribunal for Rwanda shall have the power to prosecute persons responsible for serious violations of international humanitarian law committed in the territory of Rwanda and Rwandan citizens responsible for such violations committed in the territory of neighboring States between 1 January 1994 and 31 December 1994, in accordance with the provisions of the present Statute.

Article 2: Genocide

1. The International Tribunal for Rwanda shall have the power to prosecute persons committing genocide as defined in paragraph 2 of this article or of committing any of the other acts enumerated in paragraph 3 of this article

2. Genocide means any of the following acts committed with intent to destroy, in whole or in part, a national, ethnical, racial or religious group, as such:

a) Killing members of the group;

b) Causing serious bodily or mental harm to members of the group;

c) Deliberately inflicting on the group conditions of life calculated to bring about its physical destruction in whole or in part;

d) Imposing measures intended to prevent births within the group;

e) Forcibly transferring children of the group to another group.

3. The following acts shall be punishable:

a) Genocide;

b) Conspiracy to commit genocide;

c) Direct and public incitement to commit genocide;

d) Attempt to commit genocide;

e) Complicity in genocide.

Article 3: Crimes against Humanity

The International Tribunal for Rwanda shall have the power to prosecute persons responsible for the following crimes when committed as part of a widespread or systematic attack against any civilian population on national, political, ethnic, racial or religious grounds:

a) Murder;
b) Extermination;
c) Enslavement;
d) Deportation;
e) Imprisonment;
f) Torture;
g) Rape;
h) Persecutions on political, racial and religious grounds;
i) Other inhumane acts.

Article 4: Violations of Article 3

... These violations shall include, but shall not be limited to:

a) Violence to life, health and physical or mental well-being of persons, in particular murder as well as cruel treatment such as torture, mutilation or any form of corporal punishment;
b) Collective punishments;
c) Taking of hostages;
d) Acts of terrorism;
e) Outrages upon personal dignity, in particular humiliating and degrading treatment, rape, enforced prostitution and any form of indecent assault;
f) Pillage;
g) The passing of sentences and the carrying out of executions without previous judgment pronounced by a regularly constituted court, affording all the judicial guarantees which are recognized as indispensable by civilized peoples;
h) Threats to commit any of the foregoing acts....

Article 6: Individual Criminal Responsibility

1. A person who planned, instigated, ordered, committed or otherwise aided and abetted in the planning, preparation or execution of a crime referred to in articles 2 to 4 of the present Statute, shall be individually responsible for the crime.
2. The official position of any accused person, whether as Head of State or

Government or as a responsible Government official, shall not relieve such person of criminal responsibility nor mitigate punishment.

3. The fact that any of the acts referred to in articles 2 to 4 of the present Statute was committed by a subordinate does not relieve his or her superior of criminal responsibility if he or she knew or had reason to know that the subordinate was about to commit such acts or had done so and the superior failed to take the necessary and reasonable measures to prevent such acts or to punish the perpetrators thereof.

4. The fact that an accused person acted pursuant to an order of Government or of a superior shall not relieve him or her of criminal responsibility, but may be considered in mitigation of punishment if the International Tribunal for Rwanda determines that justice so requires.

WEBSITES

Aegis Trust

www.aegistrust.org

Aegis Trust is a genocide prevention organization in the United Kingdom; good information about genocide and genocide prevention, with an emphasis on the 1994 genocide in Rwanda.

Afrol News

www.afrol.com

Afrol News calls itself "an independent news agency dedicated exclusively to Africa." To access Rwanda, go to "Rwanda." An essay written by Afrol news editor, Rainer Chr. Hennig, "The Cross and Genocide," can be found on this website.

Amnesty International

www.amnesty.org/

Amnesty International is a worldwide movement of people who campaign for internationally recognized human rights. The site provides information about human rights policies in place in Rwanda today, as well as historical data relating to the 1994 genocide.

BBC – British Broadcasting Corporation

www.news.bbc.co.uk

Search "Rwanda Genocide," on the BBC's homepage for an extensive list of pages containing voluminous information on the Rwandan genocide, including radio broadcasts, survivor accounts, and videos; good links to other sites.

Committee on Conscience – U.S. Holocaust Memorial Museum

www.ushmm.org/conscience/

The Committee on Conscience was established "to alert the national conscience, influence policy and stimulate worldwide action to confront and work to halt acts of genocide or related crimes against humanity." Excellent information about genocide, including Rwanda in 1994, photo essays, genocide alerts, and links to other websites.

From the Holocaust to Rwanda
www.holocaustmemorialday.gov.uk
This is the official government website for the United Kingdom's annual commemoration of the Holocaust. In January 2004, the theme was "From the Holocaust to Rwanda." This site has good information about the 1994 genocide, including resources for teachers and students.

Gendercide Watch
www.gendercide.org/
Gendercide Watch is an organization that seeks to confront acts of gender-selective mass killing around the world. To access information about the genocide in Rwanda, go to "Case Studies" and enter "Rwanda."

Genocide Studies Program, Yale University
www.yale.edu/gsp/
This website offers information about a number of different genocides that occurred during the last one hundred years. One of the program's projects focuses on the Rwandan genocide. The site includes satellite maps of Rwanda before and after the 1994 genocide and databases about perpetrators and victims of the genocide.

International Criminal Tribunal for Rwanda
www.ictr.org/
The internet site of the International Criminal Tribunal for Rwanda (ICTR). It is an excellent, informative site relative to legal aspects of the 1994 genocide. Good links available to other sites.

PBS – Public Broadcasting System
www.pbs.org
An excellent website with everything from interviews with survivors of genocide, news reports and teachers' guides to video documentaries and essays by well-known commentators and lesson plans about genocide and related issues. To access information about the 1994 genocide in Rwanda, enter "Rwanda" in the search option.

Prevent Genocide International
www.preventgenocide.org
Prevent Genocide International is a global education and action network working for the prevention of the crime of genocide. This site offers information in several

languages on genocides worldwide. It is an excellent resource for information regarding the tenth anniversary of the Rwandan genocide. Good links to other sites.

Remember Rwanda
www.visiontv.ca/RememberRwanda/main_pt.htm
A very good Canadian website developed to commemorate the tenth anniversary of the genocide in Rwanda. Includes a brief chronology, web resources, readings, photographs, and other information. In English and French.

Stockholm International Forum
www.preventinggenocide.com
In 2004, the Prime Minister of Sweden hosted a conference on "Preventing Genocide." This English-language site contains invaluable documentation, statements, and links about genocide, including genocide in Rwanda.

The Center for Holocaust and Genocide Studies, University of Minnesota
www.chgs.umn.edu/
This is an excellent general information site about the Holocaust and other genocides. It provides an extensive list of links to other sites concerning various aspects of the Rwandan genocide. Select "Links and Bibliography" on the home page, choose "Links," then scroll to "Rwanda."

United Nations
www.un.org
The United Nations (UN) website is filled with valuable information, documents, photographs, and other resources about countries and situations throughout the world. Click on "Search," then type "Rwanda genocide" to search the UN site for information about the 1994 genocide.

VIDEOGRAPHY

A Conversation between Elie Wiesel and Jacqueline Murekatete, New York: United Nations Video, 2003.

A poignant conversation between a survivor of the Holocaust and a survivor of the 1994 genocide in Rwanda.

A Good Man in Hell: General Roméo Dallaire and the Rwanda Genocide, Washington, DC: U.S. Holocaust Memorial Museum, 2003.

An examination of moral responsibility in the face of genocide with the commander of UNAMIR (United Nations Mission in Rwanda). Includes some background on the genocide itself.

A Republic Gone Mad: Rwanda 1894-1994, New York: First Run/Icarus Films, 1996.

Provides historic information necessary for an analysis of the genocide as it recounts Rwanda's history from 1885 to the catastrophic regime of Juvénal Habyarimana.

Chronicle of a Genocide Foretold, New York: First Run/Icarus Films, 1996.

Follows several Rwandans before, during, and after the 1994 genocide.

Crimes Against Humanity: The Search for Justice, London: BBC, 1998.

The film is about the attempt of Rwanda's Minister of Justice, Gerald Gahima, to track hundreds of Rwandans accused of perpetrating atrocities against their neighbors.

Forsaken Cries: The Story of Rwanda, Washington, DC: Amnesty International, 1997.

Insight into the class system set up in Rwanda by the Belgians in 1919; also examines human rights violations and the 1994 genocide in Rwanda.

Frontline: Ghosts of Rwanda, Washington, DC: PBS Video, 2004.

An account of the social, political, and diplomatic failures that enabled the slaughter of 800,000 people to occur unabated and unchallenged by the global community.

Frontline: The Triumph of Evil, Washington, DC: PBS Video, 1999.

Report on how the West ignored warnings of impending genocide in Rwanda and turned its back on its victims.

Frontline: Valentina's Nightmare, Washington, DC: PBS Video, 1999.

A young survivor tells about her horrific experiences during the weeks and months of the 1994 genocide, including how she hid among corpses of family and friends to survive.

Gacaca: Living Together Again in Rwanda? New York: First Run/Icarus Films, 2002.

Illuminates what is most compelling about Rwanda's quest for justice after genocide.

In Rwanda We Say ... "The family that does not speak dies," New York: First Run/Icarus Films, 2004.

An intimate and fascinating examination of how, and whether, people can overcome fear, hatred and deep emotional scars after genocide to forge a common future.

Secrets of a Thousand Hills, Laxton, Notts, UK: Aegis, 2002.

Brief overview of the 1994 genocide in Rwanda; includes interviews with survivors.

Stories from Rwanda, Washington, DC: C-SPAN Booknotes, 1998.

An interview with Philip Gourevitch, author of *We wish to inform you that tomorrow we will be killed with our families*.

The Forgotten Wars – Rwanda: The Endless War, New York: Ambrose Video, 1999.

The story of a country consumed by genocide; includes dramatic and traumatic images.

The Horror Continues, Princeton, NJ: Films for the Humanities and Sciences, 2002.

Reviews genocides in several places including Burundi and Rwanda; examines the role of the UN and discusses what the future holds in terms of trying to prevent genocide

The Last Just Man, Canada: Barna-Alper Productions, 2001.

General Roméo Dallaire, head of UNAMIR, examines whether he could have done more to stop the 1994 genocide.

The Rwanda Fund, Laxton, Notts, UK: Aegis, 2003.

Short film about the 1994 genocide; includes survivor interviews.

The Rwandan Nightmare, New York: First Run/Icarus Films, 1994.

Eyewitness accounts of the 1994 genocide as well as interviews with survivors and government figures.

BIBLIOGRAPHY

Abdulai, Napoleon, ed. *Genocide in Rwanda.* London: Africa Research and Information Centre, 1994.

Ackerman, John E. and Eugene O'Sullivan. *Practice and Procedure of the International Criminal Tribunal for the Former Yugoslavia: with selected materials from the International Criminal Tribunal for Rwanda.* The Hague: Cambridge, MA: Kluwer Law International, 2000.

Adelman, Howard and Astri Suhrke, eds. *The Path of Genocide: The Rwandan Crisis from Uganda to Zaire.* New Brunswick, NJ: Transaction Publications, 1999.

African Rights, ed. *Rwanda: Death, Despair, and Defiance.* London: African Rights, 1995.

---- *Rwanda: Not So Innocent: When Women Become Killers.* London: African Rights, 1995.

---- *The Insurgency in the Northwest.* London: African Rights, 1998.

---- *Confessing to Genocide: Responses to Rwanda's Genocide Law.* London: African Rights, 2000.

---- *Left to Die: The Stories of Rwandese Civilians Abandoned by UN Troops on 11 April 1994.* London: African Rights, 2000.

---- *Obstruction of Justice: The Nuns of Sovu in Belgium.* London: African Rights, 2000.

---- *Father Hormisdas Nsengimana: Accused of Genocide, Sheltered by the Church.* London: African Rights, 2001.

---- *Tribute to Courage.* London: African Rights, 2002.

Anyidoho, Henry. *Guns Over Kigali.* Accra: Woeli Publishing Services, 1997.

Askin, Kelly Dawn. *War Crimes Against Women.* The Hague: Martin Nihoff Publishers, Kluwer Law International, 1997.

Barnett, Michael. *Eyewitness to a Genocide: The United Nations and Rwanda.* Ithaca, NY: Cornell University Press, 2002.

Bartov, Omer and Phyllis Mack, eds. *In God's Name - Genocide and Religion in the Twentieth Century.* New York: Berghahn Books, 2001.

Baum, Gregory and Harold Wells, eds. *The Reconciliation of Peoples: Challenge to the Churches.* Maryknoll, NY: Orbis Books, 1997.

Belgrad, Eric A. and Nitza Nachmias, eds. *The Politics of International Humanitarian Aid Operations*. Westport, CT: Praeger, 1997.

Belinda, Lesley. *The Colour of Darkness*. London: Hodder and Stoughton, 1996.

Berry, Carol Pott and John A., eds. *Genocide in Rwanda: A Collective Memory*. Washington D.C.: Howard University Press, 1999.

Biggar, Nigel, ed. *Burying the Past*. Washington, D.C.: Georgetown University Press, 2003.

Bilindabagabo, Bishop Alex with Alan Nichols. *Rescued by Angels: The Story of Miracles during the Rwandan Genocide*. Brunswick East, Victoria, Australia, 2001.

Bodnarchuk, Kari J. Rwanda: *A Country Torn Apart*. Minneapolis, MN: Lerner Publishing, 1999.

Boutros-Ghali, Boutros (Introduction). *The United Nations and Rwanda 1993-1996*. New York: Dept. of Public Information, United Nations, 1996.

Chikwende, Vincent Emenike and Aimable Twagilimana, eds. *Hutu and Tutsi*. New York: Rosen Publishing Group, 1997.

Dallaire, Roméo. *Shake Hands with the Devil: The Failure of Humanity in Rwanda*. Toronto: Random House, 2003.

Des Forges, Alison. *Leave None to Tell the Story: Genocide in Rwanda*. New York: Human Rights Watch, 1999.

Destexhe, Alain. *Rwanda and Genocide in the Twentieth Century*. New York: New York University Press, 1995.

Dorsey, Learthen. *Historical Dictionary of Rwanda*. Scarecrow Press: Metuchen, New Jersey and London, 1994.

Durch, William, ed. *UN Peacekeeping: American Politics and the Uncivil Wars of the 1990s*. New York: St. Martin's Press, 1996.

Eltringham, Nigel. *Accounting for Horror: Post-Genocide Debates in Rwanda*. London: Pluto Press, 2004.

Feil, Scott. *Preventing Genocide: How the Use of Force Might Have Succeeded in Rwanda*. New York: Carnegie Commission, 1998.

Fein, Helen. *The Prevention of Genocide: Rwanda and Yugoslavia Reconsidered*. New York: Institute for the Study of Genocide, 1994.

Fisanick, Christina. *Rwanda Genocide*. Detroit, MI: Gale Group, 2004.

Frey, Robert S., ed. *The Genocidal Temptation: Auschwitz, Hiroshima, Rwanda, and Beyond*. Lanham, MD: The University Press of America, 2004.

BIBLIOGRAPHY

Gatwa, Tharcisse. "The Churches and Ethnic Ideology in the Rwandan Crises (1900-1994)." Ph.D diss., University of Edinburgh, 1998.

Gellately, Robert and Ben Kiernan, eds. *The Specter of Genocide: Mass Murder in Historical Perspective.* New York: Cambridge University Press, 2003.

Goldstone, Richard J. *For Humanity: Reflections of a War Crimes Investigator.* New Haven, CT: Yale University Press, 2000.

Gourevitch, Philip. *We wish to inform you that tomorrow we will be killed with our families.* New York: Farrar, Straus and Giroux, 1998.

Guillebaud, Meg. *Rwanda: The Land God Forgot? Revival, Genocide & Hope.* London: Monarch Books, 2002.

Gutman, Roy and David Rieff, eds. *Crimes of War: What the Public Should Know.* New York: W.W. Norton & Company, 1999.

Hinton, Alexander Laban. *Annihilating Difference: The Anthropology of Genocide.* Berkeley, CA: University of California Press, 2002.

Hirsch, Herbert. *Anti-Genocide: Building an American Movement to Prevent Genocide.* Westport, CT: Praeger, 2002.

Hochschild, Adam. *King Leopold's Ghost: A Story of Greed, Terror, and Heroism in Colonial Africa.* New York: Houghton Mifflin Co., 1998.

Human Rights Watch. *Slaughter Among Neighbors: The Political Origins of Communal Violence.* New Haven: Yale University Press, 1995.

--- *Shattered Lives: Rwanda – Sexual Violence during the Rwandan Genocide and its Aftermath.* New York: Human Rights Watch, 1996.

--- *Genocide in Rwanda: The Planning and Execution of Mass Murder.* New York: Human Rights Watch, 1997.

--- *Leave None to Tell the Story: Genocide in Rwanda.* New York: Human Rights Watch, 1999.

--- *Genocide, War Crimes and Crimes Against Humanity: Topical Digests of the Case Law of the International Criminal Tribunal for Rwanda and the International Criminal Tribunal for the Former Yugoslavia.* New York: Human Rights Watch, 2004.

Igwara, Obi, ed. *Ethnic Hatred: Genocide in Rwanda.* London: ASEN Publication, 1995.

Jefremovas, Villia. *Brickyards to Graveyards: From Production to Genocide in Rwanda.* New York: State University of New York, 2002.

Jones, Bruce D. *Peacekeeping in Rwanda: The Dynamics of Failure.* London: Lynne Rienner Publishers, 2001.

Jones, John R. W. D. *International Criminal Practice: The International Criminal Tribunal for the Former Yugoslavia, The International Criminal Tribunal for Rwanda, The International Criminal Court, The Special Court for Sierra Leone, The East Timor Special Panel for Serious Crimes, War Crimes Prosecutions in Kosovo*. Transnational Publishers: New York: Oxford University Press, 2003.

Jongman, Albert J., ed. *Contemporary Genocides: Causes, Cases, Consequences.* Leiden: PIOOM, 1996.

Kamukama, Dixon. *Rwanda Conflict: Its Roots and Regional Implications.* Kampala: Fountain Publishers, 1997.

Keane, Fergal. *Season of Blood: A Rwanda Journey.* London: Penguin, 1995.

Kent, Randolph. *After Rwanda: The Coordination of United Nations Humanitarian Assistance.* New York: St. Martin's Press, 1996.

Khan, Shaharyar. M., foreword by Mary Robinson. *The Shallow Graves of Rwanda.* New York: I.B. Tauris, 2000.

Klinghoffer, Arthur Jay. *The International Dimension of Genocide in Rwanda.* New York: New York University Press, 1998.

Klip, Andre and Goran Sluiter, eds. *Annotated Leading Cases of International Criminal Tribunals: The International Criminal Tribunal for Rwanda 1994-1999.* Belgium: Intersentia Uitgevers N.V., 2001.

Koff, Clea. *The Bone Woman: A Forensic Anthropologist's Search for Truth in the Graves of Rwanda, Bosnia, Croatia, and Kosovo.* London: Random House, 2004.

Kressel, Neil J. *Mass Hate: The Global Rise of Genocide and Terror.* Boulder, CO: Westview Press, 1996.

Leyton, Elliott. *Touched by Fire: Doctors Without Borders in a Third World Crisis.* Toronto: McClelland & Stewart, 1998.

Linden, Ian. *Church and Revolution in Rwanda.* Manchester: Manchester University Press, 1977.

Madsen, Wayne. *Genocide and Covert Operations in Africa 1993-1999.* New York: Edwin Mellen Press, 1999.

Magnarella, Paul J. *Justice in Africa: Rwanda's Genocide, its Courts, and the UN Criminal Tribunal.* London: Ashgate Publishing Limited, 2002.

Malkki, Liisa H. *Purity and Exile: Violence, Memory, and National Cosmology Among Hutu Refugees in Tanzania.* Chicago: University of Chicago Press, 1995.

Mamdani, Mahmood. *When Victims Become Killers: Colonialism, Nativism, and the Genocide in Rwanda.* Princeton, NJ: Princeton University Press, 2000.

Mbanda, Laurent and Steve Wamberg. *Committed to Conflict: The Destruction of the Church in Rwanda*. London: SPCK Publishers, 1997.

McCullum, Hugh. *The Angels Have Left Us: The Rwandan Tragedy and the Churches*. Geneva: World Council of Churches Publications, #66 in Risk Book Series, 1995.

Mcnulty, Mel. *The Media of Conflict: War Reporting and Representations of Ethnic Violence*. London: Zed Books, 1999.

Melvern, Linda. *A People Betrayed: The Role of the West in Rwanda's Genocide*. London: Zed, 2000.

---- *Conspiracy to Murder: Planning the Rwanda Genocide*. London: Verso, 2004.

Mills, Nicolaus and Kira Brunner, eds. *The New Killing Fields: Massacre and the Politics of Intervention*. New York: Basic Books, 2002.

Minear, Larry and Phillippe Guillot. *Soldiers to the Rescue: Humanitarian Lessons from Rwanda*. Paris: Development Centre of the Organization for Economic Cooperation and Development, 1996.

Moeller, Susan D. *Compassion Fatigue*. New York: Routledge, 1999.

Moore, Jonathan, ed. *Hard Choices, Moral Dilemmas in Humanitarian Intervention*. Oxford: Rowman and Littlefield, 1998.

Neuffer, Elizabeth. *The Key to My Neighbor's House: Seeking Justice in Bosnia and Rwanda*. New York: Picador, 2002.

Newbury, Catherine. *The Cohesion of Oppression: Clientship and Ethnicity in Rwanda, 1860-1960*. New York: Columbia University Press, 1988.

Newick Park Initiative. *The Churches' Role in the Restoration of Justice in Rwanda*. Cambridge, September 1997.

Nyankanzi, Edward L. *Genocide: Rwanda and Burundi*. Rochester, VT: Schenkman Books, 1998.

Off, Carol. *The Lion, the Fox and the Eagle: A Story of Generals and Justice in Rwanda and Yugoslavia*. Toronto: Random House, Canada, 2000.

Omaar, Rakiya and Alex de Waal, eds. *Rwanda: Death, Despair, and Defiance*. London: African Rights, 1995.

Organization of African Unity. *Rwanda: The Preventable Genocide*. Addis Ababa: IPEP, 2000.

Pender, John. *Rwanda: The Great Genocide Debate. Conference Papers and Transcriptions, 27 July 1997*. London: Africa Direct, 1997.

Peterson, Scott. *Me Against My Brother: At War in Somalia, Sudan, and Rwanda*. New York: Routledge, 2000.

Pottier, Johan. *Re-imagining Rwanda: Conflict, Survival and Disinformation in the Late Twentieth Century.* Cambridge: Cambridge University Press, 2002.

Power, Samantha. *A Problem from Hell: America and the Age of Genocide.* New York: Basic Books, 2002.

Prunier, Gérard. *The Rwanda Crisis, 1959-1994: History of Genocide.* New York: Columbia University Press, 1997.

Rehn, Elizabeth & Ellen Johnson Sirleaf. *Women War, and Peace.* New York: UNIFEM, 2002.

Rittner, Carol, John K. Roth, and James M. Smith, eds. *Will Genocide Ever End?* St. Paul: Paragon House, 2002.

Scherrer, Christian P. *Genocide and Crisis in Central Africa : Conflict Roots, Mass Violence, and Regional War.* Westport, Conn.: Praeger, 2002.

Semujanga, Josias. *Origins of Rwandan Genocide.* New York: Humanity Books, 2003.

Shawcross, William. *Deliver Us From Evil: Warlords & Peacekeepers in a World of Endless Conflict.* London: Bloomsbury, 2000.

Sibomana, André. *Hope for Rwanda: Conversations with Laure Guilbert and Hervé Deguine.* London: Pluto Press, 1999.

Smith, James, ed. *A Time to Remember, Rwanda: Ten Years After Genocide.* Retford, UK: Aegis Institute, 2004.

Staub, Ervin. *The Psychology of Good and Evil: Why Children, Adults, and Groups Help and Harm Others.* New York: Cambridge University Press, 2003.

Taylor, Christopher C. *Sacrifice as Terror: The Rwandan Genocide of 1994.* New York: Berg, 1999.

The International Response to Conflict and Genocide: Lessons from the Rwanda Experience. Joint Emergency Assistance to Rwanda. Copenhagen, March 1996.

Twagilimana, Aimable A. *Teenage Refugees from Rwanda Speak Out.* New York: Rosen Publishing Group, 1997.

---- *Debris of Ham: Ethnicity, Regionalism, and the 1994 Rwandan Genocide.* Lanham, MD: The University Press of America, 2003.

Uvin, Peter. *Aiding Violence: The Development Enterprise in Rwanda.* New York: Kumarian Press, 1998.

Waller, David. *Rwanda: Which Way Now?* Oxford: Oxfam, 1997.

Waller, James. *Becoming Evil: How Ordinary People Commit Genocide and Mass Killing.* New York: Oxford University Press, 2002.

CONTRIBUTORS

Editors

Carol Rittner R.S.M., a Roman Catholic nun, is Distinguished Professor of Holocaust & Genocide Studies at The Richard Stockton College of New Jersey. She is the Associate Editor of *The Genocide Forum* (USA), and Editor of *The Aegis Review on Genocide* (UK). She has published a number of books, including *The Holocaust and the Christian World* (2000), *Pius XII and the Holocaust* (2002), and *Will Genocide Ever End?* (2002).

John K. Roth is the Edward J. Sexton Professor of Philosophy and the Director of the Center for the Study of the Holocaust, Genocide, and Human Rights at Claremont McKenna College, California, where he has taught since 1966. He has published hundreds of articles and reviews and more than thirty-five books, including, most recently, *Holocaust Politics, Pope Pius XII and the Holocaust, Will Genocide Ever End?*, and a revised edition of *Approaches to Auschwitz: The Holocaust and Its Legacy*.

Wendy Whitworth, Editor of *Survival: Holocaust Survivors Tell Their Story* (2003), is Managing Editor of *The Aegis Review on Genocide* and a staff member of Beth Shalom Holocaust Centre (UK).

Contributors

Matthias Bjørnlund is pursuing a Masters degree in history, as well as working as a research assistant affiliated with the Danish Institute for International Studies, Department for Holocaust and Genocide Studies, Copenhagen, Denmark.

Roger Bowen is an Anglican priest. From 1975-1984, he was with the Church of England's Rwanda Mission (based in Burundi, 1977-84). For six years, 1991-1997, Father Bowen was General Secretary of Mid-Africa Ministries, now part of CMS. Although based in London in 1994, he was in constant touch throughout the 1994 genocide with Anglican bishops, and others, in Rwanda, doing what he could to help from London. In 1995, Roger Bowen gave the J. C. Jones Lecture in Wales, "Rwanda: Missionary Reflections on a Catastrophe."

CONTRIBUTORS

Margaret Brearley was educated at Oxford and Cambridge universities. She has been a Senior Fellow and Lecturer, Centre for Judaism and Jewish-Christian Relations, Selly Oak Colleges, Birmingham and a Fellow in Christian-Jewish Relations, Institute of Jewish Affairs, London. Dr. Brearley has many publications in academic journals, is a member of several academic advisory boards, and is currently Honorary Advisor on the Holocaust to the Archbishops' Council, Church of England.

Marie Julianne Farrington, S.S.M.N., a Sister of St. Mary of Namur, visited Rwanda frequently as General Superior of her Congregation, and especially during the early days of the 1994 genocide. In 2000, she testified at the International Criminal Tribunal for Rwanda in Arusha, Tanzania. She has led two retreat and reflection sessions on reconciliation and peace for the Sisters of her congregation in Rwanda. She gave a similar retreat in the Democratic Republic of Congo.

Jerry Fowler is the Staff Director of the Committee on Conscience at the United States Holocaust Memorial Museum, Washington, DC. He wrote and directed the short film, *A Good Man in Hell: General Romeo Dallaire and the Rwanda Genocide.*

Philippe Gaillard is the former Head of Delegation of the International Committee of the Red Cross (ICRC) in Rwanda (July 1993-July 1994).

David P. Gushee is Graves Professor of Moral Philosophy and Senior Fellow, Carl F. H. Henry Center for Christian Leadership at Union University, Jackson, Tennessee (USA). He is the author or editor of eight books, including *Righteous Gentiles of the Holocaust: Genocide and Moral Obligation* (2003).

Hubert Locke is Dean Emeritus of the Daniel J. Evans School of Public Affairs at the University of Washington (USA), where he also held the John and Marguerite Corbally Professorship in Public Service, as well as appointments on the faculties of Comparative Relation, Jewish Studies, and Sociology. He is co-editor of a number of books and author of several more, *Learning From History: A Black Christian's Perspective on the Holocaust* (2000), and *Searching for God in Godforsaken Times and Places* (2003).

Eric Markusen is a Senior Researcher at the Danish Institute for International Studies, Department of Holocaust and Genocide Studies, Copenhagen, Denmark, while on leave as Professor of Sociology and Social Work at Southwest Minnesota State University (USA). His books include *The*

Genocidal Mentality (with Robert Jay Lifton) and *The Holocaust and Strategic Bombing* (with David Kopf).

Marie Césarie Mukarwego, a Rwandan, is a member of the Roman Catholic order of the Sisters of the Assumption. Her experience includes teaching as well as administration, at various levels, for her religious order. Currently, she works in the area of development and human promotion in Rwanda. Sister Mukarwego lives in Rwanda.

Tom Ndahiro is a Commissioner of the Rwandan National Human Rights Commission. He is also a journalist. Mr. Ndahiro lives in Rwanda.

Martin (François) Neyt, O.S.B., is a Roman Catholic priest and a member of the Order of St. Benedict (Benedictines). Dr. Neyt is an art historian by training. He has traveled extensively in Africa and around the world. Dr. Neyt teaches at the Catholic University of Louvain in Belgium, and he has written several works on Central Africa and Nigeria.

Charles Petrie was the Deputy United Nations Humanitarian Coordinator in Rwanda in 1994, and special advisor on humanitarian issues to the UN Force Commander of UNAMIR during the period of the genocide. He has been responsible for policy and operational responsibilities within the UN system for almost fifteen years, in Sudan (1989-1992), Somalia (1992-1994), Rwanda (1994), the Middle East (1996-1998), Democratic Republic of the Congo (1998-2001), Afghanistan (2002-2003), and Myanmar (2003-to present).

Léon D. Saur, a historian, was Secretary General of the Belgian Christian Democrat Party (PSC), 1989-1995, in charge of international affairs. In 1997, he testified voluntarily before the Belgian Senatorial Commission of Inquiry on Rwanda. He is the author of *Influences parallèles., le rôle de L'Internationale démocrate-chrétienne au Rwanda* (Ed. Luc Pire, Bruxelles, 1998) and of *Le Sabre, la machette et le goupillon* (Bierges: Ed. Mols, 2004).

James M. Smith is co-founder and Executive Director of the Aegis Trust and Institute (UK). Dr. Smith initiated the Aegis Project in Rwanda and worked with the Rwandan Government and Kigali municipal authorities to create a national memorial centre at Gisozi, near Kigali. He is the co-editor (with Carol Rittner and John K. Roth) of *Will Genocide Ever End?* (2002), and the editor of *A Time to Remember Rwanda: Ten Yeras After Genocide* (2004).

Stephen D. Smith is co-founder of the Aegis Trust (UK). Dr. Smith is the author of numerous publications and the writer/director of several film documentaries and multi-media productions, including *Wasted Lives; Survivors: Memories of the Past, Lessons for the Future*; and, *The Holocaust and Genocide: Why Does It Happen?*

Peter Steenberg is pursuing a Masters degree in history, as well as working as a research assistant affiliated with the Danish Institute for International Studies, Department for Holocaust and Genocide Studies, Copenhagen, Denmark.

Rafiki Ubaldo, a survivor of the Rwanda genocide, is an investigative journalist. After the genocide, he taught languages at the Catholic Seminary in Butare, Rwanda. He has worked for Rwandan national newspapers and for the Rwandan Ministry of Justice. He also worked as a consultant on a Swedish television documentary on the role of the Christian churches in the Rwanda genocide.

Octave Ugirashebuja, S. J., a Jesuit priest, is professor of philosophy at Grand Séminaire de Nyakibanda in Rwanda, the author of a number of publications about philosophy and general culture, and the regional coordinator of African Jesuit Aids Network (AJAN) for Rwanda and Burundi. For six years, he was General Secretary of the Rwandan Bishops' Justice and Peace Commission, and for three years he was a member of the Unity and Reconciliation National Commission of Rwanda.

INDEX